NORTH DAKOTA

★ Theodore Roosevelt National Memorial Park

MINNESOTA

WISCONSIN

SOUTH DAKOTA

⚠ Deadwood

IOWA

IND.

Swan Land and Cattle Company Headquarters

NEBRASKA

Homestead
National Monument ★

ILLINOIS

ral City

Jefferson National Expansion ★
Memorial

KANSAS

MISSOURI

KY.

ipple Creek

LORADO

TENN.

OKLAHOMA

ARKANSAS

EW

XICO

J A Ranch ⚠

MISSISSIPPI

ncoln Historic District

TEXAS

LOUISIANA

MICHIGAN

Lake Michigan

GULF OF MEXICO

King Ranch ⚠

W9-BUT-261

# PROSPECTOR, COWHAND, AND SODBUSTER

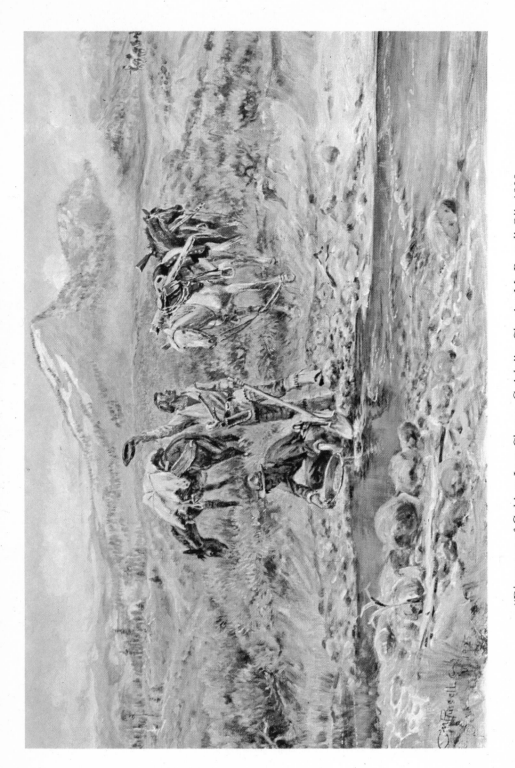

"Discovery of Gold at Last Chance Gulch."  Charles M. Russell Oil, 1925.

Courtesy, Gilcrease Institute of American History and Art, Tulsa, Oklahoma; color separations, Montana Historical Society.

# PROSPECTOR, COWHAND, AND SODBUSTER

HISTORIC PLACES
ASSOCIATED WITH THE MINING,
RANCHING, AND FARMING FRONTIERS
IN THE TRANS-MISSISSIPPI WEST

Volume XI

THE NATIONAL SURVEY OF HISTORIC SITES AND BUILDINGS

*Robert G. Ferris,* SERIES EDITOR

UNITED STATES DEPARTMENT OF THE INTERIOR

NATIONAL PARK SERVICE

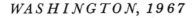

*WASHINGTON, 1967*

This volume was prepared by the Division of History Studies, National Park Service, under the general supervision of the Chief, Robert M. Utley. One of a series designed to make available to the public the studies of the National Survey of Historic Sites and Buildings, directed by John O. Littleton, it incorporates survey and evaluation reports prepared by the following National Park Service historians: William E. Brown, William C. Everhart, Ray H. Mattison, Charles W. Snell, and Robert M. Utley. These reports were reviewed by the Advisory Board on National Parks, Historic Sites, Buildings, and Monuments and the Consulting Committee for the National Survey of Historic Sites and Buildings. Members of these groups are listed in the Acknowledgments.

*The background narrative for this volume is based on studies prepared under contract by Dr. Odie B. Faulk, Arizona Pioneers' Historical Society; Dr. Benjamin F. Gilbert, San Jose State College; and Dr. Lawrence Kinnaird, University of California.*

LIBRARY OF CONGRESS CATALOG CARD NUMBER: 66–60014

For sale by the Superintendent of Documents, U.S. Government Printing Office, Washington, D.C. 20402 – Price $3.00

# Contents

[ v

Photographs are by the National Park Service except where specified

# MAPS

# Foreword

Between 1803 and 1853, the new seaboard republic of the United States acquired a vast empire of plains, mountains, and deserts west of the Mississippi River. Its borders fixed on the Pacific, it gloried in its new stature as a continental Nation. But most of the new domain lay unconquered and unknown except to scattered Indian tribes and a few explorers and mountain men. In the next half-century, soldiers, traders, road and railway builders, and other adventurers helped fill in the map of the American West. Overshadowing them all in actually subduing the land, however, were the prospector, cowhand, and sodbuster.

Though these three types of pioneers fostered exaggerated stereotypes that still live in American folklore, each shared decisively in shaping the history of the West. And each left tangible evidences of his passage across the land that recall for today's generation the contributions of frontier mining, stockraising, and farming to the making of America.

This volume surveys the legacy of historic sites and buildings bequeathed by these actors in the drama of conquering the West. It is one of a series of books designed to make available the findings of the National Survey of Historic Sites and Buildings, a nationwide program conducted by the National Park Service of the U.S. Department of the Interior under authority of the Historic Sites Act of 1935. The Survey's purpose is to identify historic and prehistoric places of significance to the Nation. Such places are studied

[ xiii

and evaluated by Service field historians and archeologists, screened by a Consulting Committee of outside scholars, and final selections recommended to the Secretary of the Interior by the Advisory Board on National Parks, Historic Sites, Buildings, and Monuments. When approved by the Secretary, sites and buildings judged of national historical significance are eligible for designation as Registered National Historic Landmarks. Upon application, their owners are provided with a certificate and a bronze plaque attesting to the distinction.

Credit for the preparation of this volume is shared widely by persons both in and out of the National Park Service. In particular, the work of the Service in the general field of historic preservation has benefited inestimably from the assistance provided by the National Trust for Historic Preservation in the United States, a cosponsor of the Survey.

The sites and buildings evaluated and described in the following pages commemorate or illustrate a vital chapter of our American heritage. Citizens who visit them will better understand and appreciate the rich history of our Nation. Now, more than ever before, urbanization and "modernization" are destroying historic places at an alarming rate. Vigilance and prudent historic preservation should be our watchwords; progress need not be made at the expense of thoughtless destruction. We hope that this volume, and others in the series, will encourage individuals, private groups, and State and local governments to join the Federal Government in making the increased efforts that are so critically needed today to preserve our historic treasures.

GEORGE B. HARTZOG, Jr.
Director
National Park Service

# PROSPECTOR,
# COWHAND,
# AND
# SODBUSTER

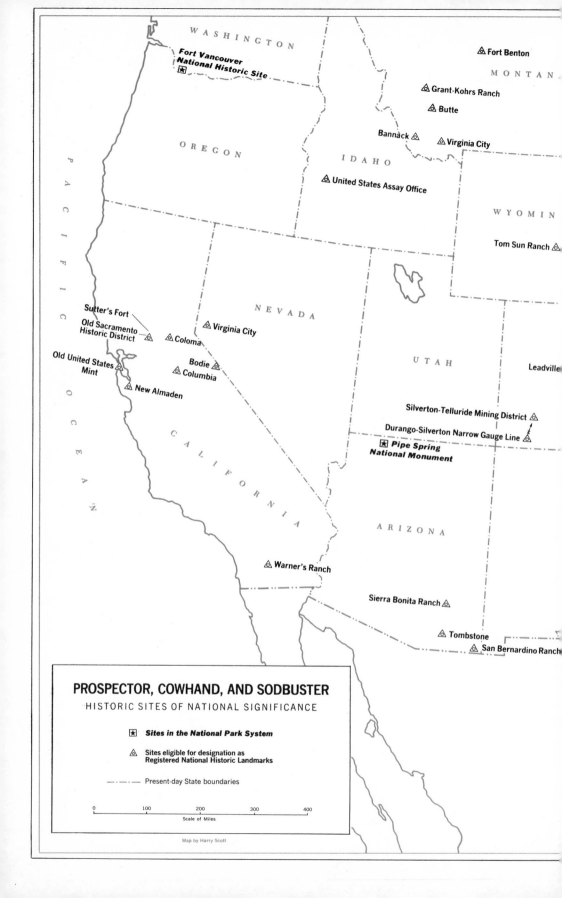

WASHINGTON

Fort Benton ⚠

MONTANA

Fort Vancouver
National Historic Site
⊡

Grant-Kohrs Ranch ⚠

Butte ⚠

OREGON

Bannack ⚠  Virginia City ⚠

IDAHO

United States Assay Office ⚠

WYOMIN

Tom Sun Ranch ⚠

PACIFIC

NEVADA

Virginia City ⚠

Sutter's Fort
Old Sacramento
Historic District ⚠  Coloma ⚠

UTAH

Leadville

Old United States
Mint ⚠

Bodie ⚠
Columbia ⚠

Silverton-Telluride Mining District ⚠

New Almaden ⚠

Durango-Silverton Narrow Gauge Line ⚠

OCEAN

⊡ Pipe Spring
National Monument

CALIFORNIA

ARIZONA

Warner's Ranch ⚠

Sierra Bonita Ranch ⚠

Tombstone ⚠

San Bernardino Ranch ⚠

# PROSPECTOR, COWHAND, AND SODBUSTER

HISTORIC SITES OF NATIONAL SIGNIFICANCE

⊡  *Sites in the National Park System*

⚠  Sites eligible for designation as
Registered National Historic Landmarks

—·—·—  Present-day State boundaries

| 0 | 100 | 200 | 300 | 400 |

Scale of Miles

Map by Harry Scott

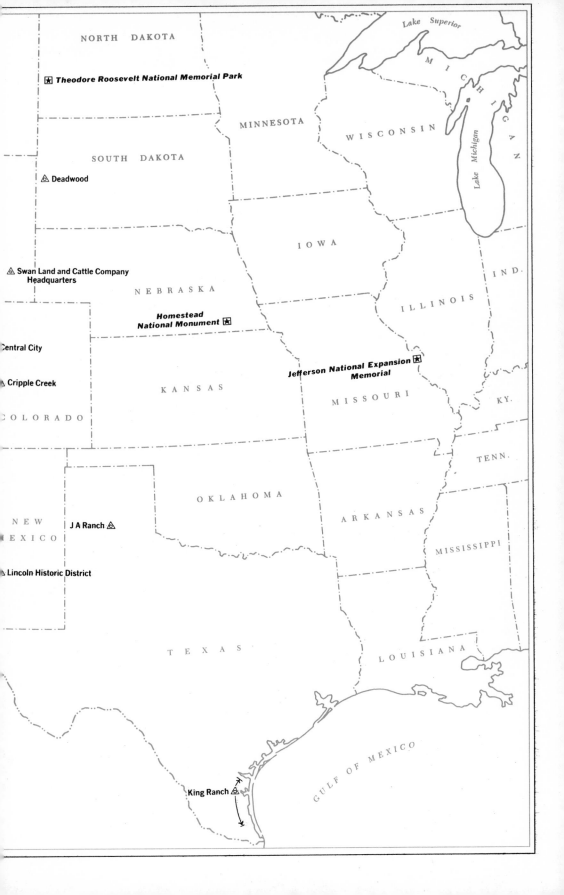

NORTH DAKOTA

⊡ **Theodore Roosevelt National Memorial Park**

*Lake Superior*

MINNESOTA

WISCONSIN

M I C H I G A N

*Lake Michigan*

SOUTH DAKOTA

△ Deadwood

I O W A

IND.

△ Swan Land and Cattle Company
    Headquarters

N E B R A S K A

**Homestead
National Monument** ⊡

I L L I N O I S

Central City

**Jefferson National Expansion** ⊡
       **Memorial**

△ Cripple Creek

K A N S A S

M I S S O U R I

KY.

COLORADO

TENN.

O K L A H O M A

A R K A N S A S

N E W
MEXICO

J A Ranch △

MISSISSIPPI

△ Lincoln Historic District

T E X A S

L O U I S I A N A

GULF OF MEXICO

King Ranch △

PART I

# Prospector, Cowhand,

# and Sodbuster:

# Historical Background

WHEN THE UNITED STATES purchased the vast Louisiana Territory in 1803, President Jefferson believed that this addition to the public domain would satisfy the needs of land-hungry Americans for at least 500 years. Yet the acquisition—roughly a quarter of the present contiguous United States— was only the first in a series that in but a few decades extended the Nation's boundary to the Pacific Ocean.

In 1819, 7 years before Jefferson died, the United States rounded out its Southeastern boundary by acquiring Florida from Spain. In 1845 it annexed Texas, which earlier had won its independence from Mexico, and the following year obtained full title to the Oregon country when Britain relinquished her claims by treaty. In 1848 the treaty that ended the Mexican War ceded to the United States approximately the present States of California, Nevada, Utah, Arizona, and New Mexico. And in 1853, by the Gadsden Purchase, Mexico yielded an additional strip of territory along the southern border of Arizona and New Mexico. Thus within only half a century after the Louisiana Purchase the small Republic presided over by Jefferson had become a giant among the nations of the world. Spanning a continent, it consisted of millions of acres of virgin forest, towering mountains, mighty rivers, forbidding deserts, and fertile valleys—and all their resources.

In the last half of the 19th century, the Nation seemingly dedicated itself to disposing of the newly acquired land and its resources as quickly as possible. It passed them into the hands of any individual or corporation who would put them to productive use. Acts designed to divest the Nation of much of the public domain rapidly followed each other through Congress. Spurred by the promise of gold and land, thousands from the teeming East and the Mississippi Valley frontier and thousands more from crowded Europe followed Horace Greeley's maxim and went west in such numbers and haste that Jefferson's estimate of half a millennium for the satisfaction of land hunger proved to be grossly exaggerated.

The settlement of the West was a continuous process—before, during, and after the five decades of land acquisition. Following the War for Independence, settlers pushed their way into the Mississippi Valley. By the time of the Louisiana Purchase, Kentucky, Tennessee, and Ohio had been admitted to the Union as States, and eager pioneers already were leapfrogging past the newly settled regions and across the Mississippi River. The motivations of these restless frontiersmen were many: Economic opportunity, free land, adventure, and escape from debts or the law.

Explorers, fur trappers, and traders quickly penetrated the newly acquired trans-Mississippi West. They charted the wilderness and exploited the natural resources and native inhabitants. But the sturdy farmers, known as sodbusters in the West, who were to break and cultivate the land, were stopped temporarily in their westward movement by the Great Plains—a region the geography books of that day called the "Great American Desert." By the mid-19th century the westward surge had come to a standstill except for the few thousand hardy emigrant-farmers who, beginning in the early 1840's, had crossed the Great Plains and moved into Oregon and California.

Then in 1848 from the Far West came exciting news. Gold had been discovered in California. Farmers abandoned their plows and hurried to the diggings. Their city cousins deserted their employment and followed. Fur trappers forgot the beaver—the silk hat

Sutter's sawmill at Coloma, California, near which James Marshall discovered gold in 1848 and stirred the Nation. From a painting by Charles C. Nahl. Courtesy, Bancroft Library, University of California.

had virtually ended their business anyway—and joined the rush. The line of settlement, which for the most part had stopped at the edge of the Plains, leaped across the deserts and mountains to the golden valleys of the Sacramento River.

Before long, the mining frontier worked its way eastward into the mineral-rich mountains from the Sierra to the Rockies. The cattlemen's empire, born in Texas at the close of the Civil War, rolled north and west to cover the Great Plains, spill over the mountains to upland plateaus, and even finger onto Southwestern deserts. At about the same time the sod house frontier of the Plains came into being. Settlers staked out the river valleys, cross-hatched the deserts with irrigation ditches, and crowded the cattlemen with whole sections of dry-land crops.

Not all those who rushed west went to the goldfields. Such an exploding population had to be fed, housed, entertained, and provided with other economic necessities. Thus mining created business, stimulated farming and ranching, fostered the west coast fishing industry, enhanced the market for lumber, spurred the establishment and growth of cities, and hastened the construction of roads and railroads.

Yet of all those who played a part in the settlement of the West, the prospector, cowhand, and sodbuster clearly stand out. They epitomize the efforts of the thousands of pioneers who gave substance and reality to the phrase—"from sea to shining sea."

## The California Gold Rush

A chance discovery by an employee of John A. Sutter, feudal baron of the Sacramento Valley, set off the rush to California. In January 1848 James W. Marshall was supervising the construction of a sawmill in Coloma Valley, about 40 miles up the south fork of the American River from Sutter's Fort. On the morning of the 24th, while inspecting progress on the excavation of the tailrace, he noticed the glint of metal on the bottom of the stream. Placing the flakes in the dented crown of his slouch hat, he excitedly rushed to the mill and shouted, "Boys, I believe I've found a gold mine."

After making tests at the mill for a few days and being unable to determine whether or not the flakes were actually gold, Marshall carried a sample to his employer at the fort. The two men tried every test that they could think of or that the *American Encyclopedia* suggested. Finally they proved that the sample was gold. In the course of time it became apparent that Marshall had in effect discovered a mammoth lode of gold-bearing quartz more than 150 miles in length that lay along the western foothills of the Sierra Nevada—the fabulous Mother Lode of California. Weathering and erosion had broken off particles of the lode, carried them down mountain streams, and deposited them in sandbars or rock crevices.

Sutter correctly foresaw that news of the gold discovery would spell disaster to his other enterprises—but such news could not be kept secret. In May an energetic San Francisco businessman and Mormon elder named Sam Brannan returned to the city from the diggings. His appearance on the streets holding aloft a quinine bottle full of glistening gold dust and bellowing, "Gold! Gold! Gold from the American River," started the stampede. Shopkeepers hung signs on their doors, "Gone to the Diggings." Schools closed as teachers and pupils alike abandoned their academic endeavors. San Francisco became a ghost town; everyone headed toward the strike.

At Monterey, Santa Barbara, San Diego, and other California settlements, soldiers deserted their posts, sailors abandoned ships,

Abandoned ships in San Francisco Harbor in the 1850's. Their crews had joined the rush to the goldfields. Courtesy, Smithsonian Institution.

lawyers left clients, and editors suspended publication of newspapers. And before the end of the year gold seekers had already arrived from Hawaii, Mexico, British Columbia, and South America.

## WESTWARD HO

Stories of the discovery gradually drifted to the Eastern United States, but most people dismissed them as rumor. Then in December 1848 they were indubitably confirmed. President Polk incorporated official dispatches from California in his message to Congress and stated, "The accounts of the abundance of gold in that territory are of such an extraordinary character as would scarcely command belief were they not corroborated by the authentic reports of officers in the public service." Two days later a Government courier arrived in Washington with a tea caddy full of gold. Sanity vanished. The tea caddy did for the Nation what Sam Brannan's quinine bottle had done for San Francisco.

Within a month, eager gold seekers chartered more than 60 ships, some of dubious vintage and condition, and weighed anchor for California. The New York *Herald*, in a special California edition, stated: "In every Atlantic seaport, vessels are being fitted up, societies are being formed, husbands are preparing to leave their

Sam Brannan, Mormon elder, brought news of James Marshall's gold strike to San Francisco. Two years earlier he had led a large group of Mormon settlers to the city. Courtesy, California Historical Society.

wives, sons are parting with their mothers, and bachelors are abandoning their comforts; all are rushing head over heels toward the El Dorado on the Pacific." Whenever and wherever men congregated that winter the talk was of California and the riches to be found there.

### ROUTES TO THE GOLDFIELDS

The gold seekers used four principal routes to California, two each by sea and land. Easterners mainly utilized the sea routes, and residents of the Mississippi Valley and southerners the land routes. For half a century "Boston" ships had been rounding Cape Horn to trade with California, and by 1849 some of the hazards of the journey had been eliminated. But the 18,000-mile voyage required 6 to 8 months—a long and tedious trip for excited forty-niners. Nevertheless in 1849 about 15,000 of them, embarking from Northeast ports, used this route.

The second water route involved a divided voyage by way of the Isthmus of Panama. In 1848 two steamship lines had begun service at each side of the isthmus. The crossing, by way of the Chagres River and an overland trek across the treacherous jungle, was a hazardous undertaking. Native guides, who supplied canoes and pack animals, were thieving, their prices exorbitant, their tempers and actions unpredictable. Cholera, dysentery, and yellow fever took a heavy toll of lives. At Panama City on the Pacific coast, the forty-niners milled about waiting for the occasional ship that managed to unload its passengers at San Francisco and return without the crew deserting to the mines. Advertised as a 6-week trip, the Panama route usually took considerably longer. Because of the hazards, however, only half as many emigrants traveled over this route in 1849 as over the Cape Horn route.

The most popular way to California was overland, either by the central or southern trails. [The overland emigrant routes, including those to the goldfields, are discussed and mapped in detail in Volume X of this series.] In 1849 some 45,000 forty-niners used the central trails and 10,000 the southern trails. The central trails followed the Platte River to South Pass, moved by various routes across the Great Basin, then labored through passes in the Sierra to the Pacific slope. This route was more convenient for Mississippi Valley residents than the ocean route—and it was much cheaper. A wagon and oxen, sufficient food and a few tools, most of which the average farmer already had, and he was ready to begin the extensive preparations for the trek.

Tens of thousands of forty-niners flocked to the embarkation towns—Independence, St. Joseph, Westport, and Kanesville—and waited until the grass along the trail was high enough to sustain the stock. Then the great wagon trains rolled out on the prairie, climbed steadily until they negotiated South Pass, then dropped down to the Great Basin desert. Those who thought that nothing was so deadly as plodding through the choking dust of the desert forgot that annoyance when they encountered the hardships of passing wagons and oxen over the Sierra and then lowering them by rope down precipitous canyons.

Other gold seekers, especially southerners, moved west by way of the southern trails. Drawing traffic from the Santa Fe Trail and the west Texas trails, the chief route followed the wagon road blazed by Lt. Col. Philip St. George Cooke from the Rio Grande by way of the Gila to the Pacific during the Mexican War. It offered the advantages of few mountain ranges and a milder climate.

Whatever their route, those who finally arrived at the diggings after the 2,000-mile overland trip, which usually required 5 or 6 months, had faced a severe test. Only the hardiest survived trail life. Asiatic cholera alone in 1849 marked the central trails with 5,000 graves before the wagons reached the Rocky Mountains. But the dangers and privations—on land or at sea—were all forgotten upon arrival at the goldfields. There the newcomers found those who had arrived earlier working every large stream along the Mother Lode, from the Feather to the Tuolumne Rivers. Tent camps sprang up everywhere as the forty-niners, washing pan in hand, set out to seek the riches so lavishly reported. A few lucky souls did find wealth, but the majority were quickly disillusioned.

### Washing pan and sluice

The free dust and nuggets of the placer deposits—surface gold, usually located in the beds of streams—could be extracted by the inexperienced with a washing pan. The miners threw a few shovels of raw earth into the pan and twirled it until water washed the earth away and left the heavier grains of gold at the bottom. Where the paydirt was especially rich, the forty-niners quickly refined their methods. The cradle was a crude box that the operator rocked with

Miners used cradles, or rockers, for especially rich paydirt. Courtesy, National Archives.

one hand while dipping earth and water in with the other; the rocking motion washed the debris out, and the gold particles settled in the cleats. The "Long Tom" was similar to the cradle, but of greater length; it was, in essence, a long box through which a stream of water was directed and into which miners shoveled raw earth.

A RUGGED LIFE

All these methods could be utilized by individuals or by small groups, for neither experience nor capital was required. But the toil was monotonous and backbreaking. Often the miners stood for hours waist deep in icy water. Laboring day by day for the yellow grains of "dust," they returned at night to. primitive shacks and uninviting meals of coffee, beans, and greasy pork. In such conditions, even in good weather, they suffered from many diseases— diarrhea, dysentery, chills, fevers, and malaria. Men who led such lives often sought solace in the saloons or the embraces of the "soiled doves."

The "cities" that sprang into being almost overnight boasted populations of many thousands. Only relatively more comfortable than the shack, lean-to, or cave of the miner, the buildings were usually constructed of juniper posts, willow branches, blankets, and rawhide. Shacks irregularly dotted the streets, which dodged at acute angles or struggled up the side of a mountain. The "restaurant" might be roofless, the walls made of flour sacks, the tables of rough planks, and the floor of mud. Newly arrived "gentlemen of fortune" slept on the floors of stores and saloons, or on the open ground. The saloons, often the most pretentious structures in town, were filled with ragged, unshaven miners, dapper gamblers and swindlers, bursts of profanity and gunfire, and the stale fumes of tobacco and alcohol.

The newspaper, always among the earliest to arrive, usually announced, "If we strike it rich, what a town you will see here." Long before the residents legitimatized a place with a name, they had platted a townsite and promoters were selling lots for $2,000. And what names these settlements had—Whiskey Bar, Skunk Gulch, Hell's Delight. The clatter of carpenters' hammers notified one and all that cultural institutions were on the way—saloons, hotels, and stores—just as soon as more green lumber and hurdy-gurdy girls could be freighted in.

Life was unsettled, animated by a nervous, crude energy. In the crowded streets men argued over ore samples, prospectors compared location notices and assay certificates, and bummers claiming to be pioneers of '49 cadged drinks from strangers in return for tales of the diggings. Men from the ends of the earth mingled and swapped rumors of the latest discoveries.

Entertainment of the nonviolent type was scarce. One miner dolefully declared, "There's nothing to do but hang around the saloons, get drunk and fight, and lie out in the snow and die." To men so lacking in ordinary diversions, the theater became a necessity. Although it could not match the action of the gaming table, the excitement of cockfights and bullbaitings, or the gaiety of the saloon, it did mark a welcome change from the monotony of camp life.

The outstanding exception to the rule of crude goldfield towns was San Francisco. Perhaps it was different because it did not owe its existence to the precious yellow metal. Founded in 1835 by the Mexicans as the village of Yerba Buena, and the site of a Spanish presidio and mission as early as 1776, it had its saloon and waterfront districts, but it also had fine residential areas, established mercantile firms, and an air of permanence. Yet it was never the same after the gold rush.

Crime and violence were common in mining camps, but nowhere more common than in San Francisco. Australian criminals, called "Sydney Ducks," fugitives from Eastern justice, and ordinary thugs mingled with gamblers and petty thieves. Life was not safe even on the main thoroughfares. Finally, in 1851, the respectable citizens, seeing laws broken with impunity, formed a vigilance association and began dispensing impromptu justice. The process had to be repeated again in 4 years, after which the city again became comparatively safe.

Far from being confined to the cities, criminal activity thrived in the goldfields. Because great sums of bullion were shipped over deserted trails, stage robberies were frequent. Claim jumping, holdups, and murders were common hazards. By nature many of the men who came to the goldfields were drifters, and the law had been left far behind. Without domestic influences and often depressed

Vigilante parade in 1856. Maintenance of law and order in San Francisco during gold-rush days required extra-legal measures. Courtesy, New-York Historical Society.

by poor living conditions, disappointment, and bad liquor, men met insult or injustice, fancied or real, with a knife blade or pistol.

## MINING JUSTICE

Because crime and violence were so widespread and the land from which the miners extracted gold was public domain, they had to pass their own laws. Not until after the Civil War did the U.S. Government attempt to govern the staking of claims or appoint officers to enforce simple justice. Under these circumstances the forty-niners took the law into their own hands. Meeting in open session at each mining camp or district, they passed miners' codes. As worked out in California, these codes were based in part on Mexican and Spanish mining laws, in part on American frontier customs. Each mining community had its miners' association, which met when the need arose. The association established rules regarding the size and registration of claims, elected community officials, and settled property disputes.

The size of a claim varied according to the district code, but ordinarily it was 50 by 100 feet. Sometimes it was as small as 10 feet square. The discoverer was entitled to a double claim; all others to one each. All claims had to be worked to be held. The water essential to placer mining belonged to the man who used it first, even though he might divert it through a sluice and leave others farther downstream waterless. When claim jumpers became too bold or criminals resorted to violence, the miners tried them in open court. With no jails—and little patience—they meted out prompt and simple justice to those they declared guilty. The types of sentences were few: Hanging, flogging, or expulsion.

### END OF THE BOOM

In 1849 the mines of California yielded $10 million. But before long the forty-niners depleted the rich placer, or surface, deposits and so thoroughly prospected every inch of ground that the chance of finding new deposits was remote. For most of the mining camps the end was oblivion—some sooner, some later. Miners, seeking new El Dorados, moved out on foot with only their picks and bedrolls or loaded their possessions onto ore wagons; the editors took their handpresses; and the merchants their stock of goods and iron cashboxes. In his last issue a California newspaper editor wrote the epitaph of a thousand Western mining camps: "The discovery of the rich mines on the other side of the mountains has carried off a large proportion of our most enterprising businessmen . . . and we have determined to pull up stakes and follow them."

In 1852 the gold yield in California reached a peak of more than $81 million. After that time, when costly underground mining and surface processing of the gold-bearing quartz became a necessity, mining became an industry that required a large capital investment and attracted speculators and Eastern investors. Nevertheless in 1853 and 1854 production dropped to about $68 million per year and during the period 1865–85 ranged from $15 to $20 million per year.

### EFFECT ON CALIFORNIA AGRICULTURE

When the miner, the saloonkeeper, the gambler, and the dance-hall girl had departed, California was far from depopulated. It was left in the hands of more permanent residents. The prospector, and those who lived directly off his labor, were transients, but the farmers and ranchers who fed them had established deep roots. Finding the soil good, the rainfall plentiful, and the climate mild, newcomers shared with older residents in inheriting the country they had come to feed—and they stayed to help build a stable State.

Ranching and farming in California predated the gold rush. The early history of the cattle industry in California was similar to that of Texas, likewise a one-time Spanish province. The first Spanish colonists, who arrived at San Diego in 1769, had brought cattle with them, and before the end of the century nearly a million head of Longhorns roamed the hills of southern California. At first they were the exclusive property of the missions, but after the Mexican Government secularized the missions in 1833 ranching became the major economic activity. Between then and 1856, during California's "golden age" of the cattle industry, the great ranchos prospered. The cattleman was an all-powerful political figure, a quasi-feudal ruler whose life of ease resembled that of the ante bellum planter of the South. The *rancheros* solved the problem of marketing their vast herds through the hide and

California *vaquero* at work in 1841 near San Jose Mission. Californians had been ranching for more than half a century before the United States acquired the region. Courtesy, Bancroft Library, University of California.

tallow trade. By the time of the gold rush, they had exported 5 million hides on "Boston" ships.

When the gold rush began in 1848, the ranchers of California found a ready market for their meat, not just the hides and tallow. The tremendous demand for food, springing from the explosive increase in population, greatly enhanced the prosperity of the *rancheros*. Drovers moved thousands of cattle the 500 miles from the vicinity of Los Angeles to San Francisco and the diggings in the Sierra Nevada foothills. By 1856, however, the large imports of cattle and sheep, mainly from Texas and New Mexico, coupled with the increase in local cattle ranches for fattening and breeding, broke the market in California and brought an end to the "golden age" of the cattle industry.

Agriculture had not been practiced on a wide scale in California before the gold rush. Despite the successful agricultural programs of the missions, most Mexican *rancheros* neglected the cultivation of crops, as did also most of the Americans who arrived in California before the Mexican War. The exceptions were almost always highly successful. Mariano Vallejo, who in 1835 founded Sonoma, grew grain, fruits, and vegetables north of San Francisco Bay. By 1840 he had about 500 acres under cultivation. Some vineyards were also located at Los Angeles and small orchards in the Santa Clara Valley and elsewhere.

The first American farmer of note in California was James Marsh. In 1838 he purchased Los Medanos (or Meganos) Ranch from José Noriega. Lying between Mount Diablo and present Brentwood, the ranch was the first in the San Joaquin Valley to achieve success. Marsh's chief occupation was cattle ranching, but he engaged in some farming.

The real founder of American agriculture in California was John A. Sutter, a Swiss immigrant who in 1840 obtained from Governor Alvarado a land grant on the east side of the Sacramento River. Sutter constructed a fort and founded the colony of New Helvetia, the forerunner of Sacramento. Though engaging in many activities—trading, trapping, distilling, tanning, milling, and ranching—he was primarily a farmer. He constructed a small irrigation system to water his crops and employed Indians, Hawaiian Islanders, and newly arrived Americans to work his farm. The parties of American immigrants arriving in California prior to the Mexican

War made Sutter's Fort their main objective. Sutter either employed them or aided them in establishing their own farms in the Sacramento Valley. By 1846 the valley was becoming a "little America," where Spanish was not spoken and Mexican officials seldom appeared.

Modern farm in the San Joaquin Valley, California. Irrigation has always been a mainstay of Western agriculture.

These Americans who settled in California during the Mexican period became acquainted with irrigated farming. Their lands were rich, but had little water. Great labor was involved in building dams and digging ditches. After the land was cleared, it had to be leveled for proper drainage. The Eastern type of plowing was not satisfactory, and eventually a new plow, the two-way sulky plow, was devised to allow a farmer to plow across a field and then back again along the same furrow.

Thus by the time of the gold rush a solid agricultural base had been established in California. The miners poured in and kept coming. By the end of 1849 the population was 100,000; 3 years later it was 250,000. Prices for food spiraled ever upward. Soon grain growing came to be more profitable than gold mining. Some of the wiser forty-niners bought ranches with gold they had extracted and began plowing and planting.

Notable among these miners-turned-farmer was John Bidwell, who after panning gold on the Middle Fork of the Feather River purchased Rancho Chico. He developed this ranch into one of the most successful agricultural establishments in the State. The estate eventually included 20 subranches, each devoted to a particular product, ranging from wheat to fruit and from sheep to turkeys. Before Bidwell's death, the fruit and nut trees numbered 65,276, and the annual production of wheat sometimes ran as high as 5½ million pounds.

During the 1850's grain growing spread southward into the San Joaquin Valley, and the era of the bonanza wheat ranches began. The valley was one of the greatest centers of irrigated agriculture in the world during the 1850's. The first to undertake extensive irrigation there was Edward Fitzgerald Beale, at El Tejon Ranch, who irrigated about 1,900 acres of wheat.

Wheat production in California was insufficient to meet the demands of a rapidly growing population until about 1854, and by 1860 wheat had become an important export. The expanding wheat acreage created a market for improved agricultural machines, such as the Stockton gang plow and the California combined harvester-thresher. Stockton became a manufacturing center for farm equipment and machinery.

During the gold-rush years cattle, sheep, wheat, and barley provided the greatest agricultural earnings. Yet farmers began experimenting with a wide variety of crops and proving that little-known ones could also be grown. For example, Benjamin D. Wilson, who owned a farm near Los Angeles, planted many varieties of fruit and grain, and in 1854 reported that all produced abundantly. He listed among his successes grapes, oranges, pears, apricots, peaches, apples, almonds, English walnuts, cherries, figs, quinces, and plums. The gold rush intensified the need for fresh vegetables and fruit to supply the thousands who were pouring in. A 150-acre garden plot near San Jose netted its owner $175,000 in profits the first year supplying vegetables to the inhabitants of San Francisco and Sacramento.

William Wolfskill, a former trapper, planted the first privately owned orange grove in California. In 1841 he transplanted trees from the abandoned gardens of San Gabriel Mission to a plot where the Los Angeles Union Railroad Station now stands. Eventually he expanded this grove to about 2,500 trees. A neighbor, Matthew Keller, imported orange trees from Hawaii and planted them. But the citrus industry grew slowly in California because of the limited market. Oranges were a novelty to most of the miners, who could not be induced to include them regularly in their diet.

Some of the forty-niners were foreigners who brought with them both knowledge and samples of crops that previously had not been widely produced in the United States. Most of the Spanish missions had vineyards and produced wine, but this fact meant little to the early American farmers in California. However, Swiss, Italian, and Hungarian miners quickly recognized the potential. Agoston Haraszthy, a Hungarian, came to California in 1851 to mine, but became more interested in the soil and climate than in the goldfields. Importing several types of European grapevines, he found that they produced fruit of excellent quality. At first he experimented with raisin grapes, but his most popular importation was the Zinfandel red-wine grape, which grew well in Napa and Sonoma Counties. By 1859 the number of grapevines in California totaled 125,000, and the foundation had been laid for a future industry. The pioneer of commercial nut raising was also a foreigner, a Frenchman named Felix Gillet, who experimented successfully with English walnuts, filberts, and almonds on a small farm near Nevada City.

EFFECT ON WESTERN AGRICULTURE

The agricultural effect of the gold rush went far beyond California. The arrival of more and more gold seekers swiftly exhausted the capacity of California's ranchers to supply enough meat, and the price of beef rose higher and higher. To meet the demand, first cattle, then sheep were driven in from Texas and even from the Middle West. One enterprising Texan who early realized that the gold rush would create a good market for beef was well rewarded for his perceptiveness. In 1848 T. J. Trimmer drove 500 head of rangy Longhorns from Washington County, Tex., to California by way of El Paso and Cooke's wagon road; the gaunt steers sold for $100 each. News of the high profits caused many Texans to disregard the hazards of the trail. Almost overnight Houston and San Antonio became jumping-off points for the California drives. By 1853 cowboys had driven an estimated 62,000 cattle from Texas to the goldfields. Sheep raisers in New Mexico also hurried to share in the golden wealth of California.

The tremendous demand for food by the miners quickly exceeded the capacity of pioneer California farmers as well as that of the ranchers. Farm commodities had to be imported from Oregon, Hawaii, and even British Columbia, whose agricultural economies were enhanced.

Indirectly the gold rush also stimulated irrigated agriculture in Utah. The Mormon sect, fleeing persecution in the Middle West, arrived in 1847 at the Great Salt Lake and immediately set to work constructing dams and irrigation ditches. By the end of the year more than 4,000 of them had settled near the southern end of Great Salt Lake, and Brigham Young spent the winter urging others to come. He told them to bring all kinds of "choice seeds, grains, vegetables, fruits, shrubbery, trees, and vines."

The Mormons established a new kind of farm frontier. Most of their early settlements were in communal groups, and their work was cooperative. The church allotted lands, and water was used on a cooperative basis. For these reasons the Mormons were more successful than many others who moved into the dry lands of the West; and the thousands who traveled to California by way of the central trails, which passed directly through the Mormon country, created a ready market for farm produce.

## Spread of the Mining Frontier

Almost as soon as the California gold rush got underway, prospectors began extending the search for new bonanzas. Eventually their hunting grounds became the entire West. For the true prospector, any other life was unthinkable. He was imbued with a feverish restlessness. For him, as for the mountain man who had preceded him, the settled and secure life was boring beyond toleration. With a washing pan, a grubstake, and endless hope, he climbed the mountains and tramped the deserts. He panned each promising stream and anxiously scanned each outcropping of rock for a telltale glint. The trial-and-error experience of California supplied the knowledge, experience, machines, and equipment needed to exploit other fields. Ex-California miners sought and found new El Dorados in the remote parts of the Rockies, the Great Basin, and the Colorado and Columbia Plateaus.

During the 1850's, while the prospectors were feverishly ranging over the hills and up and down the rivers searching for gold, politicians excitedly paced the floors of Congress as the storm clouds of the slavery and secession issues gathered over the Republic. Logic and reason yielded to inflamed passions and emotions, and ·honorable men of both the North and South turned to the sword and the gun to settle their differences. But in the West the thought of quick riches prevailed in the minds of most men, who did not lay aside the pick and shovel for deadlier weapons. California and Colorado sent token forces, but by and large it was business as usual in the goldfields. The pursuit of mineral wealth continued unabated.

When the war ended, the triumphant North did not resume its former unhurried pace. The era of frenzied finance and industrialization had arrived. Gold and silver were needed to underwrite the cost.

## ARIZONA—APACHES, SILVER, AND COPPER

The first region where ex-Californians struck it rich was the Southwest. The mineral resources of the region, unlike those of California, had been known for centuries to the Indians, Spaniards, and Mexicans. In 1825 the copper mines at Santa Rita, in the present State of New Mexico, had been leased to an American fur trapper, Sylvester Pattie. And rumors of more exciting metals—of gold and silver—had persisted from the days of the conquistadors; every locality boasted at least one "lost mine." Despite the hostility of the Apaches, the rumors continued. In 1850 the U.S. Army constructed Fort Yuma at the junction of the Gila and Colorado Rivers, and 3 years later the Gadsden Purchase added the southern parts of present Arizona and New Mexico to the United States.

Even before the United States officially took possession of the area of the Gadsden Purchase in 1856, Americans began to comb it for riches. Charles D. Poston, who came from San Francisco in 1854, and Herman Ehrenberg discovered gold and silver deposits in the mountains around Tubac, in present Arizona. They also came across the Ajo copper mines and reopened them. These mines, which portended the great mineral wealth of Arizona, had been worked by the Indians, Spaniards, and Mexicans, but had been abandoned in the 1840's. The Americans worked them from 1854 until 1861, the ore being shipped to Wales for smelting. The mines then lay idle until the 20th century.

In 1860 Sylvester Mowry, an ex-Army lieutenant and West Pointer, made a strike in the nearby Santa Ana Mountains. Soon Arizona, which became a Territory separate from New Mexico in 1863, attracted more than its share of the criminal element. Tucson, the center of mining operations, became known as the "paradise of devils," a designation not lightly won in the mining era of the West. The miners had as neighbors the fearsome Apaches, led by Cochise, who in 1861 went on the warpath and forced the miners to abandon the district temporarily.

The capture of southern Arizona by the Confederates at the outbreak of the Civil War, in 1861, temporarily ended mining, but the following year Federal troops reoccupied the area and mining activities resumed. Before the war ended, mining was further stimulated by gold strikes near Prescott and Wickenburg. Silver discoveries in 1876 near Superior and Globe caused a new silver boom. This was given special impetus in 1877 by Ed Schieffelin's bonanza strike, in the Apache-infested San Pedro Valley, which resulted in the founding of the colorful and lawless town of Tombstone.

Although Arizona gained national prominence from its production of silver, copper proved to be its most important mineral resource. The mining of copper began in 1871 in the Morenci district of eastern Arizona, and in 1877 in the Bisbee and Jerome districts. Bisbee also had gold and silver resources. In 1878 prospectors discovered copper at Globe. By the 1880's—when the coming of the railroads opened a new era in Southwestern copper mining—two copper industry giants, the Calumet and Arizona Mining Company and the Phelps-Dodge company, were production leaders.

COLORADO—"PIKE'S PEAK OR BUST"

The small initial strikes in Arizona were insignificant when compared with the discoveries in Colorado and Nevada. Gold and sil-

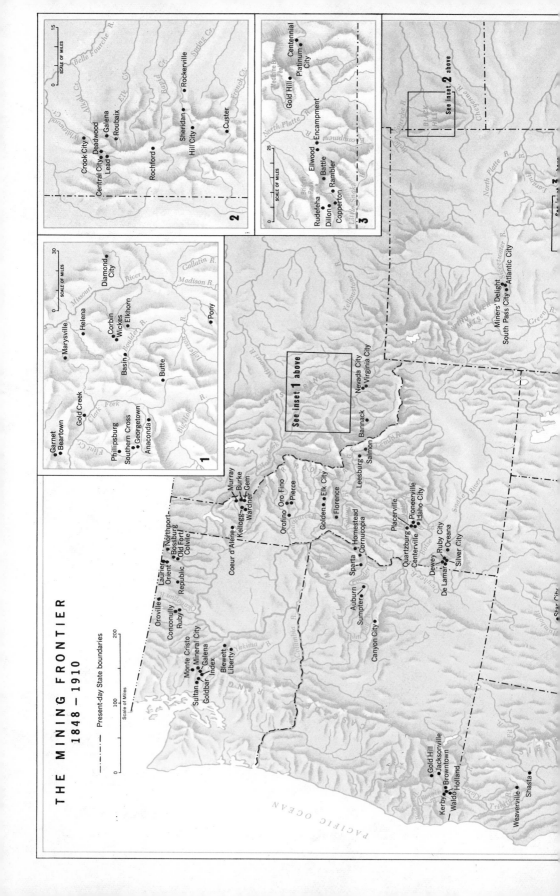

# THE MINING FRONTIER
## 1848 – 1910

–·–·– Present-day State boundaries

Scale of Miles
0    100    200

**Inset 1**

SCALE OF MILES
0    30

Diamond City
Marysville
Helena
Corbin
Wickes
Elkhorn
Basin
Gold Creek
Garnet
Beartown
Phillipsburg
Southern Cross
Georgetown
Anaconda
Butte
Pony

Missouri River
Gallatin R.
Madison R.
Boulder R.
Clark Fork
Flint Cr.
Big Hole R.

**Inset 2**

SCALE OF MILES
0    15

Crook City
Central City
Deadwood
Lead
Galena
Roubaix
Rockerville
Sheridan
Hill City
Rochford
Custer

Belle Fourche R.
Bald Cr.
Elk Cr.
Spring Cr.
French Cr.
Whitewood Cr.

**Inset 3**

SCALE OF MILES
0    25

Centennial
Platinum City
Gold Hill
Encampment
Ellwood
Battle
Rambler
Rudefeha
Dillon
Copperton

Medicine Bow Peak
North Platte R.
Encampment R.
Bridger Pass
Little Snake R.

See inset 1 above

See inset 2 above

See inset 3 above

Nevada City
Virginia City
Bannack
Leesburg
Salmon
Homestead
Cornucopia
Sparta
Golden
Elk City
Florence
Placerville
Pioneerville
Idaho City
Quartzburg
Centerville
Dewey
Ruby City
De Lamar
Oreana
Silver City
Auburn
Sumpter
Canyon City
Murray
Burke
Gem
Wardner
Kellogg
Orofino
Oro Fino
Pierce
Coeur d'Alene
Northport
Bossburg
Old Fort
Colville
Laurier
Orient
Republic
Oroville
Conconully
Ruby
Monte Cristo
Mineral City
Index
Sultan
Goldbar
Galena
Blewett
Liberty
Gold Hill
Jacksonville
Browntown
Kerby
Waldo
Holland
Weaverville
Shasta

Miners' Delight
South Pass City
Atlantic City

PACIFIC OCEAN

Yellowstone R.
North Platte R.
Green R.
Sweetwater R.
Wind River Mts.
Snake River
Salmon R.
Clearwater R.
Columbia R.
Rogue R.
Trinity R.

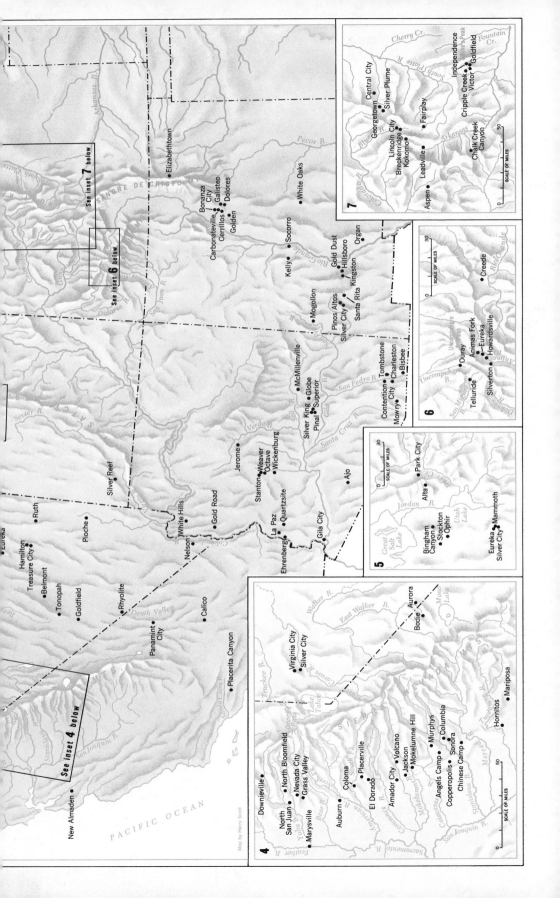

Map by Harry Scott

PACIFIC OCEAN

Cherry Cr.

Fountain Cr.

7

Georgetown • Central City
Silver Plume •
Lincoln City
Breckenridge • Kokomo
Leadville •
Aspen •

Independence
Cripple Creek • Goldfield
Victor •
Fairplay •
Chalk Creek Canyon

Arkansas R.

Blue R.

Colorado R.

SCALE OF MILES
50

6

Ouray • Animas Fork
Telluride • Silverton • Eureka • Howardsville

Creede •

Rio Grande

Uncompahgre R.
San Miguel R.
Dolores R.

SCALE OF MILES
0     30

5

Great Salt Lake

Jordan R.

Utah Lake

Alta •     • Park City
Bingham Canyon •
Stockton • Ophir
Eureka • Mammoth
Silver City

SCALE OF MILES
0     30

4

Walker R.

East Walker R.

Mono Lake

Aurora •
Bodie •

Virginia City •
Silver City •

Downieville •
North San Juan • Nevada City
Marysville • Grass Valley

Auburn •
Coloma •
El Dorado • Placerville
Amador City • Volcano
Jackson • Mokelumne Hill
Angels Camp • Columbia
Copperopolis • Sonora
Chinese Camp

Murphys •

Hornitos •
Mariposa •

Feather R.
Yuba R.
Bear R.
American R.
Cosumnes R.
Mokelumne R.
Calaveras R.
Stanislaus R.
Tuolumne R.
Merced R.
San Joaquin R.
Sacramento R.

Lake Tahoe
Carson R.
Truckee R.

SIERRA NEVADA

SCALE OF MILES
0     50

Elizabethtown •

Bonanza City • Galisteo
Carbonateville • Dolores
Cerrillos •
Golden •

White Oaks •

Kelly • Socorro
Gold Dust
Mogollon • Hillsboro
Pinos Altos • Organ
Silver City • Kingston
Santa Rita

SANGRE DE CRISTO MTS.

Pecos R.
Rio Grande
Gila R.
San Juan R.
Dolores R.

McMillenville •
Globe
Silver King • Superior
Pinal

Tombstone •
Contention City • Charleston
Mowry • Bisbee

Jerome •

Stanton • Weaver
Octave • Wickenburg

Ajo •

Gila City
La Paz •
Ehrenberg • Quartzsite

White Hills •
Gold Road •
Nelson •

Silver Reef •

Pioche •

Ruth •
Eureka •
Hamilton •
Treasure City • Belmont
Tonopah •
Goldfield •
Rhyolite •

Panamint City •

Calico •

Placerita Canyon •

Death Valley

New Almaden •

See inset 7 below
See inset 6 below
See inset 4 below

Verde R.
Santa Cruz R.
San Pedro R.
Gila R.
Colorado R.
Santa Clara R.
Sevier R.
South Platte R.
Arkansas R.
Rio Grande

Pino's Peak

ver continued to be found all over the West for more than half a
century following the strike in California, but the most exciting
discoveries were made within a decade. In the summer of 1858
several groups of prospectors—some veterans from Georgia and
California and others who were greenhorns from Kansas and Missouri—were working along the Continental Divide in western
Kansas Territory when some of them struck gold near Pike's Peak.
Before winter set in they founded Denver City.

News of the Pike's Peak discovery soon found its way eastward to
the Mississippi Valley, where the Panic of 1857 insured its welcome. Accounts of the Colorado strike spread like wildfire through
the border settlements—and with the same effect as the news
from Sutter's mill a decade earlier. Poverty-ridden frontiersmen,
unemployed workers, and unsuccessful businessmen eagerly
scanned exaggerated newspaper accounts of the new El Dorado.
Pike's Peak was only 700 miles from the Missouri River and
required no grueling trek over mountains and deserts as had the
California trip. The rush to Pike's Peak in the spring of 1859 was
one of the wildest in the Nation's history.

Gold seekers used almost every type of conveyance to get to the
scene of the strike. Some used the heavy prairie schooner wagons,
others the light carriages of the border country; some went by
horseback and carried their goods on pack animals; others, copying
the Mormon migration, pushed two-wheeled handcarts. By the end
of the summer many thousands of "fifty-niners" had passed through
Kansas and Nebraska en route to the mountains and the gold.
These enthusiastic pilgrims contributed one of the famous slogans
of U.S. history: "Pike's Peak or Bust"—crudely lettered on their
packs and wagon canvas.

When the emigrants arrived, they found that the newspapers and
guidebooks had been somewhat deceiving. Panning every stream,
chopping away at every rock outcropping, they found little. In the
jargon of the times, they had been "humbugged." One of the greatest booms in American history gave way to one of the quickest
busts. By midsummer of 1859 half of the would-be miners who had
rushed to Colorado were back home. Below the hopeful slogan on
the white canvas of the prairie schooner appeared a new one in
bolder, darker letters: "Busted, by God"—an eloquent epitaph to
one of the major fiascos of the frontier.

Ironically, soon after most of the disillusioned "fifty-niners" had returned eastward, prospectors made major gold strikes. The early boom failed not because of a lack of gold but because of its elusive location. The placer dust, panned from creek bottoms, soon played out. The rich quartz lodes from which the dust had broken loose were located upstream. These lodes, however, were so refractory that mining required major outlays of both capital and labor, which only companies could provide. As one prospector said, while watching the diggings and operations at a stamp mill, "Hell, I expected to see them backing up carts and shoveling it [gold] in." But stamp mills and tunnels were signs of the future in mining.

Prospectors in Cunningham Gulch, Colorado Territory, in 1875. They lived a rugged and lonely life. Courtesy, National Archives.

The second great Colorado boom occurred in the late 1870's, when prospectors made fabulous silver strikes at Leadville and Aspen. Colorado and silver became synonymous for a time, and the "Bonanza Kings" crashed the jealously guarded portals of the U.S. Senate. In the 1890's a third boom occurred. Gold discoveries on Cripple Creek—one of the richest of all goldfields—attracted the attention of the entire world.

NEVADA—THE COMSTOCK BONANZA

In 1858, the year of the Pike's Peak discovery, prospectors ranging over the eastern slope of the Sierra Nevada above the Carson River Valley stumbled upon a concentration of minerals rich beyond all belief—the Comstock Lode. Named for one of the discoverers and founders of the Ophir Mine, Henry T. P. Comstock, the lode did not at first seem so promising. Those lucky enough to obtain "feet" in the area were hindered in their attempts to extract gold by a blackish substance that encased the yellow metal. Sent to California to be assayed, the "black stuff" proved to be almost pure silver.

Bars of silver from the Ophir Mine, when displayed in San Francisco, brought on the usual craze to "see the elephant." By the fall of 1859 thousands jammed the tortuous roads over the mountains to Nevada en route to the Washoe District, as the area of discovery came to be called. Carson City, just off the California Trail, and Virginia City, at the site of the Ophir Mine, became leading mining centers.

The newcomers were soon frustrated. Individual miners had little opportunity. The minerals were locked in quartz veins, which could be worked only with expensive machinery. Yet scores of promoters and stock salesmen peddled "feet" in imaginary mines and sold shares in companies that did not exist. Mark Twain was one of those who arrived in Carson City soon after the initial strike and who traded "feet" with the best of them.

As capital flowed in and companies began operations, the promoters realized their wildest dreams. Less than a dozen of the 3,000 mines staked out ever produced, but their profits were such as to sustain the hopes of all, and to provide Virginia City with a group of newly rich citizens whose antics were as legendary as the profits of the mines. Ornate mansions rose from the desert hills; more than 20 theaters provided cultural relaxation. Meanwhile, every new discovery launched a period of wild trading in "feet."

In their efforts to develop the discoveries the miners altered the face of western Nevada considerably. They laid out roads over the mountains to California, for everything had to be freighted in from the outside. They almost denuded the eastern slopes of the

Decaying mine remains are scattered today over the mountain slopes of Nevada's Comstock Lode, within sight of the Sierra.

Sierra and the shores of Lake Tahoe of timber for buildings, fuel, flumes, shafts, and drifts. They hauled in machinery to construct quartz mills and formed express companies to bring in supplies.

Nevada miners were responsible for significant advances in engineering techniques. Early mining at the Comstock Lode was close to the surface, quartz being collected from open or shallow shafts and horizontal tunnels. Philip Deidesheimer, a German engineer, originated a process that made possible the mining of quartz lodes at greater width and depth. The Deidesheimer system, used throughout the Comstock, attracted the attention of European mining engineers.

Until 1873 small companies worked the lode. Then the Consolidated Virginia Company, boring straight through the flinty mountain rock, struck a lode 54 feet wide and filled with both gold and silver—the Big Bonanza, probably the richest single find in mining history. Big companies gained the ascendancy.

Until 1880 the two prime characteristics of mining in Nevada, especially in the Comstock Lode area, were wildcat speculation and expensive litigation. In this atmosphere of frantic financial manipulation and unscrupulous rigging of the market, the "Kings of the Comstock" struggled for power, bought and sold seats in the U.S. Senate, and brought ruin to the Bank of California. Speculative investment in San Francisco reached a new high. As the hectic trad-

Pioneer City, first gold camp in Montana Territory, was almost a ghost town by 1883. Like other mining boomtowns, many of which were abandoned as rapidly as they were founded, its glory faded after the nuggets were gone. Photograph by F. Jay Haynes. Courtesy, Alfred A. Knopf, Inc., and The Haynes Foundation.

ing, and prospectors joined others who trekked to Montana across the mountains and deserts from California, Oregon, and Colorado. Before long Montana, which 3 years earlier had been uninhabited by white men, had a population of 30,000.

The miners' appetites for gold were whetted in 1864, when an ex-Georgia prospector named John Cowan, who was fruitlessly panning his way down the Missouri, decided to make one more attempt at a spot he called Last Chance Gulch. The result is history—and legend. In a few months Helena was founded on the site. Nearby were a dozen gulches containing rich gold deposits. The town was strategically located on the wagon route from Fort Benton to Bannack and Virginia City. Rapidly achieving a position of eminence, it became one of the most important cities of the mining era.

Mining in Montana entered a new phase in 1874, when an Idaho miner discovered silver at Butte. Here lay one of the world's richest mineral deposits—an area less than 5 miles square that eventually produced between $2 and $3 billion in mineral wealth.

ing continued without any regulation, the wildly fluctuating market resulted in the rise and fall of many fortunes. But the Comstock Lode was not inexhaustible. In 1875 Nevada's mining stocks had a value of $300 million; 5 years later less than $7 million. Thereafter mining was lethargic until the Tonopah rush in 1900.

But the effects of the Comstock Lode on the monetary world were permanent. The lode poured wealth into San Francisco and resulted in the establishment of a stock exchange, as well as the launching of the careers of a group of silver kings, which included James G. Fair, John W. Mackay, James C. Flood, and William S. O'Brien. The output of the Nevada mines strengthened the credit of the United States during the crucial years of the Civil War, stimulated freighting, and accelerated construction of the transcontinental railroad and helped determine its route. The effects were also international. The alteration in the ratio of gold and silver probably contributed to the demonetization of silver by European nations.

## MONTANA—LAST CHANCE GULCH AND THE COPPER KINGS

The first prospectors in present Montana crossed the Continental Divide from the Idaho country and worked the headwaters of the Missouri River. In 1862 Granville Stuart, who later became an influential Montana rancher and whose father had been a fortyniner, struck minor deposits of gold. When Colorado miners learned the news, a small rush to Montana ensued. Large parties of ex-Colorado miners, bound for the Salmon River area of Idaho, hearing of the discovery, changed their plans and prospected along the Beaverhead River in Montana. William Eads and John White made the first substantial gold discovery in Montana in 1862 on Grasshopper Creek, a tributary of the Beaverhead. Soon 500 miners rushed to the site and set up a mining camp they called Bannack. The following spring prospectors made another and richer strike 70 miles to the east at Alder Gulch. There Virginia City sprang up. The gulch yielded $30 million in gold during the next 3 years.

The rush to Montana country in 1863, following the glowing reports from Bannack and Virginia City, was of the usual sensational proportions. The Snake River camps in Idaho were declin-

Butte prospered initially on the basis of its silver lodes, but along with the rest of Montana it was not on a healthy economic basis. The mines were scattered, transportation was poor, and many of the miners were leaving the region to join the rush to the Black Hills.

The strike of an Irish-born opportunist, Marcus Daly, precipitated the greatest phase of Montana's mining history—the copper era. In 1881 Daly persuaded capitalists to invest in his Anaconda Mine at Butte and began digging for silver. Disappointed when his shaft struck copper instead of silver, he persisted in his effort to locate a silver vein and finally, in 1883, struck a copper vein 50 feet wide and of unparalleled richness. Butte gained an international reputation as the "richest hill on earth." In addition to attracting miners from throughout the West, the high wages paid for labor brought workers from Ireland, England, Wales, Germany, and Italy.

Wars ensued between the copper kings of Butte similar to those between gold and silver kings elsewhere. Extreme wealth induced a frenzied struggle for even more wealth and political power. The accomplishments of Daly, who became the head of one of the world's most powerful monopolies, were similar to those of other noted benefactors who amassed fortunes from the mines. Daly was a founder and builder of cities. He mined coal for his furnaces, and acquired huge tracts of timber to supply lumber for his mines; he established banks, powerplants, and irrigation systems. And he was a force in Montana politics. His final achievement was combining a series of lumber and mining companies into an industrial giant called the Amalgamated Copper Company.

The wars between the copper kings alternated with labor battles. The men who worked the mines of Butte were also influential in State politics. As the city rose quickly to the position of the world's copper metropolis, a strong movement developed among the miners for organization. This culminated in 1893 in the founding of the militant Western Federation of Miners. Perhaps to a greater degree than in any other State, the mining industry of Montana, centered at Butte, influenced directly or indirectly every major industry in the State.

### Idaho—wealth in the wilderness

Another source of mineral wealth was the Idaho region, which became a Territory in 1863 and was admitted to the Union as a State in 1890. Late in 1859 an Indian trader, Capt. Elias D. Pierce, while prospecting in Nez Percé country along the Clearwater River just north of the old Oregon Trail, discovered gold. Soon reports of the find reached Portland. Miners from the region flocked to the diggings, despite some hostility on the part of the Nez Percés, and the mining camps of Pierce, Oro Fino, Elk City, and Florence sprang up. As the rush gained momentum, steamers began service up the Columbia and Snake Rivers from Portland to Lewiston, which developed into the principal distributing center for the region.

The miners next made strikes along the Salmon River and in mid-1862 discovered rich placer deposits in the Boise River Basin of southwestern Idaho. Within 2 years more than 15,000 people were residing in the latter district. And the next year prospectors found silver on the Owyhee River around Silver City.

Placer mining in the Coeur d'Alene country of Idaho Territory, 1884. Miners directed a stream of water through the "Long Tom," then shoveled in raw earth. Photograph by F. Jay Haynes. Courtesy, Alfred A. Knopf, Inc., and The Haynes Foundation.

Reaching the rugged Idaho wilderness was a formidable chore, even for hardy Western prospectors. They came up the Missouri to Fort Benton, or they steamed up the Columbia to Lewiston or Walla Walla. The Mullan Road, constructed between 1859 and 1862 as a military road between Forts Benton and Walla Walla, eased the problem of transporting mining supplies and helped open the entire region to settlement. To safeguard the miners from the hostile Indians of that region, the U.S. Army built Fort Lapwai near Lewiston and Fort Boise near Boise.

Mining in Idaho had a renaissance late in the century. In 1885 Noah S. Kellogg was chasing after a runaway mule in the Coeur d'Alene district of Idaho. Pausing to rest, he looked down and discovered that he was sitting on a chunk of almost pure silver. By 1905 the mine had yielded $250 million and created more than 50 millionaires. The workers who came to operate the mills and mines provided the region with a permanent population.

Violence between miners' unions and the mineowners, not restricted to the Coeur d'Alene district, broke out there in 1892 when the union dynamited the mines in retaliation for the importation of strikebreakers. Another dynamiting in 1899 caused Gov. Frank Steunenberg to declare a state of insurrection and to obtain Federal troops from President McKinley. More than a thousand miners were arrested and the unions almost destroyed. But despite the labor turmoil the wealth of the mines at Coeur d'Alene and Kellogg transformed the region.

OREGON AND WASHINGTON—MINERS
AND THE INDIAN THREAT

Although less spectacular than the earlier strikes in the West, those in Oregon and Washington attracted many miners. During the California rush, numerous Oregonians had joined the forty-niners, and many of them returned later with capital to develop the resources of their area. In the early 1850's prospectors began searching just across the California border, in southwestern Oregon Territory, but for a time irate Indians constituted a danger. Nevertheless in 1851 a strike was made at a site first known as Sailors' Diggings and later as Waldo. Successive strikes occurred in Jackson and Josephine Counties. The district flourished, and Jacksonville became the trading center. In 1861 miners opened the eastern Oregon mining district, in the vicinity of the Blue and Wallowa Mountains, and prospectors continued to make discoveries there in the 1870's and 1880's. Most of the mines in Oregon were comparatively small, and the rushes were modest in size—as were the returns.

In present Washington a strike was made in 1855 near Fort Colvile, on the east bank of the Columbia. But conflicts with the Indians were frequent, and most of the region was unsafe for prospectors for at least 3 years. When peace was finally restored, gold seekers thoroughly searched the area. They found little to repay them for their efforts.

Mining activity increased elsewhere in Washington during the 1880's as prospectors turned their attention from placer to lode mining. They discovered silver deposits in the Colville Mountains and along Salmon Creek and founded the Ruby Mining District. The discoveries in Washington and nearby Idaho caused Spokane to prosper and to become the metropolis of the "inland empire" of the Northwest.

### UTAH—GOLD AND BINGHAM CANYON

Agriculture in Utah Territory had early profited from the mining booms of the West, especially that in California, but little mineral wealth had been found there. Then in 1862 Col. Patrick E. Connor assumed command of the District of Utah. Convinced that the Mormons were disloyal, he thought that a mining rush would increase the non-Mormon population. In 1863, after soldiers and prospectors had discovered deposits of silver, lead, and copper in Bingham Canyon, Connor published a newspaper, the *Union Vidette*, which announced to one and all that the mountains were rich in minerals. He offered Government protection to parties of prospectors.

Under such a stimulus a rush started, a number of other strikes were made, and several mining camps arose. The town of Alta, in Little Cottonwood Canyon, gained almost as much fame from its Bucket of Blood and Gold Miner's Daughter saloons as from its Emma Mine.

Only a few Mormons joined the scramble to the diggings, for Brigham Young denounced the quest for easy wealth. Yet precious metals were not discovered in amounts sufficient to attract into Utah the huge non-Mormon population hoped for by Colonel Connor. Mining operations did not seriously interfere with Mormon affairs.

Unknown to the prospectors who were combing the Territory, however, the very mountain they raked for gold and silver at Bingham Canyon contained one of the largest copper deposits in the world—a major industry in 20th-century Utah.

## NEW MEXICO—"LOST" MINES AND ISOLATION

New Mexico never experienced the prosperity of other mining areas. Small-scale mining there, however, long antedated its acquisition by the United States, in 1848. The Indians, Spaniards, and Mexicans worked the copper mines at Santa Rita, gold placers in the Ortíz and San Pedro Mountains, and various other deposits.

In 1860 some Americans, pursuing the ever-present rumors of "lost" mines, discovered gold placers at Pinos Altos, just north of Santa Rita. Below the placer deposits they found gold-bearing quartz veins, and numerous miners from California, Texas, Mis-

Prospectors at work in the Cerrillos Mountains of New Mexico Territory in the 1880's. From a Henry Brown stereopticon. Courtesy, Museum of New Mexico.

souri, and Mexico rushed in. In 1861, however, Apaches forced the miners to abandon the site. Mining nearly ceased in New Mexico Territory during the Civil War, and for some time after the war transportation problems and the Indian hazard had an inhibiting effect. A silver boom occurred in the late 1870's, when several mining towns sprang up in the southern hills.

Isolation, the Apache danger, the lack of water, the predominance of base metals unsuited to simple milling, and the failure of prospectors to make any big strikes precluded any extensive mining in New Mexico until the 20th century, when uranium, oil, and natural gas became major sources of income.

### WYOMING—LESSER STRIKES

Wyoming was another region where a major boom did not occur, though prospectors made a few small strikes. In the early 1860's they discovered gold in the Big Horn country, and for a few years this region attracted some miners from Montana. In 1867 a rush to the Sweetwater River region occurred, during which South Pass City and Atlantic City were founded. The boom ended quickly, however, for the pockets proved shallow. By 1870 the miners had left the Territory. Some prospecting continued during the 1870's and 1880's, but the people of Wyoming had long since turned their attention to the cattle industry.

### THE BLACK HILLS—OPENING THE SIOUX COUNTRY

By the early 1870's only one region of the West had escaped the prospector's pick—the Black Hills of Dakota, a region occupied by the Sioux Indians and guarded by troops who barred all white men from the area. Tales were recounted of Indians who came from the Black Hills to Fort Laramie with nuggets of pure gold; of military commanders who suppressed news of gold discoveries to prevent wholesale desertions; and of Father De Smet, the pioneer Jesuit missionary who had obtained gold from the Indians before the discovery in California and warned them not to reveal this secret if they wished to retain their hunting grounds.

In 1867 more substantial proof of the riches of the Black Hills was forthcoming. A report concerning the mineral resources east of

Bull freighters arriving in Crook City, Black Hills, 1877. Pierre, Dakota Territory, was the Missouri River port of entry for the Black Hills mining region. Freighters also operated from Bismarck and other Missouri River points to interior settlements. Photograph by F. Jay Haynes. Courtesy, Alfred A. Knopf, Inc., and The Haynes Foundation.

the Rocky Mountains, drawn up at the order of the Secretary of the Treasury, was published. Asserting that explorations by Lt. G. K. Warren in 1857 and Capt. W. F. Raynolds in 1859 and 1860 had verified that the Black Hills were rich in gold and silver, as well as iron, coal, and copper, it stated: "With the pacification of the Sioux Indians and the establishment of emigrant roads, this district of Dakota would doubtless be the scene of great mining excitement, as the goldfield of the Black Hills is accessible at a distance of 120 miles from the Missouri River."

By the early 1870's, when the mines of the West were passing from the hands of the prospectors to those of Eastern capitalists, increasing pressures were brought to bear on the Government to open the Black Hills to prospecting. More and more gold seekers began congregating just outside the forbidden area. Alarmed at this buildup, the Government in 1874 organized a military expedition under Gen. George A. Custer, accompanied by a group of

Deadwood Gulch, South Dakota Territory, in 1877. One of the last great mining strikes was made at Deadwood, whose name is synonymous with "Wild Bill" Hickok and Calamity Jane. Many buildings from the town's heyday have survived. Photograph by F. Jay Haynes. Courtesy, Alfred A. Knopf, Inc., and The Haynes Foundation.

scientists, to explore the mineral resources of the region. Custer reported that gold was present in the Black Hills in profitable amounts.

The news caused gold seekers from all over the West to jam into adjacent towns, such as Bismarck, Cheyenne, and Sioux City, and loudly demand that the region be opened to miners. Many clandestinely slipped into the Black Hills, and the Army kept busy ejecting them. In 1875, after a special commission failed to obtain any concessions from the Indians, the Government, foreseeing the inevitable and unable to control the situation indefinitely, threw open the Black Hills to anyone who was willing to accept the risks involved. Nearly 15,000 miners entered the region in the next few months. They provided one of the causes of the Sioux uprising in 1876, highlighted by the annihilation of Custer's force at the Little Bighorn. In 1877 the Sioux were forced to cede the Black Hills.

The objective of the first group of prospectors in the Black Hills was French Creek, where they laid out Custer City. Then in the fall of 1875 a party of gold seekers made one of the last great strikes of the mining frontier at Deadwood Gulch. The town that grew up nearby took its name from the gulch and there the mining frontier reached its zenith. It was as wild as any in the West. The placers at Deadwood, and nearby Lead, brought fortunes to many prospectors. But the surface deposits were quickly exhausted. To extract precious metal from the quartz, heavily capitalized companies, such as the Homestake, took over, and the colorful, highly individualistic era of the prospector and placer miner came to an end in the Black Hills. With the Deadwood boom, the eastward movement of the mining frontier ended.

Wells-Fargo guards escort a gold shipment out of Deadwood, Dakota Territory. Photograph by John C. H. Grabill. Courtesy, Library of Congress.

## Drives for Self-Government

The California gold rush and the subsequent extension of the mining frontier greatly hastened settlement of the West. They resulted in a large influx of miners and many supporting ranchers, farmers, and businessmen. Creating a new interest in the West, both in Congress and the Nation as a whole, they stimulated emigration of all groups. As soon as miners and settlers moved into the almost-empty regions of many parts of the West, agitation for self-government began. Miners were particularly active and they were a decisive influence in the statehood drives of more than half of the 12 mining States. A. D. Richardson, a journalist who visited Denver in 1859 and noted the political activity there, was led to remark:

> Making governments and building towns are the natural employments of the migratory Yankee. He takes to them as instinctively as a young duck to water. Congregate a hundred Americans anywhere beyond the settlements and they immediately lay out a city, frame a state constitution and apply for admission into the Union, while twenty-five of them become candidates for the United States Senate.

Primarily because of the gold rush, California never underwent a Territorial period and became a State under the Compromise of 1850. The compromise also created New Mexico Territory, which included most of present Arizona. Arizonans, after holding a convention in Tucson, in 1856 petitioned Congress for separate Territorial status to no avail. Without success they also sent additional petitions; regularly elected delegates to Congress, who were refused seats; and even drew up a constitution and elected a full slate of Territorial officials. Finally in 1863 Congress yielded to the pressures of Arizonan mining interests, which stressed that precious metals were helping to keep the dollar sound during the war, and created Arizona Territory. Miners' groups were also very active in the long Arizona drive for statehood, which she and New Mexico did not attain until 1912.

Even though the Pike's Peak gold rush in 1859 proved to be a fiasco and the prospects of maintaining a permanent population in present Colorado seemed remote, the miners indicated in a popular referendum that they favored immediate statehood—but it was not to be achieved immediately. For 2 years, until Congress granted Territorial status, the citizens governed themselves through the provisional Jefferson Territory and an informal constitution. After rushes of miners because of new gold and silver strikes, in 1876 Congress granted Colorado statehood.

The drive for self-government in Utah had nothing to do with the development of mining, which was limited anyway and opposed by the Mormon authorities. In 1849, 2 years after the Mormons settled in present Utah, they unsuccessfully petitioned Congress to be admitted as the State of Deseret. The Compromise of 1850, however, granted Utah Territorial status and included in its boundaries most of the present State of Nevada. Friction between the Mormons and Federal officers sent into the Territory, plus controversy over the practice of polygamy, delayed Utah's admission to the Union as a State until 1896.

In 1861 Congress granted Nevada separate Territorial status from Utah, but before long the miners began agitating for state-hood. Ironically political necessity rather than mineral wealth resulted in Nevada statehood. The Republican Party, seeking electoral votes in the election of 1864, brought pressure to bear in Congress to admit Nevada to the Union, in time to return a majority for the reelection of Lincoln.

Non-mining influences also brought about Oregon statehood. In 1842 American farmer-emigrants began to move into the vast Oregon country over the Oregon Trail. The following year they formed a provisional government, the only local government except for that of the Hudson's Bay Company, whose Chief Factor, Dr. John McLoughlin, exercised feudal rights derived from the British Crown and aided American settlers. In 1848, only 2 years after Great Britain ceded the Oregon country to the United States and ended more than two decades of joint occupation, Congress created the Oregon Territory, which included present Oregon, Washington, Idaho, and a part of Montana and Wyoming. Five years later Congress removed the present State of Washington and the northern part of Idaho and the northwestern part of Montana from the Oregon Territory and included them in the newly established Washington Territory. When Oregon was admitted to the Union in 1859, the parts of the old Oregon Territory east of the present Oregon boundary were attached to the Washington

Territory. In 1863, when Congress created the Idaho Territory, the Washington Territory assumed the present boundaries of the State. Washington did not achieve statehood until 1889.

At the time of the 1860 gold rush to Idaho, it was a part of the Washington Territory. The miners soon clamored for separate Territorial status. They argued that the seat of government of the Washington Territory was too far west and that of the Dakotas too far east. Because of the development of mining and the growing agricultural population, in 1863 Congress authorized Idaho Territory, which included present Idaho, Montana, and most of Wyoming.

Because the Idaho government had difficulty in administering the eastern regions of the Territory, Congress received petitions from the mining camps there sympathetically and in 1864 created Montana Territory. Four years later it founded Wyoming Territory—more because of the completion of the Union Pacific Railroad across its breadth and the establishment of Cheyenne as an important railroad junction than the influence of miners. With the building of the railroads, the influx of population, and the growth of mining and ranching, the Territories of Montana, Wyoming, and Idaho grew rapidly. Congress admitted Montana to the Union as a State in 1889, and Idaho and Wyoming in 1890.

The Dakota Territory, created in 1861, included present North and South Dakota and much of Wyoming and Montana until 1863, when Congress founded Idaho Territory, which absorbed all of present Montana and much of Wyoming. When the Montana Territory was established in 1864, the latter area reverted to the Dakota Territory. In 1868 Congress created the Wyoming Territory and reduced the Dakota Territory to the region comprising present North and South Dakota. At that time the Black Hills region was Indian territory. When prospectors struck gold there in 1874, a rush of miners occurred. They inaugurated a drive for statehood. In 1889 Congress established the States of North and South Dakota.

## The Open Range Cattle Era

For several generations the cowboy has been a favorite among American folk heroes. He has been romanticized and glorified. In the process his fictional and television images have obscured the major contributions of the open range cattle industry to the development of the West.

## Texas origins

The cattlemen's empire of the post-Civil War period had its origins deep in south Texas in a triangle bounded by the cities of San Antonio, Corpus Christi, and Laredo. Nature seemingly had endowed this region with the specific resources for raising cattle. The climate was mild, the grass grew tall, and predatory animals were few. Northward lay a vast expanse of grassland awaiting occupation; it was guarded only by the Indians, who in a sense were tending their own herds—the buffalo.

The vast buffalo herds that ranged over the Plains supported the Indian economy. As the buffalo hunters completed their work, U.S. Army troops forced the Indians onto reservations. Shown here is part of the herd maintained today at Theodore Roosevelt National Memorial Park.

The establishment of the Texas missions by the Spaniards, beginning in 1716, marked the first effort to raise cattle in the province. By 1770 the ranches of Mission La Bahía del Espíritu Santo, near Goliad, were running perhaps 40,000 Longhorns between the Guadalupe and San Antonio Rivers. Soon the cattle constituted the principal wealth of the missions and of most of the private citizens in the province, who made long drives from Texas to Louisiana and Coahuila. In south Texas sheep increased more slowly than cattle because the area was thickly wooded and because of the shortage of trained herders.

The Spanish also introduced Longhorns into present Arizona and New Mexico at an early date, but because of the less suitable environment no significant development of the cattle industry occurred in the region until after the Civil War. In California, where Longhorns also prevailed, ranching was the basis of the economy during the Spanish and Mexican periods, but it played no real part in the development of the cattlemen's empire in the American West.

LONGHORNS: THE BASIC STOCK

The Longhorn, more a type than a breed, first stocked the ranges in what is now the United States. Despite his nondescript color, coarse and stringy meat, and wild nature, he was of distinguished ancestry. He was a direct descendant of the unseemly, lanky animals that had been reared for so long in Spain by the Moors on the plains of Andalusia.

Early American settlers in Texas considered the Longhorns to be indigenous wild animals like the buffalo. They called them "mustang cattle," "Spanish cattle," or simply "wild cattle." The cattle brought by the settlers from the Eastern United States interbred with the Longhorns. The result was an animal slightly different than the original Longhorn: the horns were longer, the body heavier and rangier, and the color variations unlimited. By the Civil War period the words "Texas cattle" and "Longhorns" had come to be synonymous.

Cowboys declared that the wiry Longhorn steer, despite his perversity and independence, was the most likely animal for trail driving that nature ever produced. They claimed that the long-legged

Vast herds of Longhorns, driven north from Texas, once grazed Western ranges. Pictured here are Longhorns at the Wichita Mountains Wildlife Refuge, near Cache, Oklahoma. The U.S. Fish and Wildlife Service maintains another herd at Fort Niobrara National Wildlife Refuge, Valentine, Nebraska. Courtesy, U.S. Fish and Wildlife Service.

animals had tougher hooves, more endurance, and the ability to range farther without water than the cattle of improved blood— the "high grade stuff" of a later period. A natural-born "rustler," the Longhorn seemed to thrive on the trail. He walked tirelessly over great distances, seemingly unaffected by heat, hunger, or the unmelodious songs of the nightriders. And above all he could walk 60 miles between waterings. These virtues compensated in part for the distressing inability of the breed to produce beef in quantity or quality.

## THE SPANISH MUSTANG

Another important contribution of the Spaniards to the cattle industry was the mustang, which, like Spanish cattle, soon had a better hold on U.S. soil than the Spaniard himself. This horse, whose bloodlines were strong like the Longhorn, was descended from stock brought into Spain from North Africa by the Moors. After the Spanish brought the mustangs to the Southwest, some of them strayed, multiplied, and formed wild herds that eventually ranged onto the Great Plains. The Indians preferred stealing from the Spaniards to catching the fleet-footed, untamed animals on the prairies.

The Texas *vaquero,* or cowboy, found the mustang a natural-born cow horse. Of scrubby appearance and slight stature, the horse had been radically changed by the Spanish. What he lost in beauty, he gained in wind and bottom. When the American cowboy first came to know him, he was a wiry, fleet, untamed little brute who could run all day and still kick his rider's hat off at night. Through selective breeding and the admixture of some imported blood, in the course of time he became larger and somewhat more tractable.

## OTHER SPANISH CONTRIBUTIONS

The Spaniards provided almost all the ingredients of the open range cattle era, except for grass and water. Besides the Longhorn and the mustang, the hackamore, or *jaquima,* was also Spanish in origin, as were the lariat, or *la riata,* the sombrero, and the chaps, or *chaparejos.* The so-called Texas saddle, almost in its present

Range crew on the Pecos River, New Mexico Territory. Courtesy, Museum of New Mexico.

form, was introduced into Spain by the Moors. Finally, Spain perfected the techniques of handling cattle on horseback.

### SEEKING A MARKET

At the conclusion of the Texas Revolution, most Mexican ranchers in south Texas abandoned their property—including cattle—and hurried southward to avoid the vengeance of the Texans. The new republic promptly declared all unbranded stock to be public property. Impoverished Texas pioneers who provided themselves with a good supply of branding irons and wielded them with vigor were soon on the way to becoming cattle barons. But Texas had insufficient markets for the cattle.

Before the Civil War the largest single market was New Orleans, reached both overland and by water, although the overland route was the more popular. In 1853 alone an estimated 40,000 head crossed the Nueces River en route to New Orleans. The California gold rush provided a new market. In the early 1850's cowboys drove thousands of Longhorns, worth $5 to $15 a head in Texas, across the desert to California, where they brought up to $150 each. The enormous difficulties encountered on the long drive to California, however, prevented it from becoming a major market.

Kansas City Stockyards in 1872, the second year of operation. Vari-colored Texas Longhorns, forwarded from railhead cowtowns over the Kansas Pacific Railroad, await shipment to Chicago and other points. Courtesy, Kansas City Stockyards Company.

Another small but promising market became apparent in the frontier towns, mainly in Missouri, where parties bound over the Oregon Trail outfitted. Texans drove herds of cattle northward and then sold them to local butchers, Chicago and Kansas City meatpackers, and the commissary department of the U.S. Army. In 1854 about 50,000 head of Longhorns crossed the Red River. But these markets were irregular and minor ones. Much better ones had to be found.

Then came the Civil War, and Texas cowboys dropped their branding irons and took up shooting irons. While they were at war, the Longhorns increased to about 5 million head. At the same time the cities of the North, rapidly expanding and becoming in-dustrialized because of the wartime boom, were hungry for meat. When Texans returned from the war, they found their Confederate currency worthless and their economy wrecked. But they did have beef—worth only a few dollars a head, or even free to anyone who was willing to go out and round it up—but beef that would bring $40 a head in Northern and Eastern markets, with which Texas had no rail connections. The $4 steers had to be connected with the $40 markets.

Such a connection was facilitated by various trends in the last half of the 19th century: The removal of the buffalo and the Plains Indians; the extension of the railroads across the West; and increased demand for meat. This demand was not only in the cities of the East, which resulted in the burgeoning of the Chicago and Kansas City meatpacking industries and the development of the refrigerator car, but also in mining areas, U.S. Army posts, Indian reservations, and railroad construction gangs in the West.

## THE GREAT DRIVES

In the spring of 1866 a few Texas ranchers drove herds of Longhorns northward over the Shawnee Trail. Their objective was Sedalia, Mo., the railhead for Eastern and Northern markets. But the first year of the "long drive" was nearly the last. Not yet experienced in trail driving, the cowboys found the half-wild cattle difficult to manage. Armed mobs of angry Missouri farmers, halting the drives at county lines, shot at and stampeded the cattle for fear that the herds would infect their own animals with the dreaded Texas fever.

It was Joseph G. McCoy who made perhaps the most important single contribution to the range cattle industry. This young, audacious cattle dealer found an effective way to bring Texas cattle to market. In 1867, when the Kansas Pacific Railroad reached Abilene, a few Texans began to drive herds there. McCoy, recognizing the economic potential of the Texas cattle drives, established shipping facilities at Abilene. He did so because he felt that it was the farthest point east that would be practicable and because it was well watered and had a good supply of grass.

Jesse Chisholm, half-breed Cherokee trader, founded the route across Indian Territory into Kansas that became a famous cattle trail, the Chisholm Trail. Courtesy, Oklahoma Historical Society.

McCoy finally persuaded the railroad that his plan was sound, and he spent the summer of 1867 building stockyards, pens, and loading chutes. He advertised the market throughout Texas and sent his agents into Kansas and Indian Territory (in present Oklahoma) to guide the trail herds to Abilene. After crossing the Red River the cowboys followed the broad trail that Jesse Chisholm, a half-breed Cherokee Indian trader, had used earlier on trading expeditions and had freshly marked while guiding a military expedition that was removing about 3,000 Wichita Indians from Kansas to a new location along the Red River. Thus was born the Chisholm Trail.

In 1867 only 35,000 head of cattle reached Abilene, but a new era had begun. Returning drovers spread the word throughout Texas of the ease with which cattle could be driven to Abilene and pointed out that few settlements, wooded areas, or angry farmers would be encountered along the way. In the next 4 years more than a million head of Texas cattle were loaded at Abilene and shipped to Chicago and Kansas City packinghouses or as feeders to Iowa, Nebraska, Missouri, and Illinois farms for fattening on corn. Then the advancing farmers' frontier made it necessary to shift the long drive westward once again. Newton and Wichita, on

Pile of 40,000 buffalo hides awaiting shipment in Dodge City, Kansas, to Eastern markets. As the buffalo hunters wrought destruction on the Plains, they destroyed the Indian way of life but opened the way for the farming and ranching frontiers. Courtesy, Kansas Historical Society.

the Santa Fe Railway, became the major termini of the drive.

The next major trail to develop was the Great Western, or more simply, the Western. Its railhead was Ogallala, Nebr., served by the Union Pacific Railroad, and by 1876 the Western had supplanted the Chisholm Trail as the major northward artery of cattle traffic. By 1880 Dodge City, south of Ogallala and located on the Santa Fe Railway, had replaced Ogallala as the major railhead of the Western Trail. But the latter city was used until 1895, and the trail was extended northward into Montana, for cattlemen had discovered that cattle could survive northern winters. Ranching was spreading, and Texas no longer was the major source of range beef for the Nation.

Despite evidence to the contrary, most Texas ranchers had long refused to believe that cattle could survive the cold winters on the northern Plains or in the mountains. Mining communities of the 1850's and 1860's in the widely separated mountain districts of the West had drawn cattlemen and sheepmen to supply meat. These ranchers usually operated on a small scale and supplied a limited market. Large-scale freighting companies that supplied the necessities of life for the miners and the Army had also brought animals West and wintered them along the overland routes. For example, during the winter of 1857–58 the freighting firm of Russell, Majors, and Waddell wintered some 15,000 head just south of the Oregon Trail.

Colorado also served as proof, for it early became a center of the cattle industry—partly as a result of the Pike's Peak mining boom that began in 1858 and partly as a result of the gradual extension northward of Texas ranches. In 1866 Charles Goodnight and Oliver Loving, two Texas drovers and ranchers, founded another major trail, the Goodnight-Loving. They trailed large herds from Fort Belknap, in Texas, into Colorado Territory via Fort Sumner, New Mexico Territory. And in 1868 Goodnight delivered a trail herd to Cheyenne, the second Texas herd to arrive in Wyoming, to feed the army of workers on the Union Pacific Railroad.

With the arrival of the Kansas Pacific Railroad late in the 1860's, ranchers in eastern Colorado Territory could ship cattle to the Eastern market or drive them to the ranges in Idaho, Montana, and Wyoming—where the nucleus of a cattle industry had already been established to satisfy local markets such as miners, overland

Chuckwagon on the move. Bedrolls stacked to the wagon bows and dishpan banging behind, the lordly cook drives to the next camp. Photograph by Erwin E. Smith. Courtesy, Mrs. L. M. Pettis and the Library of Congress.

emigrants, and Army forts, and where young stock was especially in demand. By 1869 a million cattle were grazing within the borders of the Colorado Territory and many predicted that it would become "the cattle pasture of the world."

Despite proof that Longhorns could survive cold winters, most Texas ranchers refused to believe it until they saw for themselves—and see they did. In the spring and summer of 1873 they drove several hundred thousand cattle north along the Chisholm Trail, but at Abilene they found few buyers. The Panic of 1873 had hit the Nation. Rather than drive the cattle back to Texas, the drovers left them on the prairies of Kansas and Missouri with the expectation that they would die during the winter. But in the spring, when the drovers returned, they found that the Longhorns had not only survived but had improved.

It became apparent that steers maturing in the north fattened more than in Texas. For this reason, and with proof in hand that the animals could survive, many of the bigger Texas spreads began branching out northward. They continued to use their Texas ranches as breeding places, but they maintained finishing ranges in the northern territories. Texas cattle were trailed a thousand miles to "double-winter" on the grass ranges of Wyoming, Montana, or Dakota, and then shipped to the Chicago slaughterhouses. Northern ranchers also obtained substantial numbers of cattle, English breeds, driven eastward over the mountains, from Oregon, Washington, and Idaho.

The Texas cowboys who pushed the cattle northward were full of exuberance and confidence, though they faced heat and thirst, stampedes and Indians, rustlers and armed homesteaders. They were the men who established the range cattle industry on the Great Plains and in the Rocky Mountain States. They taught their trade to the cowboys there just as they had learned it from the Mexicans and the Mexicans from the Spaniards. Such prominent cattlemen as Teddy Blue Abbott, Charlie Siringo, and Granville Stuart, along with a host of others, have testified that development

In the dust with the "drags"—weaker cattle that dropped behind the drive. As the day lengthened, so did the thirst of the cowboys. Photograph by Erwin E. Smith. Courtesy, Mrs. L. M. Pettis and the Library of Congress.

of the open range cattle industry was from first to last largely a Texas story.

The organization and routine of the trail drive was a serious business. As many as 2,500 cattle were collected in south Texas and consigned by the owners to the care and authority of the trail boss for delivery at a railhead or stocking ranch, which might be 1,500 miles or more distant. Ten to twelve hands handled the herd, along with the cook and a youthful apprentice who cared for the remuda of a hundred or more horses. The cowboys sometimes spent 14 to 16 hours a day in the saddle—hard, lonely, and monotonous work— for $30 a month and board.

The long, sinuous line of Longhorns, stretching out like a long multicolored ribbon, soon became broken to the trail, and the daily routine became automatic. The trail itself, because of the passage of hundreds of thousands of cattle, was easily recognized and easily followed. Depending in part on the grass available, it consisted of scores of irregular cowpaths that formed a single passageway, which widened and narrowed and twisted and turned according to the terrain—but led ever northward.

The number of cattle driven north each year was large. In the peak year 1871, cowhands probably drove 700,000 Texas cattle to Kansas railheads, and between 1866 and 1885 millions of head moved to the railheads and northern ranges. In the level and open country drovers were seldom out of sight of other herds. From a hilltop in Nebraska, one cowboy saw 7 herds to the rear of his own and 8 in front, while the dust of 13 more could be observed across the North Platte. "All the cattle in the world seemed to be coming up from Texas," he declared. When a thunderstorm stampeded 11 trail herds, including about 30,000 Longhorns, which were waiting to cross the Red River at Doan's Store in 1882, it took 120 cowboys 10 days to unscramble the cattle, reassemble the herds, and get them moving again.

FENCES, QUARANTINES, AND INDIANS

The trail herders usually met bitter opposition from the farmers of Kansas and Missouri, resentful because the Texas, or Spanish, fever ravaged their small herds and milk cows. The Longhorns seemed to be immune, but the fever tick that rode north with

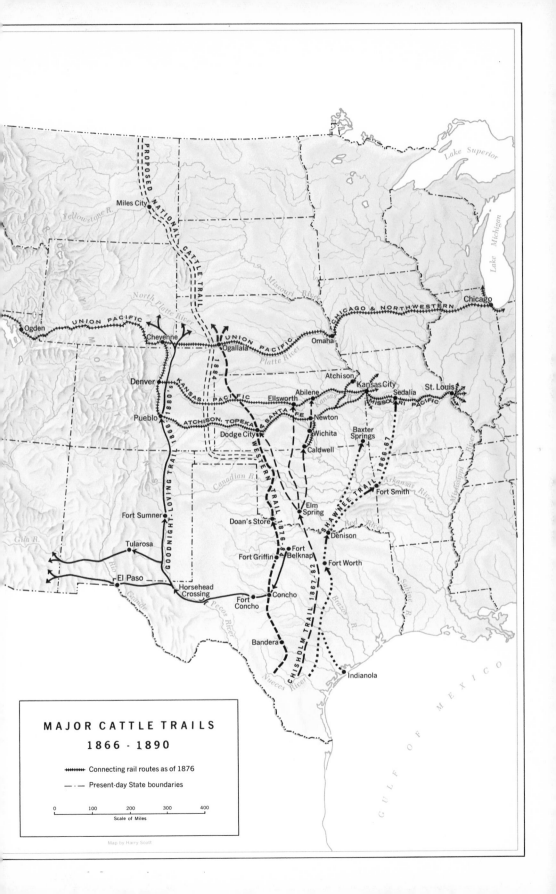

MAJOR CATTLE TRAILS

1866 · 1890

+++++ Connecting rail routes as of 1876

—·— Present-day State boundaries

0    100    200    300    400

Scale of Miles

Map by Harry Scott

them was a menace to all other cattle. To protect local herds, farmers organized vigilance committees to prevent passage of the Texas stock. Quarantine lines, established by State legislatures, were an important factor over the years in forcing the cattle drives farther and farther westward.

The westward-tending Kansas farmers became still another problem. Their small, enclosed homesteads soon began to present an almost unbroken fenceline. The farmers also plowed furrows around their farms and claimed damages when the herds were driven over these "fences." They also fenced waterholes and charged a toll for the watering of cattle. If alone, the farmer was helpless, but as agricultural settlements increased on the trail, 20 farmers armed with shotguns were sufficient to force the Texas cowboys to pay the fee.

The Indian Territory presented another barrier. The Five Civilized Tribes resided in the valleys of the Red, Arkansas, and Cimarron Rivers, squarely across the cattle trails. To protect their pasturage and raise revenue, they levied tolls and defined the trails that could be used. Conflict and friction were inevitable and frequent.

The Indian barrier, the quarantine laws, and the advance of the farming frontier pushed the trails steadily westward. The Texas Panhandle eventually became the route to the railheads, and eastern Colorado the pathway to the northern ranges. In 1884 a national convention of stockmen adopted a resolution urging Congress to establish a National Cattle Trail, a permanent road 6 miles wide extending from the Red River to Canada. But the rapid building of railroads and the fear of overstocking the northern ranges helped defeat the proposal.

THE PUBLIC DOMAIN: GRASS AND WATER

The direct cause of the widespread demand for Texas cattle in the northern territory was the ready availability of the lands of the public domain. These lands were open in the sense that they were uncontrolled and unfenced. The laws that Congress passed to encourage orderly settlement of the public domain were, to a great extent, unenforced and evaded. The open range included all or part of seven States, eight Territories, and Indian Territory. It comprised about 44 percent of the total land area of the United States.

This was land that the farmer—accustomed to the timbered, well-watered East—could not farm with his usual methods and machinery. This was land that the Plains Indians and the buffalo had called home for many generations. The demise of Indian power

Water was as necessary as "free grass and air" to the Western rancher. Most Plains streams seasonally rose and fell. Photograph by Erwin E. Smith. Courtesy, Mrs. L. M. Pettis and the Library of Congress.

in this region coincided with the slaughter of the great buffalo herds, on which the Indian economy depended. Just after the Civil War, buffalo hides became valuable for their leather, and the hide men did their bloody work exceedingly well and amazingly fast. In 1880 the last buffalo herds were sighted on the southern plains and only a few years later in the north. The Plains tribes took to the warpath, the troops clashed with them, and many soldiers and braves died before the reservations became the home of once-proud tribes of Indians.

The Government had no immediate use for these public lands, which could be appropriated by the first men to occupy them. The land constituted "free grass" and "free water," collectively known as "free air." To this open range were trailed hundreds of thousands of cattle, almost all driven up from Texas as yearlings and 2-year-olds. There they were crossed with Eastern cattle, fattened on the "free air," and sold for high prices at the nearest railhead. With little more than a few skilled cowhands and a branding iron, a man could convert the grazing land into top steers and grow rich.

RANCH LIFE

The process by which a man became a rancher was not complicated. Finding a live stream, hopefully with natural boundaries surrounding it to hold his cattle, the prospective rancher claimed the land along the stream for 10 to 15 miles and as far back as the water divide. If a waterhole was the only source of water in the vicinity, he selected his lands around the hole and effectively controlled all the surrounding acres of grass. Proof of ownership, although tenuous, was not often contested until the homesteaders arrived. Under questioning a rancher might refer to one of the Federal laws, such as the Homestead Act or the Desert Land Act, but he usually advised those so inquisitive and foolish as to ask proof of ownership to "vamoose the ranch" or "pull your freight, pronto."

At first ranch life was hard and lonely. The pioneer rancher subsisted largely on beans, bacon, and coffee. He fought Indians, wolves, blizzards, rattlers, rustlers—and his own kind. But he also watched his cattle fatten and multiply and hired cowboys to tend them. For some hands it was a 100-mile ride from the bunkhouse to the front gate. Later a ranchhouse and scattered outbuildings would replace the wickiup, and other evidences of civilization would follow.

The cattle kings were men apart—men such as John Chisum, Granville Stuart, Charles Goodnight, and John Wesley Iliff. They were strong men—men who conquered the West. What they ac-

Colorado rancher John W. Iliff purchased foundation stock from Oliver Loving and Charles Goodnight. His herds grazed thousands of acres in the South Platte Valley. Courtesy, Western History Collection, Denver Public Library.

Granville Stuart, pioneer Montana cattleman, was a leader of the Vigilance Committee, organized in 1884 by ranchers in Montana Territory to protect their stock. Courtesy, Montana Historical Society.

Charles Goodnight, cofounder of the Goodnight-Loving Trail, was one of the first cattlemen in the Texas Panhandle. Courtesy, Western History Collection, Denver Public Library.

Joseph G. McCoy, cattle dealer, established cattle shipping facilities at Abilene in 1867 and encouraged Texans to make the first drives to Kansas railheads. Courtesy, University of Illinois Library.

complished was done literally with their bare hands. They endured as many dangers and hardships as any man on any frontier. Little wonder that they later would look back with such pride at what they had done.

BOOM ON THE RANGE

About 1880 the range cattle industry entered a boom period. The rush to the cow country was in many ways similar to the rush to the goldfields. The cause certainly was the same—the prospect of quick wealth in a new country that seemed to offer unlimited opportunity for the ambitious. "Cotton was once crowned king, but grass is now," declared an Eastern livestock journal.

The stampede to the cattle lands was literally worldwide. It attracted boomers from the East, from Canada and Australia, and from the British Isles. Youths from Eastern farms and factories, savings strapped to their waists, eager for wealth and adventure, packed the trains. The mania spread to Europe. When an English parliamentary committee reported a 33-percent return to stockowners, the desire to participate in the profits of American ranching, personally or as an investor, became a craze among the British.

As British capital had been involved in the mining frontier and had helped build the American railroad system, so it figured prominently in the growth of the range cattle industry. The largest cattle companies operating in the United States in the 1880's were formed in England and Scotland. British investors followed Horace Greeley's advice to "go West"—at least they sent their money in that direction to the amount of $17 million during the short-lived boom. Gouty squires who may or may not have known the difference between a steer and a heifer discussed the niceties of the spring roundup over port and nuts.

Proper Bostonians and staid New Yorkers joined the rush to invest in the cattle industry. In a single year 20 corporations, capitalized at more than $12 million, were organized under Wyoming laws. In some transactions the buyer never saw a head of his purchase, nor possessed more than a fraction of the purchase money. Uncontrolled speculation ensued. Swindlers flourished, and paper companies without an acre of land or a single steer sold stock to a gullible and eager public.

Nor could the tally books of brokers always be trusted. When ranchers sold large herds, the transactions often represented little more than rough estimates of the cattle involved, a generous figure being inserted for the year's calf crop and on rare occasions an allowance for losses from severe winters, diseases, or other causes. Such a system gave rise to many stories, such as one that made the rounds in Cheyenne. A group of cattlemen purportedly bellied up to a local bar during a long, hard winter and were gloomily speculating on their probable losses. "Cheer up, boys," said one, setting up drinks for the house, "the books won't freeze."

After 1880 the demand for cattle to stock the northern ranges, which increased yearly, taxed the available supply and drove prices upward. Texas ranchers sent increased numbers of head northward, but the demand was still greater than the supply. "Cattle, cattle, more cattle" was the slogan of the grass country from north Texas to Canada. Answering this call, in 1884 trail drivers pointed north approximately 416,000 head of Texas cattle, the greatest number since 1871.

Some thirsty hands ride into town. The life of the cowhand was mostly work and little play. Photograph by Erwin E. Smith. Courtesy, Mrs. L. M. Pettis and the Library of Congress.

## BEGINNING OF THE END

Because of the enormous flow of capital into the cattle country, the high prices, and the spectacular profits, there could be but one result: the number of cattle would soon exceed the carrying capacity of the range. In a word, overgrazing would result. Alarmed cattlemen began to fear for the future. There was no natural limit to the number of cattle that could be bred in Texas and sent up the trail, but even the celebrated Longhorn could not fatten on air alone. The good pastures were being overgrazed, the marginal lands were crowded, and no new area of grass was available for an escape valve. The arid country, devastated by winter blizzards, could support the vast herds only under optimum weather conditions. One bad winter would ruin thousands of investors and ranch owners and kill millions of cattle. As the first half of the 1880's passed, each spring cattlemen accepted their winter losses, being thankful that the toll was no greater. But the development of the sheep industry and the invasion of the homesteaders were even greater threats than weather conditions.

Cattle raising was dangerous in arid country. In a bad year the results were disastrous. This photograph was taken in Roswell, New Mexico. Courtesy, National Archives.

Sheep have always figured prominently in the economy of the West. The sheepman led a lonely life and faced the violent antagonism of the cattlemen. Photograph by Lee Moorhouse. Courtesy, Photographic Bureau, University of Oregon.

## "Woolies" and "Wars"

Less renowned in story and song and less romantic in its appeal to the public than the cattle industry, the sheep industry was nevertheless of considerable economic importance in the historic West. During the post-Civil War period, it too struggled for a place in the Western sun. Sheepmen used the cattlemen's range and in many ways operated on the same basic principles—utilizing the grass and water of the public domain and depending on trail drives to reach markets.

The Spaniards introduced sheep into present California, Arizona, New Mexico, and Texas, usually in the mission establishments. In 1779 the Hopi pueblos probably grazed 30,000 sheep, and one California mission reported 100,000 in its herd. But New Mexico was the leading center. Between 1821 and 1846 its herders drove thousands of head annually to Mexico. The year after the United States acquired the Southwest in 1848, the California gold rush furnished a new market. In the 1850's half a million head moved from New Mexico Territory to the Mother Lode country, which paid fabulous prices until California ranches could satisfy the demand. Soon thousands of sheep landed in Pacific ports to stock California ranches. Many California counties grazed from 40,000 to 300,000 head, and some ranchers drove sheep to other States or Territories. After 1853 California ranchers found a ready wool market in San Francisco.

By 1865 New Mexican shepherds were grazing their sheep in eastern Colorado Territory, which was soon dotted with herds. In 1876, by which time sheep raising had spread to other parts of the Territory, the total number ran into the hundreds of thousands. New Mexicans also drove the first sheep into Utah from the south, and Mormons drove them in from the east. Mormon immigrants brought in spinning wheels, looms, and cards; and woolen manufacture thrived. In 1882, 10 woolen mills were operating. During the 1880's Texas assumed a position of first importance in sheep husbandry. In 1884 more than 8 million sheep grazed its ranges. Sheep ranching occurred on a smaller scale in Montana, Idaho, Wyoming, the Dakotas, Washington, and Oregon. These States had no large ranches, but many small stockmen raised sheep.

Migrants assisted at shearing time. Like harvest hands, they followed the season north from the Southwest into the Rocky Mountains and Canada. Courtesy, Photographic Bureau, University of Oregon.

The sheep industry prospered because hungry easterners showed the same inclination after the Civil War to pay high prices for mutton that they did for beef. Also the sheepmen had the additional bonus of high prices for their wool. As they spread out over the West in search of new grazing lands for their flocks, they came into conflict with the cattlemen. In the eyes of the cowboy the sheepman was low on the human scale. A person who stooped to eat mutton, according to the cowpunchers, was known to have degenerate tendencies. The fact that dogs were used to herd sheep and that the herder walked, rather than rode a horse like a man, only added to the cowboy's scorn. The cattleman's contempt for the lowly sheep and the humble herder only served to heighten his rage when he encountered the despised "woolies" contentedly grazing on the grass he claimed by right of prior use—if not by the "natural" priority of cattle over sheep.

According to cattlemen, sheep had a gland between the two halves of their hooves that secreted a foul-smelling fluid. They claimed that cattle would not graze on grass contaminated with this scent. The cattle were really not quite so sensitive. In fact they would graze side by side in the same pasture with sheep. But the hostility between cattlemen and sheepmen intensified. Perhaps the real cause of the cattlemen's hatred was the growing scarcity of grass. The "woolies" were extremely destructive to a range—especially to one that was overstocked. They industriously cropped the grass down to the roots, and their sharp little hooves destroyed the roots.

Attempts by sheepmen to find grazing lands were usually met with violence and the sheep driven from the range. Murders of shepherds and the slaughter of their flocks were not uncommon. In the Tonto Basin of Arizona a bloody range war broke out. During 5 years of hostilities, which degenerated into a feud between two families, every law-abiding rancher left the region and more than 30 cattlemen and sheepmen died. In Wyoming, along the Green River, the introduction of sheep likewise led to violence. Masked cattlemen attacked four sheep camps during the night, tied the herders up, and clubbed nearly 8,000 of the hated "woolies" to death.

In a country ruled by cattlemen the sheepmen received little protection from the law. The sheepmen quickly discovered that,

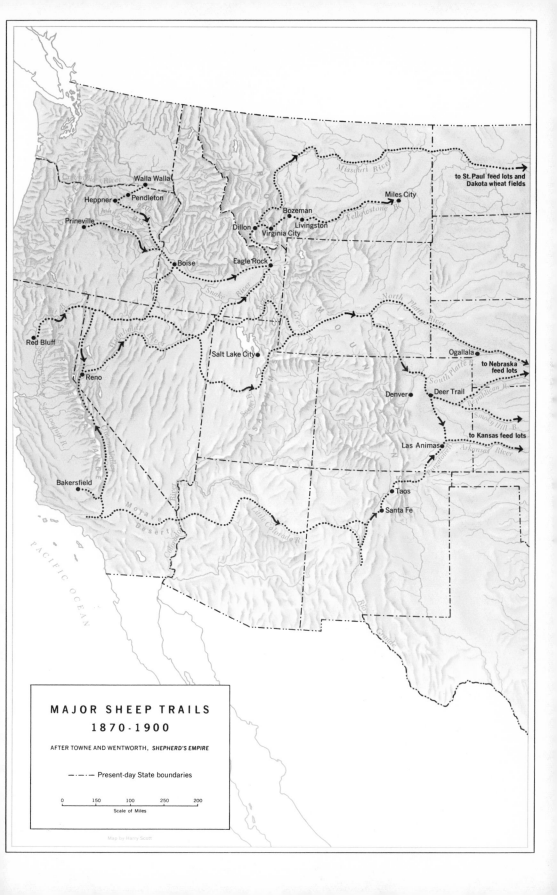

to St. Paul feed lots and
Dakota wheat fields

to Nebraska
feed lots

to Kansas feed lots

## MAJOR SHEEP TRAILS
### 1870-1900

AFTER TOWNE AND WENTWORTH, *SHEPHERD'S EMPIRE*

—··—·· Present-day State boundaries

0    150    100    250    200
Scale of Miles

Map by Harry Scott

Sheep, like cattle, were driven to markets or railheads. When streams barred the way, sheep required special bridges. Specially trained wethers or goats led the crossings. Courtesy, Photographic Bureau, University of Oregon.

though the meek might inherit the earth, if they carried loaded 30-30's, shot first, and then talked humbly, they and their sheep stood a better chance of living to collect the inheritance.

The sheepmen, in common with the ranchers, had the problem of getting their animals to railheads or markets. The sheep drives began, as did the cattle drives, shortly after the Civil War. Most of the sheep, in herds numbering as many as 7,500, were trailed eastward from California and Oregon, some to the Rocky Mountain mining camps, but most to the feedlots and railheads of Kansas, Nebraska, and Minnesota (St. Paul). As the railroads moved westward, the trails grew shorter.

The number of "woolies" trailed eastward during the period from 1865 to 1900 was about 15 million. Many difficulties were involved in the driving of sheep such great distances, over mountains and deserts and through the domain of hostile cattlemen. Yet the success of these drives guaranteed the ascendancy of the West over the East in sheep husbandry—a decisive influence on the economy of the trans-Mississippi country.

## The Sodbusters' Frontier

Running the sheepherder a close race for the title of "most despised" in the eyes of the cattlemen was the farmer. The cowboy disdained any labor that he could not perform on horseback, and almost everything connected with farming was done afoot. Despite the cattlemen's scorn, crop failures, Indians, and many other hazards the farmers continued to move into the West. And where they went they built schools and churches and established towns. In short they wanted civilization and brought it with them. After the farmers settled the West the frontier was gone.

### AGRICULTURE AND THE MINING FRONTIER

The California rush and subsequent mineral strikes stimulated the development of agriculture, as well as ranching, in many parts of the West. They brought in a large population, which had to be fed, and they increased interest in Western settlement in the East. In most mining areas, farmers and ranchers moved in, or expanded their operations if they had already settled in the region, and cowboys made cattle drives to many of the areas.

Montana homesteader breaking the sod. Courtesy, U.S. Bureau of Reclamation and National Archives.

The substantive effect of the California rush on agriculture in that State and on the rest of the West has already been discussed. Many of the other mining rushes had a similar result. Utah Territory is a good example. For many years it was an agri- cultural island, surrounded by mining-created Territories and States. Taking advantage of these markets, the Mormons extended their farming into the mining areas and prospered as traders and suppliers. Before the Civil War they founded settlements in Ne- vada, California, Arizona, New Mexico, Wyoming, and Idaho. Ev- erywhere they had notable success with irrigation, which in- fluenced other settlers to utilize it.

In various non-Mormon areas of the West, where major strikes occurred, the pattern that had developed in California was re- peated. First would come the miners and then ranchers and farmers. When the miners left in search of a new El Dorado, the farmers and ranchers stayed to form a stable population.

Even in the unfruitful desert country of Nevada, the mining boom caused an expansion of agriculture. Farms increased from 91 in 1860 to 1,404 in 1880, when the Nevada mines began to fail. In the arid Southwest, agriculture was also affected to some de- gree. For example, in Arizona Charles D. Poston irrigated a small plot beside the Santa Cruz River to feed the employees of his So- nora Exploring and Mining Company. Just outside of present No- gales, Pete Kitchen established his famous farm-ranch in the 1850's. Noted for his ham and bacon, he pioneered in large-scale pig farm- ing and was rewarded with handsome profits—and Apache attacks.

In varying degrees, the mining frontier stimulated agriculture in many other sections of the West, sometimes only in certain parts of States or Territories and at different times and places in response to specific local mining strikes.

OTHER AGRICULTURAL DEVELOPMENT

The initial agricultural development of some parts of the West had little or no relationship to the mining frontier. A notable example is the Oregon country, a vast region north of California which stretched from the Rocky Mountains to the Pacific Ocean and which Great Britain ceded to the United States in 1846 after more than two decades of joint occupancy. During the 1840's, beginning 6 years before the California gold rush, a few thousand restless emigrant-farmers followed in the steps of Methodist missionaries, who had laid the groundwork for settlement during the previous decade, and crossed the vast and agriculturally forbidding Plains into the Oregon country. Most of them settled in the Willamette Valley, where they engaged in wheat farming.

Disillusioned because the back country of Iowa, Missouri, and Arkansas had not proved to be the shining paradise of their dreams and troubled because the Panic of 1837 had shriveled the value of their land and the price of their crops, the emigrants were lured by reports of rich farm country in Oregon much like they had known in the East. Venturesome and courageous and pioneering a long and dangerous overland trek, they refused to accept the Plains as an agricultural barrier as did most other farmers.

In trekking so far the Oregon emigrants of the 1840's, as well as the few thousands who also traveled to California, broke the established pattern of westward advance. From the Atlantic coast to Iowa, Missouri, and Arkansas that advance had usually proceeded in small increments of 50 to 100 miles. Now in one great bound it leaped some 2,000 miles. Arid, treeless plains and intermontane basins made up most of the distance—regions isolated from rivers and railroads that were inhospitable and foreign to farmers from humid woodlands. The farmers, who even in the East had avoided the open prairies and grasslands as long as possible, believed that grassland was too sterile to grow trees and hence to grow crops; agriculture had been mainly conducted in previously forested areas and rural life was based on an abundant supply of wood.

Not for many years would the dry farmer subdue the steppelands west of the 95th meridian with barbed wire, the windmill, new mechanical equipment, and a unique cultural adjustment. For the land-hungry emigrants of the 1840's, who lacked the technology and knowledge necessary for the conquest of the Plains environment, the Oregon country was the next stop.

Montana is another example of an area where agricultural development was not fostered by mining activities. Farming began there in 1842, some years before the discovery of gold. The Jesuits at St. Mary's Mission, near present Stevensville, were such successful agriculturists that they sold their surplus produce to trading

Well-drilling outfit at work on the Plains. Water was a scarce commodity. Either the settler hauled water from the nearest stream or called on itinerant well drillers to solve his problem. Photograph by W. D. Johnson. Courtesy, U.S. Geological Survey.

posts along the Missouri. About 1850 they leased the mission to Maj. John Owen and moved to another location in Montana. Major Owen continued to cultivate the land and sold his produce to emigrants using the Mullan Road.

For another example, in Arizona the first extensive irrigation system had little connection with the mining industry. In 1867 Jack Swilling and several associates began to construct the Salt River Valley Canal, around which the thriving agricultural community of Phoenix arose.

### FREE LAND AND OPPORTUNITY ON THE PLAINS

While agriculture was developing on the Pacific coast, in the Intermountain Basin, and through the Rocky Mountain valleys, the Great Plains to the east had remained largely unsettled because of the harsh and strange natural environment and the presence of

Accustomed to hilly, forested country, most settlers were awed by the emptiness and loneliness of the Plains. Photograph by W. D. Johnson. Courtesy, U.S. Geological Survey.

vast buffalo herds and hostile Indian tribes. Eventually, after the buffalo hunters had done their work, the U.S. Army removed the Indians by force, but the troops could do nothing about the weather, the periodic plagues of grasshoppers, or the other problems.

To encourage farmers to move onto the Plains, the Federal Government passed a series of land laws. Before 1861 settlers who pushed into the West to acquire land were governed, theoretically at least, by a series of laws that never seemed entirely satisfactory. The laws either did not fit the conditions of soil or climate or they favored speculators and large landholders rather than small farmers. The Land Law of 1820—the basic land law until 1862—had reduced the price of public land to a low of $1.25 an acre and permitted the sale of 80-acre tracts. Thus anyone with $100 cash could buy a farm from the Government.

Despite the cheapness of land, thousands of settlers could not raise the necessary cash. They simply squatted where they chose without benefit of title. As the squatters became more numerous, they pressured Congress to legalize their occupancy by establishing "preemption rights." Prior to 1840 Congress yielded gradually to these demands by granting relief to special groups. Then in 1841 it enacted a general preemption law that gave squatters the right to purchase the lands on which they had settled, and specified that the sale should be at the minimum price.

The sodbuster brought his bride to a sod house on the Plains and raised a family. Beyond the tree belt, sod was the basic building material. Photograph by S. D. Butcher. Courtesy, Nebraska State Historical Society.

The act of 1841 did not completely satisfy the squatters. It did provide that their lands could not be sold to speculators without ample warning, but landgrabbers seriously abused it and often hired counterfeit farmers to preempt the best lands. The genuine farmers had their demands satisfied in 1862, when the Homestead Act became law. This act provided that any American citizen or person in the process of becoming naturalized could obtain 160 acres of Government land by paying only a registration fee. Before the settler could pay the fee he had to live on the land for 5 years, make improvements, and begin cultivation. He also had the option of obtaining title at the end of 6 months by paying the minimum price at that time, but few settlers chose this alternative.

When Congress passed the Homestead Act, it was also engaged in deeding large portions of the public domain to railroad companies, especially to the transcontinental lines that would become avenues of frontier advance after the Civil War. Between 1850 and 1871, to stimulate railroad construction, Congress granted to various companies an area approximately three times the size of Pennsylvania. Notable among these grants were a total of 40 million acres, made in 1862 and 1864, to the Union Pacific and Central Pacific Railroads. The Northern Pacific and the Southern Pacific also fared well at the hands of Congress. In many instances settlers found it more advantageous to purchase railroad land than to establish a homestead.

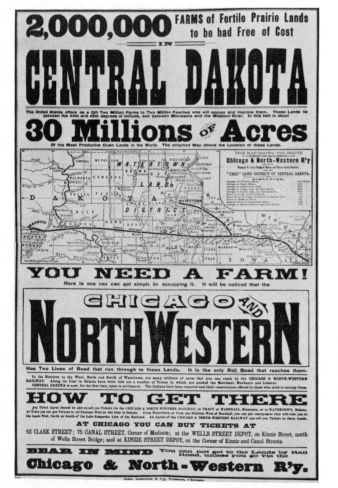

Railroad advertisements lured thousands of emigrants to the West. Many settlers chose to purchase railroad land rather than establish a farm under the Homestead Act. Courtesy, Chicago and Northwestern Railway.

However, large numbers of citizens, the bulk of them from the Mississippi Valley region, and newly arrived foreigners took advantage of the free land offered by the Homestead Act. As one farmer said, "The government bet us 160 acres against five years of our lives that we could not stick it out." The opportunity to acquire a farm at no cost except for the registration fee encouraged farmers and would-be farmers to venture out onto the Great Plains in the face of drought, dust, grasshopper plagues, and blizzards.

Because the 160 acres allowed by the Homestead Act proved to be an insufficient number to earn a living in the arid and semi-arid West, in 1873 Congress passed the Timber Culture Act, which entitled a farmer to acquire an additional quarter section of land simply by planting 40 acres of trees within a specified period of time; later the requirement was reduced to 10 acres. Then in 1877 the Desert Land Act offered sections of land in the desert regions for $1.25 an acre if the farmer could irrigate it within 3 years of the filing date. Only 25 cents an acre was due at filing time; the balance was not due until the conclusion of the 3-year waiting period.

Finally, in 1894 the Carey Act provided for the transfer of Government lands in arid regions, up to a million acres that could be irrigated, to any one State. States accepting the land had to agree to irrigate at least 20 acres of each 160 actually farmed within 10 years. Many Western States accepted these conditions. They usually contracted with private companies for the construction of irrigation projects; these companies then sold or leased water rights to the farmers.

## THE GREAT MIGRATION

The flow of farmer-settlers to the West was hastened by a number of favorable circumstances—many of which also stimulated development of the open range cattle industry. These circumstances included the conclusion of the Civil War, removal of the buffalo and the Plains Indians, free land under the Homestead Act, a period of adequate rainfall, increased immigration, the introduction of improved farm machinery, and the building of the railroads. In fact the railroads had as much or more to do with the westward migration as the Government itself. Recipients of millions of acres of Government land, the railroad companies set up "land departments" and "bureaus of immigration," which lured customers and arranged prices, sales, and credit. They spent millions on advertising, much of it not closely related to the truth, and sometimes used high-pressure selling methods.

In the 1870's Kansas gained 347,000 people, Nebraska 240,000, and other Plains States and Territories in proportion. Then came the great deluge of immigrants from Europe. Railroads, steamship companies, and the Western States and Territories themselves promoted the immigration. From northern Europe came Germans, Dutch, Swedes, Norwegians, and Danes. The Minnesota and Dakota regions appealed especially to the Scandinavians. In some areas of the northern Plains, the farmers' frontier was more European than American, even as to the language spoken.

Despite the hardships and financial risks faced by the immigrants, the population of the Plains States increased rapidly. By 1880 Kansas had 850,000 people and Nebraska 450,000. Dakota boomed with the removal of the Indians and the arrival of the railroads. Equally important in the settlement of the Dakota region were the spectacular efforts of Oliver Dalrymple. When the Panic of 1873 forced the Northern Pacific Railway into bankruptcy, com-

A harvester-thresher at work in the Imperial Valley, California. Newly invented machinery facilitated the conquest of the Plains and produced increased yields. Courtesy, National Archives.

pany officials decided to promote the sale of railroad lands. They engaged Dalrymple, a skilled wheatgrower from Minnesota, to establish demonstration farms. They provided him with 18 sections of land in the Red River Valley and adequate funds for the purchase of machinery. Using methods similar to those on California's bonanza wheat ranches, Dalrymple imported gangs of laborers and used the best agricultural machinery. With extremely low production costs—about $9.50 per acre—he produced a high yield, for which he obtained a good price. His profits were more than 100 percent. As a result, within 4 years large wheat farms covered most of the Red River Valley, and the population of the Dakotas increased rapidly.

Wyoming, natural cattlemen's country, began to attract a few farmers after 1867, when the Union Pacific Railroad arrived. The farmers achieved some success along the eastern border of the Big Horn Mountains. where water could be diverted for irrigation. Between 1880 and 1890, after the Indian danger ended, considerable development took place; the farmers constructed about 5,000 miles of ditches to irrigate approximately 2 million acres of land. Yet the population of Wyoming grew slowly, and cattle ranching remained the dominant industry. A similar situation existed in eastern Montana.

As the population of the northern Plains increased, farmers also moved into the southern Plains. In Texas, where the State owned the public domain, during the 1870's the number of farms increased by approximately 113,000. Land-hungry settlers then began looking toward the Indian Territory, where millions of acres had been assigned to 22 tribes. Pressure from prospective settlers, as well as from land speculators and railroad companies, eventually forced Congress to modify its Indian policy and open the country to settlement. The pressure of would-be settlers to get into the area was so great that the Army had to keep them out. Finally, in January 1889 the Government compelled the Creeks and Seminoles to sell an unsettled part of their land, and Congress authorized the President to announce that on April 22 the Oklahoma District, as the land was called, would be open to settlement under the Homestead Act.

On that date occurred probably the wildest land rush in American history. Within half a day, settlers claimed 1,920,000 acres for homesteading. Guthrie and Oklahoma City sprang into existence before nightfall. The new settlers immediately began to agitate for self-government, and in 1890 Congress created Oklahoma Terri-

Sod schoolhouse in Grant County, Oklahoma Territory. When pioneer farmers moved onto the Plains, they built schoolhouses as well as homes of sod. Courtesy, National Archives.

tory, essentially the part of Oklahoma settled by whites. Gradually the Government opened the lands of other tribes to settlement. On September 16, 1893, it allowed settlers to homestead the Cherokee Outlet, the unoccupied part of Cherokee land, and 100,000 settlers entered that area in one day. In 1907 Oklahoma became a State, numbering half a million inhabitants and combining what had been Oklahoma Territory and Indian Territory. The advance of the farmers onto the Great Plains had been completed.

### NEW METHODS AND MACHINERY

The first settlers to venture onto the Plains were forced to invent new techniques to replace the ones they had worked out in the East. Soon exhausting the basically inadequate timber supply, they had to turn from wood to other raw materials to build their cabins and fences. With inventive genius, they cut the tough prairie sod into slabs and built their homes in much the same manner as residents of the Southwest used adobe bricks. They

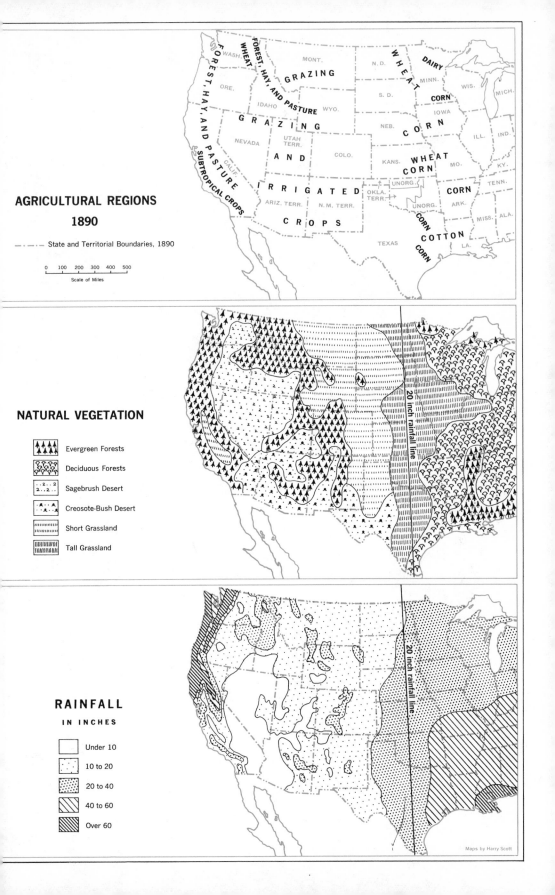

**AGRICULTURAL REGIONS**

**1890**

— ·· — ·· — State and Territorial Boundaries, 1890

0  100  200  300  400  500
Scale of Miles

FOREST, HAY, AND PASTURE
WASH.
WHEAT
FOREST, HAY, AND PASTURE
ORE.
GRAZING
IDAHO
MONT.
N.D.
DAIRY
MINN.
WIS.
MICH.
WHEAT
S.D.
WYO.
CORN
IOWA
GRAZING
NEVADA
UTAH TERR.
NEB.
ILL.
IND.
FOREST, HAY, AND PASTURE
CALIF.
COLO.
CORN
AND
KANS.
WHEAT CORN
MO.
KY.
CORN
TENN.
SUBTROPICAL CROPS
IRRIGATED
ARIZ. TERR.
N.M. TERR.
OKLA. TERR.
UNORG.
UNORG.
ARK.
CORN
MISS.
ALA.
CROPS
CORN
COTTON
CORN
TEXAS
LA.

**NATURAL VEGETATION**

| | |
|---|---|
| ▲▲▲▲ | Evergreen Forests |
| ♈♈♈ | Deciduous Forests |
| ..2..2 2..2.. | Sagebrush Desert |
| ·▲·▲ ·▲·▲· | Creosote-Bush Desert |
| |||||||| | Short Grassland |
| |||||||| | Tall Grassland |

20 inch rainfall line

**RAINFALL**

**IN INCHES**

| | |
|---|---|
| ☐ | Under 10 |
| ∴ | 10 to 20 |
| ∷ | 20 to 40 |
| ╱╱ | 40 to 60 |
| ▨ | Over 60 |

20 inch rainfall line

Maps by Harry Scott

constructed barns and other structures in like manner, and even used sod occasionally for building fences.

Thirsty plainsmen knew that water was a farmer's salvation. Only a few lucky farmers on the Great Plains possessed land adjoining rivers or streams, and they faced the danger of spring floods. Until well-drilling machinery came into common use in the 1880's, the rest had the problem of getting any water at all—even for drinking and for the farm animals. Water was hauled to outlying farms in barrels; it was collected in ponds and in cisterns. Impure ground water caused epidemics of "prairie fever," or typhoid.

While bonanza farmers worked extensive fields of wheat, small landholders improved their harvests with a Marsh self-binder, drawn by oxen. Across the expanding wheat country in the 1870's sodbusters bought the newly invented agricultural machinery, in a variety of types and models. Photograph by F. Jay Haynes. Courtesy, Alfred A. Knopf, Inc., and The Haynes Foundation.

From the beginning, Plains farming required improved machinery. Without a new type of plow to replace the cast-iron plow the prairie sod could not even be broken. John Deere answered this need; by 1857 more than 10,000 of his steel plows, invented in

1837, were being sold annually to prairie farmers. James Oliver's "chilled-iron" plow, an improved model, was invented in 1868. Within a decade more than 175,000 of these plows were in use, and production had soared to 60,000 a year. The next significant innovation was the breaker plow, which differed from the Eastern plow in that it turned over the sod in rather shallow but very wide furrows. Because this plow required more power, oxen instead of horses were required to pull it.

McCormick twine binder float, ready for a Fourth of July parade in Fargo, North Dakota. The exhibition of farm machinery was almost a carnival affair. Photograph by F. Jay Haynes. Courtesy, Alfred A. Knopf, Inc., and The Haynes Foundation.

The groundwork for the mechanized agriculture that became a necessity on the flat Plains, which lent themselves so well to mechanization, had been laid in the East during the first half of the 19th century and the Civil War. Wartime labor shortages and high prices stimulated the use of machinery. Even before the war began the cutting of wheat by hand had ceased on almost all large farms, which ·used Cyrus H. McCormick's mechanical reaper, patented in 1834. Competition between manufacturers and the labor scarcity during the war brought the self-rake reaper to perfection and encouraged experimentation with harvesters and automatic binders. In 1873 the wire binder came into use but it proved unsatisfactory, and by 1880 William Deering had put 3,000 twine binders on the market.

Along with the improved machinery came a new technique of tilling the land, a system known as "dry farming" that evolved at the end of the 19th century. Soil moisture was conserved by careful cultivation. Usually a field was cultivated continuously, but only planted in alternate years. By keeping a dust mulch over the surface at all times, a 2-year supply of moisture could be stored in the ground, provided a windstorm did not blow away the topsoil. Dry farming required extensive tracts of land and the efficient use of farm machinery.

Thus farmers trying to make a start on the Plains had to go heavily into debt for farm machinery, unless they had a great deal of money to begin with—which few had. The use of the new and improved agricultural machinery—common in California's great central valley and later in the "inland empire" of Washington and Oregon—enabled a farmer to increase his acreage and production with less manpower. But the Plains farmer took a greater risk of

Group of farmhands during the busy season on the Barnes bonanza farm at Glyndon, Minnesota, just east of Fargo, North Dakota. Most were itinerants. Photograph by F. Jay Haynes. Courtesy, Alfred A. Knopf, Inc., and The Haynes Foundation.

becoming a slave to his machines, or rather to the mortgage company that lent him the money to buy them, than did farmers elsewhere. For him mechanization was a necessity, but often it failed to raise his standard of living.

The agricultural development of the Plains was based to a considerable extent upon the work of scientists and inventors who perfected a new process of milling. The Plains, especially in the north, were unsuited for raising the soft winter wheat previously sown in the United States. Hard-kerneled wheat, known as "Turkey Red," imported from the Crimea, grew well in Kansas and Nebraska, while other varieties of spring wheat from Northern Europe produced excellent yields in Minnesota, Dakota, and Montana. But old methods of milling were not effective with spring wheat. Then inventors came to the rescue of the growers. Corrugated, chilled-iron rollers were substituted for millstones and solved the problem. By 1881 Western mills were using the new process and producing fine grades of flour from spring wheat. And grain elevators were constructed by the railroads so that grain could be stored for shipment and loaded into cars mechanically.

## GRASSHOPPERS, DROUGHT, AND BLIZZARDS

New methods and machinery did not solve all the problems posed by the Plains environment. Most of the homesteaders ventured onto the Great Plains with the courage of complete ignorance. They planted corn, but it did not grow. They also tried to raise barley, sorghum, and millet, but with only limited success. Finally, wheat became the staple crop, but in dry years serious failures occurred. The inhospitable climate ranged from blizzards to searing heat. Many farm animals froze to death or died from heat and thirst. Recurring droughts turned much of the region into a desert, and grasshopper plagues filled the prairie farmer's cup of frustrations. The worst invasion occurred in 1874, when the whole area, from the Dakotas to Texas, was devastated. The grasshoppers ate everything, leaving, as one farmer said, nothing but the mortgage. But many farmers continued to fight the battle with nature. Many others did not; their byword was "In God we trusted; in Kansas we busted."

Ready to begin harrowing on the Grandin farm, Red River Valley of Minnesota-North Dakota. Photograph by F. Jay Haynes. Courtesy, Alfred A. Knopf, Inc., and The Haynes Foundation.

Settlers in Custer County, Nebraska. They brought with them everything they owned—a few horses or oxen, a coop of poultry, seeds for planting, a plow. Photograph by S. D. Butcher. Courtesy, Nebraska State Historical Society.

Typical sod house in the Cimarron Valley, in southwestern Kansas. The adjustment to a new way of life on the Plains was not easy for most settlers. Photograph by W. D. Johnson. Courtesy, U.S. Geological Survey.

### RECESSION, ALLIANCES, AND POPULISM

Farmers on the Plains faced serious problems other than the natural environment. They suffered from the post-Civil War agricultural recession that affected all farmers and had been set in motion by increased agricultural production and the end of wartime inflation and special demand. Adversely affected by the high transportation rates to vital Eastern markets and low prices for their products, they had to pay high prices for manufactured articles, produced by Eastern plants that were enjoying high postwar demand. They were thus forced to buy supplies and farm implements on credit and mortgage their crops and farms at high interest rates. After the disastrous Panic of 1873, creditors foreclosed mortgages, and the money supply tightened severely.

The farmers, attributing many of their misfortunes to corporate monopolies, especially the railroads, took steps to advance their economic interests. The Grange, the first nationwide farm organization, founded in Minnesota in 1868, provided them with a focus for their grievances. It sought by educational and quasi-political means to eliminate the middleman through cooperative buying practices and to initiate State legislation to control the railroads.

But Western farmers, feeling that the Grange was not sufficiently aggressive, in the middle 1870's began to turn to various other alliances, which prospered throughout the 1880's. [The nationwide development of the Grange and other farmers' alliances will be treated in detail in the volume of this series dealing with the history of U.S. agriculture.] The Populist Party, formed in 1890, synthesized the aims of these alliances, as well as those of the Greenback movement, which had been active from about 1868 to 1884 and had sought to increase farm profits and eliminate debts by convincing the Government to increase the amount of paper money in circulation. The Populist Party was gradually absorbed by the Democratic Party and collapsed in 1896, when the Democrat William Jennings Bryan supported free silver, a key plank in the Populist Party platform.

## End of the Open Range Cattle Era

The movement of homesteaders, or nesters, into the Great Plains and Rocky Mountain States had started at approximately the same time as that of the cattlemen. Almost unnoticed at first, the nesters soon offered a formidable challenge to the cattle kings and eventually triumphed over them. Increasing steadily in numbers, they closed in around the large spreads, staked claims to prime grass and water, and established farms or small ranches. Finding a place along a stream where the cattleman had been unable to preempt every bit of adjacent land, a farmer would stake his claim and dig an irrigation ditch to supply his fields. A second farmer would homestead at the rear of the first, and the ditch would be extended to the second farm—and so the farms multiplied. Farmers shot trespassing cattle and drew upon the herds for their beef supply; they called such meat "slow elk." Then they began to fence the open range.

### BARBED WIRE AND "WARS"

For years an answer to the need for a cheap fencing material for the open West had been sought. Farmers at first had planted the thorny Osage-orange and black locust, hedges that were drought resistant and reasonably stock-proof. Then in 1873 Jacob F. Glidden, a De Kalb, Ill., farmer, invented barbed wire. Slow to sell at first, the new two-strand wire gradually found a market when it was proven that cattle actually were kept in—or out—by it. Homesteaders began fencing their acres and small ranchers their grass, and the proponents of the open range were brought face-to-face with their greatest challenge.

The first lands to be fenced were those with a supply of water. The owner naturally kept out those animals that did not belong to him and pushed them back on the overcrowded open range. Once fencing got underway on a wide scale, the large ranchers had to make a choice: they could join the movement, or they could fight it. To do nothing would bring ruin.

By 1883 fence-cutting "wars" were widespread. In Texas, for example, in more than half the 171 organized counties fence cutting assumed epidemic proportions. In some counties the proponents and opponents of barbed wire were so evenly divided that civil war seemed imminent. Gov. John Ireland was forced to call

Working the roundup. Cutting out cattle without unduly disturbing the herd required great proficiency on the part of the rider as well as his horse. Photograph by Erwin E. Smith. Courtesy, Mrs. L. M. Pettis and

out the Rangers and invoke a special session of the legislature to consider the problem. The legislature made fence cutting a felony and ruled that the enclosing of any land not owned or leased was illegal. Finally, public opinion swung against the fence cutters, and the "war" drew to a close.

The Texas experience was repeated elsewhere, until the cattle kings were forced to join in the enclosure movement. Other factors hastening the spread of fencing—and the end of the open range era—were the extension of the railroads, the discovery of more adequate ground water, and the use of windmills to obtain it. The large cattle companies, most of them owned by Eastern capitalists, led in the fencing movement, and gradually the lesser cattle kings followed suit.

### STOCKMEN'S PROTECTIVE ASSOCIATIONS

To protect themselves from the homesteaders—and from cattle rustlers among their own ranks—the fiercely individualistic cattlemen succumbed to necessity and formed protective stockmen's associations. Few other frontier organizations ever achieved the power and efficiency of these associations. They employed a large force of range detectives to keep an alert eye on everyone and everything in the cattle business. They organized and supervised roundups, administered grass and water rights, and investigated cattle diseases. And they exerted strong influence on State and Territorial legislatures to assure laws favorable to the welfare of the large cattlemen. By 1885 they blanketed the Great Plains and Rocky Mountain States.

The strength and efficiency of the stockmen's associations ultimately resulted in the development of a violent antagonism on the part of the townsmen and small ranchers, who joined the farmers in fighting the associations. In time even the brazen larcenies of cattle rustlers went unpunished because grand juries in the towns would not indict anyone harassing the large ranchers.

Against this rising tide of popular sentiment the Wyoming Stock Growers Association, the most influential and successful of the cattlemen's groups, made a last desperate bid to regain its authority. In the Johnson County War of 1892, it used imported gunmen to eliminate opposition. Public opinion was inflamed against the members of the association, and for a time it seemed likely that every head of stock owned by the large companies in Wyoming would be slaughtered. The Johnson County War and its disastrous outcome demonstrated to cattlemen that range wars were not the solution to their problems.

### OVEREXPANSION

The closing of the cattlemen's frontier was finally brought about, not by barbed wire or by homesteaders, but by overexpansion and nature. Until about 1885 most of the larger outfits were returning at least a paper profit despite the crowding of herd upon herd, absentee and often inefficient management, and wholesale thievery. That year the arrival of 200,000 cattle from the Indian Territory, removed from the Cheyenne-Arapaho Reservation by proclamation of President Cleveland, smothered the already crowded ranges of Kansas, Colorado, and the Texas Panhandle.

The year 1886 was one of crisis. Ranchers in the Southwest, who had suffered heavy losses the preceding winter, unloaded what was left of their herds on the falling market. The editor of the *Rocky Mountain Husbandman,* noting that the market was growing weak-

Branding scene. After the ropers and heelers got the calf in position, the brander applied the iron and another puncher slit the ears for further identification. Despite Hollywood prototypes, these cowboys seemed to find suspenders more helpful to their work than sixguns. Courtesy, National Archives.

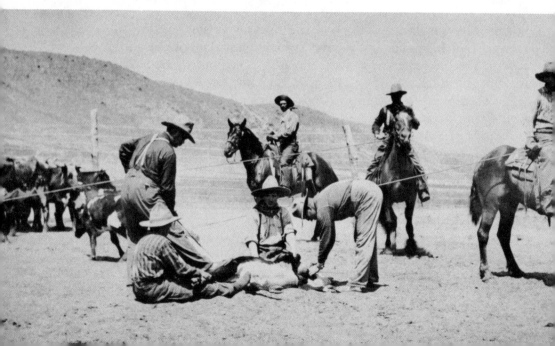

er by the day, advised that "it would be better to sell at a low figure than to endanger the whole herd by having the range overcrowded." The summer of 1886 was hot and dry. The grass withered and streams disappeared. Cattle were in exceptionally poor condition for the coming winter. Some ranchers forestalled disaster by driving their herds across the Canadian border and leasing new grazing lands. Others shipped cattle to Iowa and Nebraska for fattening.

## THE WINTER OF 1886–87

Then came the catastrophic winter of 1886–87, probably the most severe ever experienced on the Plains. The storms came early. A chinook that blew up from the south in January, melting snow and bringing hope, was immediately followed by a howling blizzard. Cattle, driven by a merciless wind, piled up against fences and died by the thousands. A numbing cold followed the storm, and the thermometer dropped out of sight. Cowboys, imprisoned for weeks around bunkhouse stoves, dared not think of the starving, freezing herds, helpless to find food or shelter.

When spring finally came, cattlemen saw a sight that they spent the rest of their lives trying to forget: Carcass piled upon carcass, gaunt cattle staggering about on frozen feet, and trees stripped bare of their bark. Perhaps the most expressive description of the catastrophe is artist Charlie Russell's celebrated painting "The Last of the 5,000," which shows a single, starving cow in deep snow, a hungry coyote waiting nearby. Rancher Granville Stuart said that the cattle business, which "had been fascinating to me before, suddenly became distasteful," and estimated his loss at 66 percent of his herd. Most stockmen had severe losses; many were wiped out.

The range was still as good as ever, and stood an excellent chance of recovering from the overgrazing. But cattlemen had lost their confidence—the unshakable optimism that had lured them into taking chances in the expectation of wealth. Outside capital, freely supplied in the days of easy profits, low operating costs, and rapidly expanding herds, was no longer available. Those cattlemen who remained in business did so by developing new methods. All realized that they had been mistaken in believing that the grass of the open range was sufficient to build a lasting empire.

That disastrous winter had another far-reaching effect. Bankruptcy broke up many of the great corporate ranches and to a large extent ended the period of absentee ownership. The Swan Land and Cattle Company, largest of all the companies on the northern range, went into receivership in May 1887. Many of the small ranchers and a few of the larger pioneer ranchers remained, and some of them purchased the stock and land of the large companies that went bankrupt. Even so enthusiastic a cattleman as Theodore Roosevelt, whose own herds on the Little Missouri had been decimated, believed it "right and necessary" that the era of the open range should pass, and that the future of the country should lie with the small agriculturist—be he farmer or rancher.

And that fateful winter brought an end to the romantic era of the great trail drives. Farmers fenced in the trail and plowed it under. The open range cattle era had faded into the mists of history.

## Epilogue—A Bygone Age

The golden age of the West is gone. But it was an age so rich in achievement, romance, courage, and adventure that it will always have a prime place in our history and folklore. In the process of taming and settling the West the prospector, cowhand, and sodbuster changed the face of the wild land. They brought civilization, established towns, forced the nomadic Indians onto reservations, drove the game into the hills, and wrested whatever they could from the land—be it gold, silver, cattle, or wheat.

As time passed and men adapted to new conditions and tried to better their lot, the West changed. Individual effort yielded to corporate endeavor. In the early days one man panned a stream for gold or silver. He ignored the other metals and felt that their retrieval was not worth the effort. By the turn of the 20th century mining was in the hands of large corporations, whose stock was traded on Wall Street. These industrial giants were not interested only in gold or silver; they mined any metal that promised a profit. The electrical revolution created a demand for copper, and the railroads made it possible to transport low-grade ores at a reasonable cost. The mining corporations turned to copper and other minerals, which brought them far more return than gold or silver ever had to the lone prospector. The miner became a day laborer, he entered some other occupation, or he wandered to the far corners of the earth.

After the range was fenced, ranchers could experiment with improved breeds of cattle. Most of them replaced Longhorns with Herefords and other breeds. The cowhand, who was used to living in a line camp dugout a hundred miles from nowhere and who trailed many a herd out of Texas, got married, took a homestead, kept milk cows, and raised vegetables along with a few "whitefaces."

The subsistence farm of the Plains gave way to large, highly mechanized, one-crop establishments that produced for the world market. The farmer became a businessman, who in order to survive had to turn from the pioneer independence of his forebears to cooperatives for economic and political protection. As time passed, climatic factors, economic conditions, new machinery and equipment, and trends in government brought a new face to the West.

Accustomed to the comforts and conveniences of the 20th century, we today can only dimly appreciate the hardships encountered and overcome by the pioneer prospector, cowhand, and sodbuster—who had far more sinew and spirit than have the romanticized versions we see in television and movies. These men went west with high hopes and dreams. They worked and they fought. They looked upon their children and hoped for something better for them. Some sought adventure and found it; some tried to start over again and busted again; some hoped to get wealthy, but few did. But they fulfilled their destiny. They kept faith with their dreams. They transformed the West from a frontier into a vital part of the United States and helped mold the character of the Nation.

PART II

Prospector, Cowhand,

and Sodbuster:

Survey of Historic

Sites and Buildings

ISTORIC PLACES associated with the mining, ranching, and farming frontiers—with the prospector,
cowhand, and sodbuster—are spread across the
vast open face of the trans-Mississippi West. They
are usually as separated by great distances as are the towns that dot
the endless horizon—with its wide plains, open sky, rugged mountains, sparkling streams, and arid stretches. This land, which both
thwarted and nurtured the pioneers, is itself the greatest monument of all to their individualistic efforts.

The face of the land reflects what man has done. The prospector
and miner left the most enduring physical remains because the nature of their operations required more extensive structures than
did those of the rancher and the farmer. Remains of the mining
frontier are distributed throughout 12 of the States in the trans-
Mississippi West—Arizona, California, Colorado, Idaho, Montana.

Nevada, New Mexico, Oregon, South Dakota, Utah, Washington, and Wyoming. Many of them are in villages that are no longer inhabited—ghost towns whose dusty streets are flanked by weather-beaten, unpainted structures that were used by the thousands who eagerly rushed to each discovery in the hope of finding quick riches.

It is impossible to list or even locate more than a fraction of all the mines that once yielded fortunes, or all the towns that sprang up in the vicinity of such mines. In the gold-mining region of California alone, more than 500 towns were probably established in the period 1848–60, of which more than half have disappeared, even from maps. Time has done the same damage to the towns that it has to the sluice boxes, machinery, and cabins that dotted the vicinity of each camp. A prominent feature of the landscape is the debris left behind—mile after mile of stark and unsightly waste, mounds of boulders lining the streams and canyons, and the colorless rockpiles spewed out by countless dredges.

Some mining towns have continued to the present, and a few are today prosperous modern cities. Others have continued their existence as lumbering towns, trading centers, or cowtowns. Those that have become ghost towns vary widely in their state of preservation. Because of widespread interest, as well as local pride, in the relics of the frontier mining days, the preservation of individual structures, groups of buildings, even entire towns is done on a wide scale—by State park commissions, towns, municipalities, individuals, and private foundations. At least one well-preserved town is located in almost every important mining State in the West.

In contrast to the prospectors and miners, the ranchers and sodbusters left few material remains. The pioneer ranchers built a limited number of structures, for their investment was in cattle and their natural resources were grass and water. Much of their range, now fenced, is little changed in appearance from the time they first saw it, although Herefords and other breeds of cattle have replaced the distinctive Longhorns. Fortunately for those interested in the history of the West, the Fish and Wildlife Service, U.S. Department of the Interior, maintains two representative herds of Texas Longhorns: one at the Wichita Mountains Wildlife Refuge near Cache, Okla., and the other at the Fort Niobrara National Wildlife Refuge near Valentine, Nebr. The two herds contain about 500 animals. Both of the refuges are open to the public.

Few cowtowns today give much indication that they once welcomed the boisterous cowboy at the end of the long drive. Thrown up hurriedly, many of them have long since disappeared. Others have destroyed all traces of the early days as they have modernized. The same is true of the original ranch headquarters of the great cattle spreads. The early buildings were rudimentary and most of them did not even survive the era of the range cattle industry. As the cattlemen lost parts of their vast landholdings, they often abandoned the old headquarters. Most of the buildings that have survived have been modernized to provide more comfortable living quarters than the early cattlemen enjoyed.

The famous cattle trails—the Chisholm, the Western, the Goodnight-Loving, and the Shawnee—were dug out by the hooves of millions of Texas cattle. Most traces of them have long since disappeared. Almost the only surviving remains are of the forts that served as way stations for the drivers and their herds. Fort Gibson, Okla., Fort Griffin, Tex., Fort Belknap, Tex., and Fort Sumner, N. Mex.—names familiar to thousands of cowboys—today are preserved as visitor attractions.

As for the ranchers, few physical evidences remain of the activities of Western farmers. Pioneers reached valleys untouched by man, farmed a year or two, moved on because of advancing civilization or in a search for more fertile fields, and left little of permanence behind. Because of the nature of the land and his rudimentary tools, the frontier farmer could cultivate only on a limited scale. He built the bare minimum—a rude shelter and barn—so that when he moved on little was left except the land. Such structures as the sod house, built by most homesteaders on the Plains, did not last long; and wild grass soon re-covered the plowed fields. Today, when agriculture has become a mechanized big business, it is difficult to find anywhere in the agricultural belt west of the Mississippi a farmstead that bears much resemblance to one in the days of the homesteader.

Unfortunately no attempt has been made to re-create the life of the pioneer farmer of the West on a scale such as is being done at the Farm Museum in Cooperstown, N.Y. Popular interest in the agricultural phase of Western history has never been great. Writers have seldom seen fit to romanticize the life of the farmer, as they have those of the cowboy, gunman, miner, and mountain man.

Many of the sites and buildings associated with the era of the prospector, cowhand, and sodbuster are described in the following pages. They are arranged alphabetically by State within the following four categories: pertinent units of the National Park System; sites eligible for the Registry of National Historic Landmarks; Historic Districts eligible for the Registry; and sites of sufficient importance to merit attention but which are not considered nationally significant when measured by the special Landmark criteria (pp. 269–270). A number of general agricultural sites that have some association with Western agriculture, as well as irrigation and reclamation sites, will be included in the volume of this series dealing with the development of U.S. agriculture.

# A. Sites in the National Park System

The principal aim of the National Survey of Historic Sites and Buildings is to identify nationally important historic sites that are not units of the National Park System, but no such survey would be complete without mention of sites in the System. The sites described below are those administered by the National Park Service that have primary or secondary associations with the phases of history treated in this volume. Further information about a particular site may be obtained by writing directly to the superintendent at the address indicated.

## 1. Pipe Spring National Monument, Arizona

*Location: Mohave County, on Ariz. 389, about 15 miles southwest of Fredonia; address: c/o Superintendent, Zion National Park, Springdale, Utah 84767.*

The Mormon extension southward from the Salt Lake Basin and the achievements of the Southwestern pioneers are exemplified in this National Monument. In the 1850's the Mormons began dispersing from the basin to locations in southern Utah and northern Arizona that provided water. As centers of defense against Indian attacks and way stations for travelers, Brigham Young established forts at strategic locations. Pipe Spring National Monument contains probably the best remaining example of such a fort.

Although the Escalante expedition of 1776 passed nearby, the first white men known to have visited Pipe Spring were members

Pipe Spring National Monument, Arizona. Strategically located frontier forts, such as Pipe Spring, helped extend Mormon settlement southward from the Great Salt Lake into Arizona.

of the Jacob Hamblin party, who camped there in 1858. They had been sent out by Young to explore and report on the Colorado River country and try to negotiate a treaty of peace with the Navajos living on the south side of the river. Between 1863 and 1865 Pipe Spring was the headquarters of a Mormon cattle ranch, but a marauding band of Navajos killed the inhabitants.

The Mormon Church then acquired the property. Between 1869 and 1871 Bishop Anson P. Winsor built the fort that became known as "Winsor Castle." The fort consisted of two redstone buildings, two stories high, that faced each other across a courtyard. Sandstone walls and heavy gates enclosed the courtyard on either side of the buildings. The firing platform just below the top of one wall and the associated loopholes that remain today were planned for use during Indian attacks. A continuous flow of water was insured, for one of the buildings stood directly over a spring. Bishop Winsor left Pipe Spring about 1875. The place then became important as a cattle ranch and as the starting point for cattle drives to the railroad at Lund, Utah, more than 100 miles away.

Pipe Spring, consisting of 40 acres, was established as a National Monument in 1923. In addition to the fort and outbuildings, it features displays of pioneer tools and furnishings. Many interesting forms of vegetation and wildlife prosper in the vicinity. Park rangers conduct tours daily.

## 2. Jefferson National Expansion Memorial, Missouri

> *Location: St. Louis, downtown; address: 11 North 4th Street, St. Louis, Mo. 63102.*

This memorial celebrates the vision of President Jefferson, the great architect of westward expansion, and all aspects of that vital national movement.

St. Louis, "gateway to the West," was founded in 1764 by Frenchmen from New Orleans and became a center of French-Canadian culture and Spanish governmental control. Conveniently located in relation to the mouths of the Ohio, Missouri, and other Mississippi tributaries, it became the hub of midcontinental commerce, transportation, and culture—the place where East met West and jumping-off point to the wilderness beyond. A base of operations for traders, travelers, scientists, explorers, military leaders, Indian agents, and missionaries, it was also headquarters of the Western fur trade and focus of advanced scientific and political thought in the West.

Along the St. Louis waterfront, hulking steamboats from the East and South met the smaller river boats that served the frontier communities and outposts on the upper Mississippi and Missouri Rivers. At this major transfer point, a small but teeming city, mercantile establishments, boatyards, saloons, and lodginghouses served and supplied the westbound settlers and other frontiersmen who congregated there before setting out across the Plains. Oregon and California pioneers and gold seekers bought tools, wagons, guns, and supplies; lumbermen, planters, farmers, and fur dealers sold their products; and artisans fashioned Newell & Sutton plows, Murphy wagons for the Santa Fe trade, Grimsley dragoon saddles, Hawken "plains" rifles, and the cast-iron stoves of Filley, and Bridge & Beach.

To dramatize westward expansion and the great cultural, political, economic, and other benefits that followed in the wake of the Louisiana Purchase of 1803, an extensive development program for the memorial is being undertaken by the National Park Service and the Jefferson National Expansion Memorial Association, a nonprofit organization of public-spirited citizens. Crowded, obsolescent industrial buildings have been cleared away as part of a broad urban renewal program.

The dominant feature of the memorial—on the site of the original village of St. Louis—is a 630-foot-high stainless steel arch, designed by the noted architect Eero Saarinen, and completed in 1965. Rising from the west bank of the Mississippi River, it symbolizes the historic position of St. Louis as gateway to the West. It contains an elevator system enabling the visitor to reach an observatory at the top. Scaled to the heroic dimensions of such structures as the Washington Monument, the Eiffel Tower, and the Statue of Liberty, it ranks with them in size and grandeur.

An underground visitor center, featuring a Museum of Westward Expansion—temporarily located in the Old Courthouse—is planned at the base of the arch. Museum exhibits portraying the experiences and contributions of Western explorers, fur traders, statesmen, overland emigrants, soldiers, miners, Indians, cattlemen, and farmers will present our Western heritage in new dimensions. Guided, as well as self-guided, tours for visiting groups will be provided. The devices and services used in telling the story of westward expansion will be enriched through the years by continuing historical research.

Two historic buildings are preserved at the memorial. One is the Old Courthouse, constructed during the period 1839–64. It was the scene of the first trial in the famous Dred Scott case and the dominant architectural feature of the town during the years that St. Louis was "emporium of the West." Its rotunda resounded with the oratory of Thomas Hart Benton and other famed speakers of the 19th century. At the courthouse Senator Benton delivered his famous oration, using as his theme Bishop Berkeley's poetic phrase "Westward the course of empire." The second historic structure is the Old Cathedral, built during the years 1831–34 on church property set aside at the time of the founding of St. Louis. It was at one time the seat of the archdiocese, but is now a shrine and place of worship.

The Jefferson National Expansion Memorial was designated as a National Historic Site by Executive order in 1935. It occupies an area of more than 80 acres.

Restored Palmer-Epard log cabin at Homestead National Monument, typical of thousands of such homes built by sodbusters.

## 3. Homestead National Monument, Nebraska

*Location: Gage County, on Nebr. 4 about 40 miles south of Lincoln and 4½ miles northwest of Beatrice; address: Beatrice, Nebr. 68310.*

This monument commemorates the free land policy that governed the settlement of the Western Plains and the hardy pioneers who endured frontier conditions while settling the West. Vast amounts of cheap land induced native and foreign-born emigrants to join the vanguard of the westward expansion of the United States. Free land as a reward to pioneer settlers for their part in converting undeveloped lands into farms was gradually recognized by law. Disposal of the public domain to private owners, partly to provide governmental revenue, continued until well after 1900.

In the decades just prior to the Civil War, Congressmen, newspaper editors, political leaders, antislavery groups, and individuals cried out for free land. Nonsectarian both in origin and during its early history, the homestead movement attracted diverse support as it gained force and popularity. First minor, and later major, political parties advocated free homesteads in their platforms.

Between 1840 and 1860 the movement for a homestead law slowly crystallized. At first it received some support from the Southeastern States. As the alliance between the agrarian West and the industrial East grew stronger, however, the slave States increasingly opposed homestead proposals and several bills failed of passage in Congress.

Finally, in 1862, President Lincoln signed the Homestead Act, under which any citizen or citizen-to-be could obtain 160 acres of unappropriated Government land free of charge, except for a small filing fee. To become full owner, the settler was obligated to live on the land and cultivate it for 5 years.

Later acts made land more easily obtainable, especially for Civil War veterans. At the end of the war thousands of men sought a livelihood in a country disrupted by 4 years of upheaval. Many took advantage of the free public lands offered by the Homestead Act. Europeans were lured to seek new homes in the United States because they could obtain a free farm, as well as enjoy the other opportunities of a democratic Nation. The influx of land seekers— aiding significantly in peopling Kansas, Nebraska, the Dakotas, and Montana—was a major factor, along with industrial development, in doubling the Nation's population during the 40 years following passage of the Homestead Act.

Homestead National Monument is on the site of Daniel Freeman's homestead, located on a T-shaped quarter section. Freeman was one of the first applicants to file under the Homestead Act; he filed Homestead Entry No. 1 at the Brownville, Nebr., Land Office during the early hours of January 1, 1863, the day the act went into effect. Several applications were filed at the other 29 Land Offices as early or earlier than Freeman's. Freeman and his wife are buried near the monument's eastern boundary, the highest point on the homestead. From the gravesites the entire Freeman homestead may be viewed.

In 1936 Congress designated the Homestead National Monument of America as "a proper memorial emblematical of the hardships and the pioneer life through which the early settlers passed in the settlement, cultivation, and civilization of the great West." On exhibit at the National Monument are pioneer objects and graphic displays of life during settlement of the public domain. The Palmer-Epard homestead cabin, erected in 1867 in a neighboring township, has been moved to the monument. Its furnishings and tools suggest the pattern of life followed by the homesteaders on the tall-grass prairie. A 1-mile self-guiding trail, beginning at the visitor center, leads to the Palmer-Epard and original Freeman cabins and the sites of later Freeman buildings, including the brick home of 1876. Side trips may be made to the graves and the site of Squatters Cabin, near Cub Creek.

## 4. Theodore Roosevelt National Memorial Park, North Dakota

*Location: Billings County, off U.S. 10 and 85, just north of Medora; address: Medora, N. Dak. 58645.*

Roosevelt's part in developing the open range cattle industry of the Northern Plains and his contributions to the conservation of the Nation's resources are memorialized in this vast park. Roosevelt first came to the Dakota Badlands, on the Little Missouri River, in 1883, at the age of 25, to hunt buffalo and other game. Within a few weeks, however, he purchased some 400 cattle and made arrangements to graze them on the Chimney Butte Ranch, owned by two local ranchers, before he returned to the East; the ranch was

The Maltese Cross Cabin, Theodore Roosevelt's first residence in the Badlands, is now exhibited at Theodore Roosevelt National Memorial Park, in North Dakota.

also known as the Maltese Cross Ranch because of its distinctive brand. The next summer, after Roosevelt's election to the New York State Assembly and the death of his wife and mother, he returned to his property in the West. The following year he stocked the Elkhorn Ranch. Soon he became an influential cattleman, though he had a small number of cattle compared to many ranchers in the area, and was elected to lead the local livestock association. Meantime he continued his study and writing. He wrote much of his *Life of Thomas Hart Benton* while residing at the Elkhorn Ranch. One of his neighbors was the Marquis de Mores, a French nobleman who founded the town of Medora.

Along with most cattlemen, Roosevelt suffered severe losses in the disastrous winter of 1886–87. Probably 60 percent of his herd perished—and with it most of his large investment. Yet he continued to visit the ranch every few years until 1898, when he sold out just before leaving for Cuba with the Rough Riders.

Years later Roosevelt wrote, "I have always said I never would have been President if it had not been for my experience in North Dakota." Certainly he always regarded his life on the range as an idyllic interlude, a place where "the romance of my life began." He admired the rough virtues and the rugged integrity of the men with whom he rode in the Dakotas, and from them he drew his inspiration for organizing the Rough Riders—the group that made him famous and furthered his political career.

Established by Congress in 1947, the memorial park consists of about 110 square miles. It is divided into three units: the South Unit, near Medora; the North Unit, near Watford City; and the Elkhorn Ranch site, along the Little Missouri River west of and about midway between the other two units. The Elkhorn Ranch site is accessible only by rough dirt road, and local inquiry should be made before attempting to reach it. Neither the ranchhouse nor any other original buildings remain at the site today, but a diorama at the Medora visitor center is an accurate reproduction. The site has been excavated and nearly all the original Elkhorn Ranch features have been located.

Motorists entering the South Unit at the Medora entrance should first stop at the visitor center, which features exhibits on the history and natural history of the park. Also located at the Medora entrance is the Maltese Cross cabin, which has been authentically restored and furnished as it was in Roosevelt's day.

The park is open all year but spring, summer, and autumn are the best seasons to visit. Campgrounds and picnic grounds are located in the North and South Units. The badlands landscape in the park has great scenic beauty and is of geologic interest—tablelands, buttes, canyons, and rugged hills. Although the climate is semiarid, much interesting plantlife may be seen. Of special interest among the animal life is a small herd of buffalo that has been introduced in the park.

## 5.  Fort Vancouver National Historic Site, Washington

*Location: Clark County, in the area bounded by East and West Reserve Streets, Vancouver; address: Vancouver, Wash. 98661.*

This fort served for two decades as the headquarters and depot for all activities of the Hudson's Bay Company west of the Rocky Mountains. As such, it was the economic, political, social, and cultural hub of an area now comprising British Columbia, Washington, Oregon, Idaho, and western Montana.

Fort Vancouver, founded in the 1820's by the Hudson's Bay Company, served as headquarters and depot for all activities of the company west of the Rocky Mountains. For two decades it was one of the most important settlements in the Pacific Northwest and pioneered in widescale agriculture. This photograph is from a watercolor made about 1845 by an unknown artist and now part of the Coe Collection of Western Americana, Yale University.

The fur resources of the Pacific Northwest were discovered by British seamen who visited the coast about the time of the American War for Independence, traded with the Indians, and discovered that the furs brought fantastic prices in China. Soon traders from several European countries, Canada, and the newly formed United States were vigorously competing in the trade. After years of bitter contest, the Hudson's Bay Company, a British firm chartered in 1670, won a dominant position.

In 1824 the company decided to move its western headquarters from Fort George, at the mouth of the Columbia River, to a site about 100 miles upstream. The shift was made to strengthen British claims to the territory north of the Columbia and to obtain better farming lands. Built in 1824–25, the fort was named for Capt. George Vancouver, the famous English explorer. In 1829 the company built a new fort a mile to the west, closer to the Columbia River.

For the next 20 years the fort was the most important settlement in the Pacific Northwest. Under the leadership of Chief Factor John McLoughlin, it monopolized the fur trade in the Oregon country and became the nerve center of a vast commercial empire that ranged from the Rockies to the Pacific and from Russian Alaska to Mexican California.

In addition to trading activities, the Hudson's Bay Company fostered farming and manufacturing. In 1825, using seeds and grain imported from England, personnel at the fort made the first plantings on 300 acres in the vicinity and later cultivated thousands of acres of land along the north bank of the Columbia River. They also established orchards. The fort milled enough flour to supply the company's needs in the entire region and also processed salmon and lumber. As mills, drying sheds, forges, and shops sprang up, it developed into a large-scale agricultural and industrial community, a pioneer in such activities in the Pacific Northwest.

Around the fort a village formed. Tradesmen, artisans, boatmen, and laborers built homes on the plains to the west and southwest. McLoughlin's encouragement to American pioneers and missionaries emigrating to the Oregon territory fostered the growth of an American population in the region, which the British then controlled.

According to the treaty of 1846 between the United States and

Great Britain, which established the 49th parallel as the southern boundary of Canada, Fort Vancouver was in U.S. territory. Thereafter the influence of the fort and the Hudson's Bay Company declined rapidly. U.S. settlers began to take over the land near the fort, and the village surrounding it expanded. In 1849 the U.S. Army organized a post at the fort. Within a couple of decades a fire destroyed all traces of the old stockade.

Fort Vancouver National Historic Site, established in 1954, contains 89 acres. Archeologists have uncovered a large quantity of artifacts, as well as remains of the stockade and building foundations.

# B. Sites Eligible for the Registry of National Historic Landmarks

The historic sites in this group have been judged by the Advisory Board on National Parks, Historic Sites, Buildings, and Monuments to meet the criteria of "exceptional value" for commemorating or illustrating the phases of U.S. history treated in this volume. As historic sites of national importance, they have been declared by the Secretary of the Interior to be eligible for inclusion in the Registry of National Historic Landmarks. Some have already been designated Registered National Historic Landmarks, and others will receive the designation upon application of the owners. A few have been proposed for addition to the National Park System.

## 1. San Bernardino Ranch, Arizona

*Location.* Cochise County, on an unpaved road, 17 miles east of Douglas.

*Ownership and Administration.* Privately owned.

*Significance.* One of the oldest cattle ranches in Arizona, San Bernardino had its origins in Spanish colonial days. A well-known watering place on the Spanish military trail from Chihuahua to Tucson, it was visited by Juan Bautista de Anza and Father Francisco Garces. For a while it was the site of a presidio and a hacienda, whose owners may have done some ranching. Reminiscent of presidial days is the name of a mesa near the ranch—*Mesa de la*

Ranch buildings at San Bernardino Ranch, in the San Pedro River Valley of Arizona. John Slaughter built them in the 1880's and 1890's.

*Avansada* (Mesa of the Advance Guard).

In 1822, during a period of peace with the Apaches, Lt. Ignacio Perez applied to the Mexican Government for a large tract of land surrounding San Bernardino Springs on which to graze cattle. He bought four *sitios* of land, 73,240 acres, but he controlled more than 1 million acres. At the peak of his prosperity, the ranch supported 100,000 cattle, 10,000 horses, and 5,000 mules. It was a sumptuous establishment, patios and flowering gardens surrounding its spacious adobe buildings. But all too soon the Apaches resumed their attacks, and in 1831 Perez abandoned the ranch. The cattle, left untended, soon went wild. Though the Apaches preyed upon them, they multiplied and overran the vicinity. Some attacked Lt. Col. Philip St. George Cooke's wagon train while it was en route to California during the Mexican War.

The American phase of ranching at San Bernardino began in 1884, when John Slaughter purchased the grant. Slaughter had arrived in Arizona from Texas and then worked for 7 years as a contractor and wholesaler of beef. He subsequently purchased the ranch, built his headquarters near the old Perez hacienda, and began running his cattle on both sides of the international boundary line. He dammed the springs and built irrigation networks.

About 30 families living on the ranch harvested his hay, vegetables, and fruit.

In 1886 Slaughter formed a partnership with George W. Lang, a famous trail driver who owned the Bato Pico Ranch on the Bavispe River of Sonora. The Bato Pico adjoined San Bernardino on the south, and the two partners purchased cattle in Sonora and held them on the San Bernardino until they could be shipped to California markets. They even operated a slaughterhouse in Los Angeles for much of this beef. In 1890 Slaughter bought the Bato Pico from Lang, along with all the cattle, and the partnership was dissolved. Slaughter, who also achieved fame as the sheriff of Tombstone, died in 1922; and, because he had no sons, Mrs. Slaughter sold the property.

*Present Appearance.* The ranch is presently owned by Marion L. Williams of Douglas, Ariz. Most of the headquarters buildings, dating from the 1880's and 1890's, are still intact and in use. These include the main ranchhouse, a stone-and-adobe cookhouse, a bunkhouse, and utility buildings. Ruins of the houses Slaughter erected for his Mexican farmers still stand at various points in the valley. Evidences of the Perez Ranch may also be seen nearby—ruined foundations and traces of adobe walls. San Bernardino Ranch is not open to the public.[1]

## 2.  Sierra Bonita Ranch, Arizona

*Location.* Graham County, on an unpaved road, 10 miles southwest of Bonita.

*Ownership and Administration.* Privately owned.

*Significance.* This ranch—in the shadow of the Graham Mountains overlooking Sulphur Springs Valley—was founded in 1872 by Col. Henry C. Hooker. Marking the penetration of U.S. cattlemen into the grasslands of southeastern Arizona Territory, an area where the Spanish-Mexican cattle empire had already risen and fallen, it was the first U.S. cattle ranch in the Territory to survive the Apache terror. It was also the first to introduce graded stock in the region.

The resumption of the campaign against the Apaches, at the end of the Civil War, brought an influx of troops to Arizona's 14 military posts. Feeding these men called for beef and laid the basis for

Early adobe barn at Sierra Bonita Ranch, Arizona.

Arizona's cattle industry. As the Army rounded up the Indians, a demand also arose for beef at the reservations, as it did also at the mines in the Territory. As early as 1867 Colonel Hooker became the leading military beef contractor. From Texas, New Mexico, California, Oregon, and Idaho, he drove as many as 15,000 cattle a year to holding ranges in Arizona Territory for resale to the Army camps and Indian agencies. In 1872 he established Sierra Bonita ("Beautiful Mountains").

Hooker built his ranch buildings on the site of a Spanish hacienda that had been abandoned in the early 1800's because of Apache raids. His main house was large and rectangular, 80 by 100 feet, and had thick adobe walls and gunports in the parapets. The water supply was plentiful and consisted of five springs, creeks that flowed in the spring and fall, and an underground river easily tapped by wells. This water gave Hooker control of a range approximately 30 miles long and 30 miles wide. Situated at 4,000 feet elevation, the ranch escaped extremes of heat and cold, and thus provided an ideal breeding range. In the 1880's Hooker improved his herds by importing Hereford graded stock. He also fenced portions of the land and planted alfalfa and other hay crops. Gradually he built his holdings until he controlled 250,000 acres that carried 20,000 head. So soundly did he build that he was one of the few Arizona ranchers to survive the disastrous drought of 1891. When he died in 1907, he was still the cattle king of Arizona.

*Present Appearance.* The Sierra Bonita is an operating cattle ranch, presently owned by Mrs. Harry Hooker, granddaughter of Colonel Hooker. The adobe ranchhouse has been remodeled inside, but it still retains the fortress-like appearance of early days. It is shaded by giant cottonwoods and surrounded by the original adobe corrals, bunkhouses, and barns. The integrity of the site is exceptional for three reasons: Continuity, appearance of the buildings, and the same magnificent setting that first attracted Hooker. The ranch is not open to the public.[2]

## 3.  Tombstone, Arizona

*Location.* Cochise County.

*Ownership and Administration.* Various private owners; and State of Arizona, State Parks Board.

*Significance.* In the summer of 1877 soldiers at nearby Fort Huachuca advised prospector Ed Schieffelin that all he would find would be his "tombstone," not the rich mineral deposits he sought. Because of hostile Apaches in the vicinity the advice seemed sound. But Schieffelin persisted in his search and found a silver bonanza, which attracted droves of miners, gamblers, gunmen, and others. By 1881 Tombstone was a booming town of 7,000 people. When Wyatt Earp served as a lawman there in the early 1880's, the famous Earp-Clanton feud made the town a battleground of warring factions and culminated in the celebrated fight at the O. K. Corral. Later, rancher John Slaughter became sheriff and made progress in cleaning up the town.

In the mid-1880's water began to fill the mining shafts. The expensive pumping equipment that was imported failed to solve the problem. By 1888 mining was at a virtual standstill, and by 1890 the town was well on the way to oblivion. In 1914 the Phelps-Dodge company took over the mining properties and still mines some ore. The total value of the silver taken from the vicinity of Ed Schieffelin's "tombstone" is estimated at approximately $80 million.

*Present Appearance.* Tombstone has advertised itself as "The Town Too Tough to Die," and indeed it is. Except for the addition of some neon signs and paved streets, it retains much of its

Tombstone, Arizona, was the site of one of the great silver bonanzas. Ed Schieffelin constructed this hall with the proceeds from his fabulous strike.

Tombstone retains much of its frontier flavor. The Bird Cage Theatre is one of the many Territorial buildings still standing.

frontier flavor—and is recapturing even more. Among the more important buildings still standing from Territorial days are the Bird Cage Theatre, the Tombstone City Hall, the Cochise County Courthouse, Schieffelin Hall, the office of the Tombstone *Epitaph,* and St. Paul's Episcopal Church. Boot Hill Cemetery is another attraction; the grave markers are periodically refurbished. Recently the Tombstone Historic Associates, a private group, renovated Schieffelin Hall and provided a number of other visitor attractions.

In 1957 a group of local citizens formed the Tombstone Restoration Commission and began gathering material to establish a museum in the old Cochise County Courthouse. Two years later, the State took over the courthouse and designated it as a State park. The courthouse contains authentic period furniture, weapons, mining machinery, assayers' equipment, photographs, and documents relating to the famous Earp family.[3]

### 4.  Bodie, California

*Location.* Mono County.

*Ownership and Administration.* State of California; Division of Beaches and Parks.

*Significance.* As yields from the California Mother Lode decreased in the 1850's, prospectors crossed the Sierra Nevada and explored the eastern slope. The first strike at Bodie, of gold placers, occurred in 1859, but difficulties in transporting supplies and

From a distance the well-preserved ghost town of Bodie, today a California State historical park, appears to be a small, active village.

equipment over the mountains and deserts restricted activities. Then in the late 1870's prospectors discovered a gold zone "bigger than the Comstock"—2½ miles in length and nearly 1 mile in width. The town mushroomed to 10,000 people and the usual assortment of gambling dens and saloons. Because of the shootings, stabbings, and brawls that occurred nightly, the town came to be known as "Shooters Town." While the boom lasted, the Bodie mines produced approximately $400,000 in bullion monthly. The Standard Mine alone yielded nearly $15 million over a 25-year period. The mines began to play out by the mid-1880's, but mining continued intermittently until World War II. Since that time the town has been deserted.

Bodie is significant not so much because of the estimated $70 million mined in the vicinity but because its history is typical of the strike, boom, and decline cycle of Western mining communities. In location, setting, and isolation, it may be considered a prototype of the Western ghost town.

*Present Appearance.* Situated in the high desert country near Mono Lake, Bodie is unusual because so many original buildings have survived in good condition. From a distance, it still appears to be a small, active village. More than a hundred dwellings, mostly of wood and weathered a dust-brown color, are still standing. Bodie is today a State historical park.[4]

## 5. Coloma, California

*Location.* El Dorado County.

*Ownership and Administration.* State of California; Division of Beaches and Parks.

*Significance.* The discovery of gold in January 1848 by James Marshall in Coloma (Culluma) Valley, about 40 miles from Sutter's Fort, while he was constructing a sawmill on the south fork of the American River, decisively affected the course of U.S. history. It touched off the great gold rush to California and brought about California statehood in 1850. The town of Coloma, which grew up around the gold discovery site, was the first white settlement in the foothills of the Sierra Nevada. When the local goldfield was exhausted, the town began to decline and eventually disappeared. It will always be remembered, however, as the site of one of the historic milestones of westward expansion.

James Marshall statue at Coloma, California, erected by the Native Sons and Daughters of the Golden West. Marshall points to the site of his discovery.

*Present Appearance.* Today only a cluster of dilapidated buildings remains at the original townsite. In 1890 the State of California, at the instigation of the Native Sons and Daughters of the Golden West, erected a statue of James Marshall about half a mile from the sawmill site at the gold discovery site; and in 1924 the Society of California Pioneers placed an 18-foot-high stone monument at the sawmill site. In 1947 University of California archeologists, in cooperation with the National Park Service and the California State Park Commission, established the dimensions and structural details of the old sawmill and recovered several hundred artifacts. The sawmill site, including Marshall's cabin and other structures, is preserved today as a State historical monument.[5]

## 6.   Columbia, California

*Location.* Toulumne County.

*Ownership and Administration.* Various private owners; and State of California, Division of Beaches and Parks.

*Significance.* The gold strike at Columbia was made comparatively late for the California Mother Lode country—in 1850. But the district proved phenomenally productive, and within a few weeks several thousand miners had taken up claims. Yet the peak did not come until after 1852, when miles of flumes and canals were built to bring water to the dry region. One aqueduct wound 60 miles through the mountains. By 1853 the town had become the third largest in California and was known as the "Gem of the Southern Mines" because it was the wealthiest and largest mining camp in the Mother Lode area. The district probably yielded a total of about $90 million in gold. In 1854 a fire destroyed much of the town, which the residents rebuilt largely of brick. About 1860 mining and population began to decline. The population finally settled at approximately 500, where it has remained over the years.

Because the major buildings were constructed of brick and have been continuously occupied and maintained, the town is one of the best preserved mining camps in the Mother Lode country. It probably has more historic and fewer modern buildings than any other mining town in California today, and provides a vivid picture of life in the land of the first and most fabulous of all gold rushes.

*Present Appearance.* Although Columbia contains a substantial number of private residences and businesses, it is a quiet town. Most of the historic section and the surrounding area is included within the boundaries of a State historical monument. Outside the town, rocks, pits, and hummocks indicate where the earth was washed away from the gold-bearing rock. Thirty-nine important structures—stores, saloons, churches, and residences—have survived. Some are still privately owned, and many have been restored.[6]

### 7. New Almaden, California

*Location.* Santa Clara County.

*Ownership and Administration.* Various private owners; and New Almaden Community Club, Inc.

*Significance.* Quicksilver (mercury) was first discovered on the American continent near the site of New Almaden long before the white man ever visited California. Santa Clara Indians used the bright red, eye-catching mineral known as cinnabar, which they obtained from the deposit, to paint themselves. In 1824 information provided by the Indians led Antonio Surol, a Mexican, to the deposit, where he unsuccessfully sought to find silver. In 1845 Andreas Castillero, a Mexican army officer, proved that the cinnabar ore contained mercury. The mine, named after the famous Almaden mine in Spain, the world's greatest producer of mercury, was developed with English capital. By 1848 crude refining methods were yielding a limited production.

The discovery of gold at Sutter's mill and the resulting mining boom led to an enormous demand for New Almaden's output because mercury was essential to the amalgamation process used to extract gold from ore. In 1850 the mine produced more than 7,000 flasks, each containing 76 pounds; the following year, 30,000 flasks. By 1881 it had produced a total of 54,378,418 pounds. Over the years production fluctuated as ore pockets were discovered and exhausted. Mining ceased in 1927 for the first time since 1849, but resumed during World War II. Today the mine is generally inactive, but ore bodies probably still exist untapped because of low prices and high mining costs. But the New Almaden, which produced more than $70 million in quicksilver, was the most valuable single mine in the entire State of California.

*Present Appearance.* Numerous and well-preserved remains of the mining era are still apparent today in New Almaden. Near the northern entrance to the town stands Casa Grande, a palatial three-story structure of brick, adobe, and wood erected in 1854 by Henry Halleck, the mine superintendent, as his residence. It serves today as a clubhouse. Lining the town's main street, which forms a loop in the canyon, are 29 other structures erected in the 1850's. All are original, little changed on the exterior, and are now being utilized as private residences. Because the mine is still occasionally worked, the Mine Hill area is not usually open to visitors.[7]

## 8. Old United States Mint, California

*Location.* San Francisco County, Fifth and Mission Streets, San Francisco.

*Ownership and Administration.* U.S. Government; General Services Administration.

*Significance.* The Old Mint had an important relationship with the mining frontier. The Government established it in 1854 as a branch of the Philadelphia Mint to accommodate the enormous bullion production of the California Mother Lode. The added influx of silver from the Comstock Lode of Nevada, which began to flow into the San Francisco branch office in 1860, soon overtaxed the facilities there. The Government then initiated plans to construct a new and larger mint. In 1867 it purchased land for the site, in 1869 began construction, and in November 1874 completed the

The Old United States Mint, in San Francisco, was built in the classic tradition of the mid-19th century and is one of the finest examples of Federal architecture of the period in the West. During the boom mining days, it received a large part of the gold and silver produced in the West. The building is used today for U.S. Government offices.

building. Within a year the mint had become the principal one in the Nation. For example, out of a national total of $83,888,900 in gold and silver coined in 1877, it accounted for about $50 million. Thereafter coinage began to fall off because of declining gold and silver production, and averaged only about $22 million per year between 1884 and 1892. Minting operations continued at the Old Mint until 1937, when they were transferred to a new building in San Francisco.

*Present Appearance.* Designed by the noted architect Alfred B. Mullet, the Old Mint was constructed in the classic tradition of public buildings of that day at a cost of $2,358,636. The massive structure, two stories high above a raised basement, measures 220 by 160 feet and is built around an interior courtyard. The concrete foundation is 5 feet thick, and the exterior brick walls 3 feet thick. For this reason the building was one of the few in San Francisco to survive the earthquake and fire of 1906. In 1939 the Government remodeled it for use as an office building. This involved the installation of temporary partitions, modern lighting, and other improvements. In spite of these changes, the basic exterior and interior design remains unaltered, and the Old Mint is one of the finest examples of Federal architecture of the period in the West.[8]

## 9.   Sutter's Fort, California

*Location.* Sacramento County, 28th and L Streets, Sacramento.

*Ownership and Administration.* State of California; Division of Beaches and Parks.

*Significance.* This fort was the headquarters of an agricultural colony, managed by John Augustus Sutter, that figured prominently in the early agricultural development of California, during the period 1840–48. Sutter, a Swiss-German, arrived in the United States in 1834. Four years later he traveled with a caravan of fur traders to Fort Vancouver, and then sailed to the Hawaiian Islands. From there he took passage on a trading vessel and, after visiting the Russian colony at Sitka, Alaska, came to San Francisco in 1839 planning to develop a vast empire in the California wilderness.

In 1840 Sutter became a naturalized Mexican citizen. The following year he obtained from the Mexican Government a provi-

Around Sutter's Fort grew the farming colony of New Helvetia, important in the early agricultural development of California. John Augustus Sutter, Swiss-German immigrant who was naturalized a Mexican citizen in 1840, was ruined after the discovery of gold on his property near Coloma. This lithograph is from a sketch made in 1847 by John W. Revere, a U.S. Navy officer. Courtesy, Bancroft Library, University of California.

sional grant of 11 square leagues of land (48,818 acres) and purchased Fort Ross and its equipment from the Russians. His herds then totaled 4,500 head of cattle, 1,500 horses, nearly 2,000 sheep, and a large number of hogs. American employees at New Helvetia, as the colony was called, supervised approximately 200 Indians. In 1842 the Indians planted the first crops. By 1845 Sutter controlled ranches, a tannery, gristmill, spinning and weaving shops, a hat factory, a blacksmith shop, a carpenter shop, a shoemaker shop, sawmills, and a salmon saltery.

For his headquarters and protection from the Indians, during the period 1841–44 Sutter constructed a large quadrangular adobe fort near the confluence of the American and Sacramento Rivers on a knoll overlooking the vicinity. The fort was 330 feet long and varied in width from 120 to 183 feet. Its walls were 2½ feet thick and 18 feet high and had bastions. Within the walls Sutter erected one large building and several smaller ones, including a bakery, mill, and blanket factory.

The Mexican War and the gold rush, touched off by the chance discovery of gold at his sawmill at Coloma, about 40 miles from the fort, brought ruin to Sutter. In October 1848, to avoid foreclosure for debt, he transferred all his property to his oldest son. Late that same year the son surveyed and laid out what was to be the town of Sacramento, about 2 miles from the fort, and soon offered lots for sale. By November 1849 the town had grown to almost 10,000 residents. Forced to sell his fort through his son in 1849 for $40,000 to meet payments on his debts, Sutter moved to Hock Farm, his ranch on the Feather River. There he lived until 1865, when he moved to the East. He died in 1880, still harassed by creditors.

*Present Appearance.* Sutter's Fort deteriorated until 1890, when the Native Sons of the Golden West purchased it. During the next couple of years the State of California restored it. In 1937 it became a part of the State park system and is now a State historical monument consisting of 6 acres of the original fort site. Exhibits include items of the Reed-Donner emigrant party, pioneer firearms, stagecoaches, mining tools, and furniture and objects associated with Sutter. Numerous exhibits also interpret the story of the fort.[9]


## 10. Warner's Ranch, California

*Location.* San Diego County, on San Felipe County Road, off Calif. 79, about 4 miles south of Warner's Hot Springs.

*Ownership and Administration.* Various private owners.

*Significance.* Although famous as a way station for almost all pioneers entering southern California over the Gila Trail and as a Butterfield Overland Mail stage station, Warner's Ranch was also a pioneering cattle ranch.

Jonathan Trumbull Warner, a native of Connecticut, in 1830 joined a trading party bound from St. Louis to Santa Fe. The following year he accompanied a party of fur trappers to California, where he spent 2 years trapping beaver. From 1834 to 1841 he operated a store in Los Angeles, by which time he had become a naturalized Mexican citizen and changed his name to Juan José

Warner's Ranch, California, was the stopping place for forty-niners bound for the goldfields on the southern trails. Pictured here is the adobe ranchhouse Warner erected in 1849.

Warner. In 1844 and 1846 he obtained two land grants from the Mexican Government. These grants totaled about 44,322 acres and were located in what is now eastern San Diego County. In 1845 Warner built a two-room adobe house with thatched roof on his new estate, at the Indian village of Agua Caliente, now known as Warner's Hot Springs.

Because of the influx of travelers over the Gila Trail in 1849, Warner moved from the house at Agua Caliente about 4 miles to the south, where he erected the adobe ranchhouse that still stands, as well as a store to trade with the immigrants. Warner resided at this location until 1857, when the U.S. District Court reawarded one of his claims, Rancho Agua Caliente, and his house to an earlier claimant of the land. Warner then moved to Los Angeles. From 1858 to 1861, his former home served as a stage station on the Butterfield route. In 1861 by mortgage foreclosure Warner lost the other portion of his ranch to John Rains, capitalist and cattle baron of Los Angeles and San Bernardino Counties. Rains moved up his vast herds of cattle from his ranches at Chino and Cucamonga, and the Warner property became a great ranch.

*Present Appearance.* A part of the original ranch land has been covered by Lake Henshaw, but most of the remaining part is little changed from the way it appeared in 1849. Private cattle raisers have leased the valley. At the ranch headquarters are the remains of two original adobe structures, Warner's ranchhouse of 1849 and a barn erected in 1858. Both of these structures have been partially covered with weatherboard. They are now being preserved and restored by the Vista Irrigation District, in cooperation with several historical societies of southern California.[10]

## 11. Central City, Colorado

*Location.* Gilpin County.

*Ownership and Administration.* Various private owners, and the Central City Opera House Association.

*Significance.* Central City originated during the first great mining boom in Colorado, in 1859. When the Missouri frontier received reports of gold in Colorado Territory, thousands packed up and started for the Rockies to the cry of "Pike's Peak or Bust." During this rush John Gregory found gold placers in the gulch that came to bear his name. A boom occurred and miners laid out Central City in the gulch. They soon exhausted the placer beds, but the town maintained a stable population and in 1873 ranked second in size only to Denver in the Territory. Silver booms in the 1870's and 1880's caused further population increases. Central City became the cultural center of the region and on the stage of the Opera House appeared some of the finest talent in the country, including Emma Abbott, "Fanny" Janauschek, Edwin Booth, and Joseph Jefferson. But by 1919 production in the vicinity ended and the city declined.

Opera house at Central City, Colorado, erected in 1878. In recent years it has been restored by the University of Denver.

*Present Appearance.* Central City is the best preserved of the old mining towns of Colorado, and still retains much of its historic atmosphere. A fire in 1874 destroyed all but six of the original buildings, but the inhabitants reconstructed the city more solidly and it now contains a number of the reconstructed buildings, including the St. James Methodist Church; the home of Henry M. Teller, one of the first U.S. Senators from Colorado; the restored Opera House; the Mines Hotel; the Old Armory, later occupied by the Belvidere Theatre; and St. Paul's Episcopal Church. The Opera House and the Mines Hotel are owned by the Central City Opera House Association; the other buildings are privately owned. During the festival each year the plays that are presented in the Opera House draw audiences from all parts of the country.[11]

## 12.  Cripple Creek, Colorado

*Location.* Teller County.

*Ownership and Administration.* Various private owners, except for the railroad depot, which is municipally owned.

*Significance.* In the declining years of the Colorado silver boom, prospectors discovered one of the world's largest goldfields along Cripple Creek near Pike's Peak. This strike, made in 1891, was one of the greatest of all time in the amount mined and the number of people involved. The district yielded about $400 million, and the population at one time probably numbered 50,000. Other towns in the district besides Cripple Creek included Victor, Goldfield, Gillett, Anaconda, Independence, Cameron, and Altman. Development of the placer deposits was comparatively slow until the miners discovered that the deeper they went the richer the veins became. Unlike most mining districts, Cripple Creek prospered over the years. The treasure continued to pour forth for almost two decades; declines were checked by new strikes. A long period of stagnation followed World War I, but in the 1930's production once again rose to more than $5 million yearly. Some mining is still done in the district today.

*Present Appearance.* Because of a fire in 1906 that destroyed most of the original town, few buildings from the early boom period have survived. The five railroads that served the town at its height have abandoned it, and the old depot serves as a municipal museum. At the Imperial Hotel, plays of the 1890's are produced each summer.[12]

### 13.   Durango-Silverton Narrow Gauge Line, Colorado

*Location.* La Plata and San Juan Counties.

*Ownership and Administration.* Denver and Rio Grande Western Railroad; administered as a branch line.

*Significance.* During the frantic years of the gold rushes in Colorado, transportation of ore caused many problems. Railroaders finally discovered the many economies and advantages of the narrow gauge—3 feet wide instead of the standard gauge of 4 feet, 6 inches. This gauge could be built in the Colorado mountains at 37 percent less cost than standard gauge; it could accommodate sharper curves; the equipment was lighter for each ton of freight; the rails were lighter and easier to install; and fuel efficiency was higher. For these reasons in 1882 the Denver and Rio Grande Western Railroad built the 45-mile Durango-Silverton Line, which connected with its main line at Durango. The first passenger train arrived at Silverton on the Fourth of July 1882. Thereafter the line carried ore from Silverton to Durango, where it was reduced. Freight operations continued through World War I. Today a narrow gauge freight line still operates between Alamosa and Durango, but the Durango-Silverton freight line is a historic relic of a bygone age.

*Present Appearance.* The Durango-Silverton Narrow Gauge Line is the only passenger railroad of its kind still operating in the United States. The track follows the gorge of the Las Animas River from Durango, elevation 6,500 feet, to Silverton, elevation 9,032 feet. It passes through some of the finest scenery in the Rocky Mountains. In recent years the trip has become popular with summer visitors.[13]

## 14.   Leadville, Colorado

*Location.* Lake County.

*Ownership and Administration.* Various private owners, and the State of Colorado.

*Significance.* After the discovery of gold placers near the site of Leadville in the late 1860's, a short-lived boom ensued. Then in the 1870's prospectors made a series of incredibly rich silver strikes

The Dexter Cabin in Leadville, Colorado, is an ordinary two-room miner's cabin. Built in 1879 of square-hewed logs, it is now a State museum.

along California Gulch. Almost overnight the desolate pine flat just below the timberline sprouted into a rugged mining camp that came to be known as Leadville. The town consisted of the usual assortment of pine-bough shelters, tent hotels, banks, grocery stores, saloons, and mine dumps. In 1879 the population was 20,000 people, most of whom were proud of the town's "wide open" reputation—enhanced by a hundred licensed saloons and a dozen gambling houses that operated around the clock. In the late 1890's, below the silver-bearing strata, miners ran across quartz veins heavily seamed with gold. Thus, despite the Panic of 1893 and the end of the silver boom, Leadville prospered. Since the turn of the century, lead, zinc, manganese, and molybdenum have been mined in the district.

*Present Appearance.* Still an active town, Leadville contains a number of historic structures that commemorate its once tempestuous life. Outstanding among these are the Vendome Hotel, the Elks Opera House, the Old Pioneer Bar, Healy House, the Dexter Cabin, St. George's Episcopal Church, and the Tabor House. The Healy House and Dexter Cabin are administered by the State.[14]

## 15.  Silverton-Telluride Mining District, Colorado

*Location.* San Juan and San Miguel Counties.

*Ownership and Administration.* Various.

*Significance.* In the early 1870's prospectors found silver in the Silverton area and by the end of 1873 had staked out nearly 4,000 claims. The area did not boom, however, until the following year, when a treaty with the Ute Indians made it safe for miners to enter the area. Soon the towns of Silverton, Mineral Point, Animas Fork, Eureka, and Howardsville dotted the hillsides and valleys of the San Juan Basin. In 1876 miners founded Telluride, 15 miles north of Silverton, but it grew slowly until the narrow gauge Rio Grande Southern Railroad passed through in 1890. It then became one of the busiest gold-mining camps in Colorado. For a time its population was 5,000. Silverton and Telluride were the principal towns in the area, which was rich in gold, silver, lead, and copper. Silverton and Telluride have each been accorded Landmark status, but are treated here collectively because of their proximity and historical relationship.

Telluride, Colorado, today. Silverton and Telluride were the principal towns in a historic mining area rich in gold, silver, lead, and copper.

*Present Appearance.* A few of the mines in the Silverton-Telluride district are still operating. Of the many mining camps and towns in the district, Silverton has the most impressive early buildings, including the Imperial Hotel (1882); the Methodist Church (1881); the gold-domed courthouse (1907); and the City Hall (1908).[15]

## 16.  United States Assay Office, Idaho

*Location.* Ada County, 210 Main Street, Boise.

*Ownership and Administration.* U.S. Government; Department of Agriculture, Forest Service.

*Significance.* The discovery of gold on the Clearwater River in 1860 brought the usual rush of miners, and 2 years later prospectors found new placers on the Salmon River and in the Boise Basin. These activities soon led, in March of 1863, to the creation of Idaho Territory. Between 1861 and 1866 the Territory's gold output totaled about $52 million, or about 19 percent of the Nation's total, but shipping costs to the U.S. Mint at San Francisco were high. For these reasons a strong demand arose for a Federal mint or assay office in Idaho. In 1869 Congress responded by appropriating $75,000 to erect a building for a Federal assay office in Boise.

A. B. Mullett, Supervising Architect of the Treasury Department, directed the preparation of plans and specifications. Construction began in July 1870 and required about a year. The building was of dignified design and measured 48 by 46 feet. It had a basement and two stories, and its exterior native sandstone walls were more than 2 feet thick. The coursed stone face was marked by ashlar corner quoins. The architectural style is difficult to classify, but has been described variously as "Italian Villa," "French Chateau," and "provincial." The building cost a total of $77,252. A delay in the receipt of machinery prevented the first assay from being made until March 2, 1872.

By the time the assay office began to function, the rich surface placers of gold in Idaho had been almost depleted and production underwent a considerable slump until 1883, when miners opened the Coeur d'Alene region. They sank deep shafts, built stamp mills, and opened new mines, including silver and lead mines. By 1895 annual deposits in the assay office had reached more than a million dollars. For the next 11 years they averaged a million and a half dollars. By 1917 the Idaho mines had yielded $400 million—one-fourth in gold, one-fourth in silver, and one-half in lead. The assay office continued operating until 1933, when the U.S. Forest Service acquired the building as headquarters for the Boise National Forest and remodeled it.

*Present Appearance.* Originally the offices and assayer's laboratory were located on the first floor. The second floor contained the living quarters of the chief assayer. Despite slight alterations to the exterior and interior during the remodeling in 1933, the basic structure and general appearance are essentially the same as those of the original building.[16]

## 17. Bannack, Montana

*Location.* Beaverhead County.

*Ownership and Administration.* Various private owners; and the State of Montana, State Park Commission.

*Significance.* In 1862, after a gold strike in Montana on Grass-

Bannack, Montana, the first Territorial capital and site of one of the earliest strikes in the Territory.

hopper Creek, the usual rush occurred and miners founded the town of Bannack—later the first Territorial capital of Montana. Because of richer discoveries elsewhere and the lack of water, however, most of the population soon drifted to other camps, such as Alder Gulch (Virginia City). Then between 1866 and 1870 five ditches brought the water that made placer mining possible. In 1895 an electric dredge was first used. Mineral production was steady, but never spectacular. Bannack gained widespread fame, however, because of the activities of the Plummer gang in the vicinity and the ensuing vigilante action, in which Virginia City shared. In 1864 the residents hanged Plummer at Hangman's Gulch near Bannack. A few mines still operate in the vicinity, but the town ceased to exist in 1938 and the post office was closed.

*Present Appearance.* Bannack is an excellent example of a Western ghost town. The main street, a dirt road, is lined with weatherbeaten one-story log cabins, partially hidden by sagebrush and greasewood, frame false-fronted stores, and a church. Two imposing structures are a two-story frame schoolhouse and a red brick structure that served as the first Territorial capitol of Montana. Of special interest is the old jail, a solid wooden building that has a sod roof and dirt floor, small barred windows, and tiny cells. A path leads through the sagebrush to Hangman's Gulch, where a replica of the gallows may be seen. Overlooking Outlaws' Cemetery are two other burial grounds, where lie many gold seekers. Recently Bannack became a State park.[17]

## 18. Butte, Montana

*Location*. Silver Bow County.

*Ownership and Administration*. Various.

*Significance*. Mining began in Butte in 1864, when miners from the Virginia City area found placer deposits of gold in Silver Bow Creek. By the end of the decade, however, a shortage of water was seriously hampering operations. In 1874 a new arrival, Marcus Daly, while prospecting for silver, found copper—a vein 50 feet wide and of unparalleled richness. Two years later the town of Butte was laid out. In 1881, when the first railroad, the Utah and Northern Railroad, reached the city and Daly formed the Anaconda Copper Company to develop his find, the great copper boom was underway. In 1883 Daly founded the city of Anaconda. By 1885 the population of Butte had reached 14,000. At the end of the century the city was the copper metropolis of the Americas. In addition to being the center of the famed wars between the copper kings—men such as Marcus Daly, William A. Clark, and Frederick A. Heinze—it was also the scene of violent struggles between labor and management.

*Present Appearance*. Butte, a melting pot of nationalities, is still a typical mining town, surrounded by enormous yellow and gray ore dumps and mine shafts. Its era of great mineral production has not yet ceased. Among the historic structures is the home of Senator W. A. Clark. The suburbs of Centerville, Walkerville, and Meaderville contain most of the mines and the homes of the miners— weathered frame structures clinging to steep hillsides and surrounded by sagging picket fences and grassless yards. The whole area is pockmarked by the surface workings and structures of one of the world's richest copper mines.[18]

Steamboat discharges freight at Fort Benton, head of navigation on the Missouri River, in the 1860's. Courtesy, Montana Historical Society.

## 19. Fort Benton, Montana

*Location.* Chouteau County.

*Ownership and Administration.* Various.

*Significance.* Fort Benton, an important post on the Missouri River during the late fur trade era, was also the hub of traffic from the East to the goldfields of Idaho, Montana, and Canada. At the head of steamboat navigation on the Missouri, it was the eastern terminus of the Mullan Road, which ran westward to Fort Walla Walla. Established in 1847 by Alexander Culbertson as Fort Lewis, it became known in 1850 as Fort Benton and was soon the most important fur trading establishment in Montana. It was a military post from 1869 to 1875.

After the arrival of the first steamboat, the *Chippewa,* in 1859, a new era began. A town grew up around the fort, and steamboats arrived regularly. After the Montana gold strike in 1862, miners rushed to the town by steamboat and then traveled overland to Bannack, Virginia City, and other mining camps that were located in the interior. Ox teams and pack trains carried food, clothing, ammunition, and whisky from Fort Benton to Idaho, Montana, and Canada. Much of this traffic passed westward over the Mullan Road, opened in 1863 as a military road from Fort Walla Walla. The Mullan Road was also used by emigrants en route to the Northwest and gold seekers traveling to Idaho and Montana. By the middle 1860's its importance increased as keen competition developed between St. Louis, Mo., and Portland, Oreg., for trade with Montana settlements. From each of these cities cargo was shipped to the termini towns on the Mullan Road, from which mule pack trains carried cargo into the mountains.

In 1868 downriver shipments from Fort Benton totaled $1,200,000, and inbound shipments $1,394,000. When the railroads arrived in the region, the river traffic declined and the town lost its importance as a shipping center.

*Present Appearance.* All that remains today of the early fort itself are a blockhouse and a portion of the adobe walls. The riverfront, along which the steamboats once docked and unloaded their cargoes, is little changed. Several brick and stone commercial buildings of 19th-century vintage give a historic flavor to the town.[19]

## 20.  Grant-Kohrs Ranch, Montana

*Location.* Powell County, adjoining the town of Deer Lodge on the north.

*Ownership and Administration.* Privately owned; now known as the Warren Ranch

*Significance.* This ranch is highly significant in the history of the range cattle industry. John Grant, the original owner, was the son of a Scottish employee of the Hudson's Bay Company, and is sometimes credited with being the founder of the cattle industry in Montana. In 1853 he began his career in Deer Lodge Valley. Acquiring rundown cattle in the vicinity of Fort Hall, about 240 miles to the south, he fattened them on his ranch and sold them at a good profit. By 1863 the ranch was running 4,000 head of cattle and nearly as many horses, and was providing most of the beef for the miners at Bannack and Virginia City.

Modern view of the Grant-Kohrs Ranch headquarters, Deer Lodge, Montana. One of the earliest ranches in the State, it pioneered in selective breeding.

In 1866 Conrad Kohrs purchased the ranch. He had been employed in a butcher shop in Bannack, had borrowed money to go into the cattle business, and had risen quickly. As soon as he purchased the ranch, he stocked it with Shorthorn bulls to improve the blood of his stock—the first constructive cattle-breeding effort in Montana. Becoming one of the foremost cattle kings of his era, he figured prominently in the organization of the Montana Stockgrowers Association. In 1883, with Granville Stuart and another associate, he bought out the interests of the Davis brothers and Hauser in the DHS (Davis, Hauser, and Stuart Company) Ranch, a $400,-000 transaction that involved 12,000 cattle, and launched the Pioneer Cattle Company. The disastrous winter of 1886–87 reduced his herd from 35,000 to 3,000, but he borrowed heavily and recovered. Until his death in this century he remained a leading Montana cattleman.

*Present Appearance.* The Grant-Kohrs Ranch is now owned and operated by Conrad Warren, a grandson of Kohrs, and is known as the Warren Ranch. In the tradition of his grandfather, Warren raises purebred cattle. The original frame ranchhouse, erected by Grant in 1862, is still standing, though in the 1890's Kohrs built a large brick addition on the west side. Other old structures include several log cabins, probably built in the 1850's and 1860's, and old corrals. The ranch is not open to the public.[20]

Virginia City, Montana, sprang into existence after prospectors discovered gold at Alder Gulch. It was the Territorial capital from 1865 to 1875. A large number of buildings from the gold-rush period survive in the modern town, pictured here.

## 21. Virginia City, Montana

*Location.* Madison County.

*Ownership and Administration.* Various.

*Significance.* The strike at Alder Gulch was a memorable episode in frontier mining history. Virginia City, the camp established after the strike, became the center of the Montana gold rush and served as the Territorial capital from 1865 to 1875. At its peak it had a population of 10,000, and mines in the vicinity yielded about $70 million in gold. Virginia City is also closely associated with one of the most famous vigilante actions of the mining era—the hanging of Henry Plummer and his gang of road agents near Bannack. Little mining is done in the vicinity today.

*Present Appearance.* Lower Wallace Street, the historic section of Virginia City, has been restored in an outstanding manner by millionaire rancher Charles A. Bovey. It has numerous false-fronted stores, wooden sidewalks, and old-fashioned street lamps. The stores are even stocked with antique merchandise. Some of the structures, such as the Wells-Fargo express office and the dress-maker's shop, contain life-sized figures dressed in the historic fashion. The barber shop, built in the 1870's, appears ready for business.

Among the older buildings, constructed of brick and native stone, are the Territorial capitol and the building that housed the office of the *Montana Post*. At the Bale of Hay Saloon are nickelodeons and large clanging music boxes. Beyond it stands the old stone barn, now used as a theater; during the summer months, the Virginia City Players enact old-time melodramas. Nearby is the famous Boot Hill Cemetery, where several of Henry Plummer's agents are buried.[21]

## 22. Virginia City, Nevada

*Location.* Storey County.

*Ownership and Administration.* Various.

*Significance.* In its feverish heyday Virginia City was the prototype of all boomtowns on the mining frontier, and for a time seemed likely to achieve its boast that it would become the most cosmopolitan city on the Pacific coast. The major city in the Comstock Lode area, it was laid out in 1859, and by early the next year

Virginia City, Nevada, in the heart of the Comstock Lode country, as it appeared in the 1860's. The "Bonanza Kings" made their fortunes from the Comstock Lode. Courtesy, National Archives.

some 20,000 miners had arrived. Life in the city reflected the dazzling wealth of the mines and the frenzied search for still another big bonanza. The first boom ended just after 1865, when the surface deposits played out. The mines, which had yielded $45 million in gold and silver, closed down one by one, and the population of 15,000 dwindled.

But the main vein was yet to be discovered. In 1873 John W. Mackay and James G. Fair struck the "Heart of the Comstock," an underground vein about 400 feet deep and 150 to 320 feet wide. A second and much larger boom occurred. It reached its peak in 1877, when production was netting the mining companies more than $1 million a month and 750 miles of mine tunnels were burrowed under the city.

The theaters, restaurants, and saloons of Virginia City, a desert metropolis, rivaled those of San Francisco. While other mining camps have become ghost towns or neon, aluminum, and glass cities of the 20th century, Virginia City has retained much of its original flavor.

*Present Appearance.* Interest in Virginia City in preserving the past is high. Many saloons and business establishments of boomtown days are clustered on C Street; other historic structures are scattered throughout the city. Piper's Opera House, in which appeared Lawrence Barrett, Edwin Booth, Joseph Jefferson, and the Red Stocking Blondes, still stands. Other surviving structures are the Miners Union Hall, St. Mary's in the Mountains Catholic Church, the Episcopal and Presbyterian churches, the *Territorial Enterprise* building, and the Storey County courthouse. Nearby are yellowing mine dumps and the ruins of mineworks.[22]

## 23. Deadwood, South Dakota

*Location.* Lawrence County.

*Ownership and Administration.* Various private owners.

*Significance.* The Black Hills region was one of the last strongholds of the mining frontier, and it marked the end of the eastern advance of the prospectors. Because of the discovery of gold there, in 1875 the U.S. Army was finally forced to withdraw its opposition to the entry of whites into the Great Sioux Reservation.

Deadwood, South Dakota, retains much of the early mining atmosphere and many original buildings still stand. The town of Lead, 3 miles distant, was the site of one of the greatest mines in the Territory—the Homestake.

Thousands of miners poured in and made strikes. By the following spring Deadwood, a ramshackle town catering to the voracious appetites of 7,000 miners, was the center of activity. Among those whose names were associated with its heyday are "Wild Bill" Hickok, Calamity Jane, Poker Alice, and the legendary Deadwood Dick. In 1876 prospectors discovered approximately 50 mines in the vicinity of the town of Lead, 3 miles distant. That same year miners uncovered near Lead a gold lode that became the greatest mine of all in the Territory—the Homestake—which George Hearst purchased the following year. Becoming the biggest and most profitable in the United States, the mine has yielded most of the $550 million in gold that has been produced in the Black Hills since 1875.

*Present Appearance.* Deadwood is one of the few early mining towns to survive in the Black Hills. It retains much of the atmosphere of its early days, and many original buildings and the famous cemetery remain. At Lead a large number of buildings that comprise the Homestake property dominate the scene. Old two- and three-story framehouses are propped up on the gulch to keep them from slipping down to the stream at the bottom. The Homestake Mining Company provides guided tours of its mine.[23]

## 24. JA Ranch, Texas

*Location.* Armstrong County, Palo Duro Canyon, Paloduro.
*Ownership and Administration.* Privately owned.

*Significance.* In 1876, only a year after the Kiowas and Comanches had been forced onto a reservation, Charles Goodnight became the first of many cattlemen to bring herds onto the Llano Estacado, the high plains of the Texas Panhandle. The first Goodnight spread—the Old Home Ranch—was located in Palo Duro Canyon a few miles below the site of Col. R. S. Mackenzie's battle with the Comanches in 1874. It consisted of corrals and picket houses built from timber cut in the canyon. In 1877 Goodnight formed a partnership with John G. Adair, an Irish country gentleman whose penchant for hunting had attracted him to the buffalo plains. With Adair furnishing financial backing and Goodnight managing the spread, the JA began a long and profitable history.

In 1879 Goodnight moved the ranch headquarters to Turkey Creek, farther east, to be closer to the railroad. There he built new ranch and residential buildings of logs; later he built a stone house for the Adairs to live in when at the ranch. Under Goodnight's management, the JA grew to encompass 700,000 acres and 40,000 head of cattle. An advocate of herd improvement, Goodnight developed outstanding cattle by mixing Herefords and Longhorns, and he also built up a large herd of domesticated buffalo. In 1880 he helped found the Panhandle Stockmen's Association. Foreseeing the end of the open range, in 1889 he ended his association with Adair and the JA Ranch and settled on a smaller ranch of his own, whose headquarters was at the village of Goodnight.

*Present Appearance.* Of the three sites associated with Goodnight in the Texas Panhandle, the JA Ranch headquarters probably best commemorates his activities and contributions to the cattle industry. Located in a wide section of the Palo Duro Canyon, the ranch is still a large and active concern, owned by Mrs. Adair's surviving grandson by her marriage to Montgomery Ritchie. Some of the original buildings, erected in 1879, are still standing. The big house built for the Adairs, now modernized and expanded, still

Ranchhouse of the JA Ranch, Texas. Though renovated in modern times, it probably dates from the 1890's.

Bunkhouse at the JA Ranch, Texas. Charles Goodnight founded the ranch in 1876 and the next year went into partnership with John G. Adair.

Surviving early stable buildings at the JA Ranch, Texas.

dominates the cluster of buildings at the ranch headquarters. Although changed by the addition of new buildings and the improvement of the old, the ranch still possesses the essential flavor of the original, and the vast areas of surrounding rangelands remain as they were in Goodnight's day.

Two related sites of importance are nearby. The original Goodnight ranch headquarters—the Old Home Ranch—is farther up the canyon at a site not easily reached. The buildings burned in 1904, but the foundations are still visible. The Panhandle-Plains Historical Society of Canyon, Tex., has marked the site. The framehouse where Goodnight lived from 1889 until his death in 1929 is still standing in the nearby town of Goodnight, and is used as a private residence. The JA Ranch is not open to the public.[24]

## 25. King Ranch, Texas

*Location.* Nueces, Kenedy, Kleberg, and Willacy Counties; headquarters in Kingsville.

*Ownership and Administration.* Privately owned.

*Significance.* This mammoth and historic ranch ranks as one of the most outstanding—and certainly the best known—of all cattle enterprises in the history of the Southwestern cattle frontier. It was founded on July 25, 1853, when Capt. Richard King purchased from Juan Mendiola a Spanish land grant, the Rincon de Santa Gertrudis, consisting of 15,500 acres. From 1860 to 1868 King operated the ranch in partnership with Mifflin Kenedy. At the time of King's death in 1885, his youngest daughter Alice was engaged to Robert J. Kleberg. The wedding was postponed until the following year, when Mrs. King asked Kleberg to manage the ranch. When Kleberg retired in 1933, his son, Robert J. Kleberg, Jr., took over. When Mrs. King died in 1925, she left her land in a 10-year trusteeship, at the end of which the heirs would obtain title as specified in her will. In 1935 Mrs. Robert J. Kleberg formed the King Ranch Corporation, which managed the land she inherited, as well as that which she bought from the other heirs.

The King herd grew from Longhorn stock imported from Mexico, but about 1893 Kleberg began purchasing British breeds—Shorthorns and Herefords. He later purchased Brahman cattle and bred them with Shorthorns to produce the famous Santa Gertrudis cattle, which the Department of Agriculture in 1940 recognized as a new and distinct breed of beef cattle. The ranch gradually grew until it included at its peak almost 1,225,000 acres. By the mid-20th century it encompassed 826,000 acres and covered most of four south Texas counties.

*Present Appearance.* Although the business offices of the King Ranch today are at Kingsville, the original headquarters area is 2 miles west. In 1911 fire destroyed the first ranchhouse. The present white brick mansion and most of the surrounding structures date from 1912, although the original commissary building still survives. To accommodate visitors, the management of the ranch has generously laid out a 12-mile tour that has numbered posts keyed to a self-guiding trail leaflet.[25]

## 26.   Swan Land and Cattle Company Headquarters, Wyoming

*Location.* Platte County, Chugwater.

*Ownership and Administration.* Privately owned.

*Significance.* The Swan Land and Cattle Company was one of several well-known foreign companies that engaged in the cattle

Built in 1876 as headquarters of the Swan Land and Cattle Company, this residence also served as a stopping place on the Cheyenne-Black Hills stage route.

The Tom Sun Ranch, part of which is portrayed in this modern photograph, was one of the first ranches in Wyoming. It was a typical medium-sized ranch.

business in the United States; and it was one of the largest in the Nation. Organized in Scotland in 1883 with a capital of $3 million, it at one time held more than 600,000 acres of land. Its cattle ranged as far as from Fort Fred Steele in Wyoming in the west to Ogallala, Nebr., in the east, and from the Union Pacific Railroad on the north to the Platte River on the south. Its principal range ran along the Chug and Sybille Creeks and over the mountains to the Laramie plains. The company books carried more than 113,000 head when the severe winter of 1886–87 struck, but by spring the number was only 57,000.

Going into bankruptcy following the disaster, the company reduced its inventory, and the capable John Clay, well-known stockman of the northern Plains, took over the management. He reduced the capital and in 1893 cut the herd to 40,000. Though he resigned in 1896, the company continued to run about 40,000 head until 1904, when it went into the sheep business. At the peak of its sheep operations, in 1911, it was running about 112,000 head. Continuing to operate until 1945, it then began liquidating.

*Present Appearance.* The home office of the Swan Land and Cattle Company, along with a small parcel of land around the old headquarters at Chugwater, is still being operated, under the management of Russell Staats. The surviving remains of the headquarters ranch consist of: The ranchhouse, in excellent condition, which was built in 1876 and served as a hotel and stage station prior to the coming of the Colorado and Southern Railway to Chugwater in 1887; the barn, also constructed about 1876; the store, constructed in 1913 to serve as a commissary; and the brick Hiram Kelley House, erected in 1877 and located about a half mile below the headquarters.[26]

## 27.  Tom Sun Ranch, Wyoming

*Location.* At the junction of Natrona and Carbon Counties, on Wyo. 220, about 6 miles west of Independence Rock, in the south-central part of the State.

*Ownership and Administration.* Privately owned.

*Significance.* This ranch is one of the best preserved that dates from the boom period of the range cattle industry on the Plains.

Its site is historic and scenic, for Sun chose his range on the Oregon Trail along the Sweetwater River near Devil's Gate and Independence Rock. A French-Canadian who had been a mountain man and knew the Wyoming country from his trapping days, Sun tried prospecting in the early 1870's at the sodium deposits near Casper, but Indians burned his cabin. Sun then turned to cattle raising. His ranch consisted of about 14 square miles, which was well-watered. Soon it was running about 6,000 head.

Like many cattlemen of Wyoming and Montana, Sun obtained his cattle from the Oregon country—fine Durham stock that were trailed over the Cascades and Rocky Mountains through South Pass. A cowboy who accompanied Sun on the drive from Oregon wrote: "We followed the Oregon Trail, swam the rivers, climbed the mountains, and then followed the Indian river. We were five months making the return trip." He added that the signs posted at the Tom Sun Ranch "No women or barbed wire allowed" were accurate.

During the 1870's and 1880's the ranch was typical of the medium-sized ranching operations in the cattle country. The Cheyenne *Daily Leader* remarked in 1882 that "the eastern person of inquiring turn of mind who writes to his friends out west to ask what a ranch is like would find his answer in a description of Tom Sun's."

*Present Appearance.* The Tom Sun Ranch has continuously been in the Sun family. The present owner, Bernard, a grandson of Tom, runs about 3,000 head of Herefords. A considerable number of the original ranch buildings have survived. The low-roofed ranchhouse is the original log structure built by Sun in 1872, though it contains log additions. Several of what are believed to be original outbuildings are still standing. The setting of the ranch is practically the same as when Sun first staked his claim. The ranch is not open to the public.[27]

# C. Historic Districts Eligible for the Registry of National Historic Landmarks

In some instances groups of historic buildings located in proximity, when considered collectively, provide outstanding illustrations of a past era. These groups are designated Historic Districts and declared eligible for the Registry of National Historic Landmarks. Such districts sometimes include individual structures that are eligible on their own merits for Landmark designation. The following Historic Districts illustrate the phases of history treated in this volume.

## 1. Old Sacramento Historic District, California

*Location.* Sacramento County, Sacramento; area bounded by the Sacramento River and Front Street on the west, Capitol Avenue on the south, Second Street between L and I Streets on the east, and the I Street bridge and its approach on the north.

*Ownership and Administration.* City of Sacramento; the Redevelopment Agency of Sacramento is purchasing properties from various private owners.

*Significance.* Founded in 1848 by John Augustus Sutter's oldest son on the lower Sacramento River not far from Sutter's Fort, headquarters of Sutter's agricultural colony during the period 1840–48, the city of Sacramento soon had a population of 10,000 and emerged as the great interior distribution and transportation center for the mines in the Mother Lode country. Beginning in

Sacramento, the present capital of California, grew from humble origins, as indicated by this 1850 lithograph. Beginning as a squatters' town near Sutter's Fort, within 1 year after its formal founding it had 10,000 residents. Courtesy, Bancroft Library, University of California.

1858 it served as the western terminus of the national communication and transportation systems that linked the East and the West, including the Pony Express, the Central Overland Mail and Stage Line, and the first transcontinental railroad, the Central Pacific. Periodically razed by fires and floods, it was rebuilt time and again with locally manufactured brick. In 1854 it became the capital of California.

*Present Appearance.* Old Sacramento has the largest collection of structures dating from the gold-rush days of any major city on the Pacific coast. Still standing in the Historic District are 44 original buildings—including banks, express offices, hotels, restaurants, saloons, various shops and stores, as well as a firehouse, newspaper office, and telegraph office. Many of the buildings have been altered over the years, but the basic structures are largely intact. Plans are now underway to reemphasize the historic character of this District by means of a State park and an urban renewal project.[28]

## 2. Lincoln Historic District, New Mexico

*Location.* Lincoln County.

*Ownership and Administration.* Various private owners except for the courthouse, which is State-owned.

*Significance.* Lincoln typifies in many ways the cowtowns that

Lincoln County Courthouse about 1900. A Historic District today, in the 19th century Lincoln, New Mexico Territory, was a raucous cowtown, scene of cattle feuds and clashes between badmen and lawmen. Courtesy, Museum of New Mexico.

sprang up on the advancing cattlemen's frontier after the Civil War. Not a railhead town but a business and social community for the surrounding ranches, it attracted cowboys, gunfighters, badmen, rustlers, soldiers, and lawmen, and was the scene of conflicts over water, Government beef contracts, and grazing rights.

Lincoln originated in the early 1850's as a Mexican village called La Placita del Rio Bonito. In 1869, when Lincoln County was created, the village was renamed Lincoln and became the county seat. At this time the cattle frontier was advancing westward, as well as northward, from Texas. Lincoln County—270,000 square miles in area—provided a natural home for these cattle because of its fine grass ranges and the ready market for beef at the nearby military posts and reservations. The king of the county was John Chisum, who alone owned 80,000 head of cattle.

At Lincoln occurred one of the most famous cattle feuds in the history of the West, the Lincoln County War in 1878. The rival Murphy and Tunstall-McSween factions fought a battle that lasted for 5 months and culminated in a 3-day gunfight on the streets of Lincoln, in which half a dozen men were killed. A prominent participant was William H. Bonney, better known as "Billy the Kid." Three years later, in 1881, killing his two guards, he dramatically escaped from the Lincoln County jail. But he was shot and killed several months later at Fort Sumner by Pat Garrett.

*Present Appearance.* Aside from its dramatic history and its importance in the development of the cattle industry in southeastern New Mexico, Lincoln is historically important primarily because of its excellent state of preservation. It is probably the least spoiled surviving example of the frontier cowtown. Virtually the entire town of 1878 has survived with comparatively few modern additions.

The focal point of interest is the old county courthouse, built in 1874. This large two-story adobe structure was, until 1880, "the big store" of L. G. Murphy and Company, but it also housed offices, a billiard room, post office, living quarters, and a visitors' bunkroom. After Murphy went bankrupt as a result of the Lincoln County War, the county bought the building for a courthouse and jail. Minor repairs have been made to the building, but otherwise it is entirely the original construction. Now a State monument, it is also headquarters for the Old Lincoln County Commission, and it houses a county historical museum.

Another building of outstanding importance is the old Tunstall store, a long rambling adobe that figured prominently in the Lincoln County War. Numerous other business houses and residences dating from the 1870's and 1880's are also still standing. The Old Lincoln County Commission has placed markers throughout the town to identify important structures and sites.[29]

McSween Store at Lincoln, New Mexico Territory, as it appeared about 1900. It figured prominently in the Lincoln County War, in which Billy the Kid participated. Courtesy, Museum of New Mexico.

# D.  Other Sites Considered

In the process of selecting the comparatively few historic sites of such outstanding character as to merit recognition as Registered National Historic Landmarks for the phases of history treated in this volume, a great many throughout the Nation were carefully studied, compared, and evaluated. The sites described below were among those deemed by the Advisory Board to possess noteworthy historical value but not "exceptional value" (national significance) within the special Landmark criteria. Some of them, however, may satisfy the criteria for other volumes in this series. In addition to the Landmark sites and those described below, many others— far too numerous to list—were judged to be of lesser importance.

## 1.  Ajo Mines, Arizona

*Location: Pima County, Ajo.*

In 1854 a group of Californians entered present southwestern Arizona, and found evidence of Mexican prospecting at the site of Ajo. They founded the Arizona Mining and Trading Company, the first company formed to exploit the mineral resources of Arizona, and began extracting copper ore. At first mule teams hauled the ore to San Diego, from where it moved by boat to Wales for smelting. Beginning about 1858 Yuma replaced San Diego as a shipping point, and barges carried the ore from there down the Colorado River to the Gulf of California. Because of low-grade ore, transportation difficulties, and protests by the Mexican Government that

Ajo lay south of the Gadsden Purchase, the mines yielded only small profits. By 1861 the surface ore had played out, and the Ajo mines then lay idle for many years.

Early in the 20th century the St. Louis Copper Company found that the deposits were low-grade overburden that covered an enormous sulphide ore concentration of some 50 million tons. It went bankrupt, however, and another company unsuccessfully tried various methods of extracting the ore. In 1911 the Calumet and Arizona Mining Company took over the mines. After removing the overburden, it began the great Ajo open-pit copper mine. In 1931 the Phelps-Dodge company acquired the mine. Ajo today is a modern company town.

## 2. Bisbee, Arizona

*Location: Cochise County.*

Center of one of the richest and most extensive copper, gold, and silver mining districts in Arizona, Bisbee traces its origin to a discovery made by Hugh Jones in 1875 while he was prospecting in the Mule Mountains. Jones was looking for silver, and the copper he found so disappointed him that he did not even file a claim. In 1877 an Army scout, Jack Dunn, did so. Miners arrived, began operations, and founded the mining camp of Bisbee. Not until 1881, when Phelps-Dodge purchased much of the property, did large-scale mining get underway. Through mergers and litigation, the Copper Queen Consolidated Company, controlled by Phelps-Dodge, emerged as the dominant enterprise.

Bisbee today is a company town much like other Phelps-Dodge mining centers in Arizona, but it retains many of the traditions of its earlier days. Nearby abandoned mines recall its history, and producing mines emphasize the foundations of its present economy.

## 3. Globe, Arizona

*Location: Gila County.*

A silver strike in the Pinal Mountains in 1876 led to a boom and the establishment of Globe, a mining camp in a nearly impenetrable area in the heart of Apache Indian country. Within a year the camp had a population of a thousand. The silver supply lasted only 4 years, but large deposits of copper ore insured the prosperity and growth of the town.

In 1881 the Old Dominion Company acquired the best ore fields in the area. Profitable large-scale operations, however, were delayed for two decades by the difficulty of freighting the ore 120 miles by ox team over rough mountain trails, infested with hostile Apaches, to the Southern Pacific Railroad terminal at Wilcox. When a branch line reached Globe in 1898, the Old Dominion Mine became one of the greatest copper mines in the world. Although it closed down in 1931, other mines in the area had opened. The town's economic foundations still rest upon the copper industry.

Modern Globe only remotely suggests its early history. A mile to the north, however, the concrete foundations, ruins of the smelter plant, and other remains give some idea of the extent of the Old Dominion.

## 4. Jerome, Arizona

*Location: Yavapai County.*

A famous and picturesque mining town, Jerome originated soon after 1876, when John Rufner and August McKinnon discovered rich copper ore nearby. Not until the Atlantic and Pacific Railroad reached the area in 1882, however, did extraction become profitable. That year the United Verde Copper Company was formed, with Eastern financial backing, to exploit the deposits. One of the New York financiers involved, Eugene Jerome, gave his name to the town that had sprung up on the side of Mingus Mountain. In 1885 a group led by William A. Clark, the famous Montana copper king, purchased the mines and profitably expanded them. In the early 1930's, when the price of copper was at a low, Phelps-Dodge bought out the United Verde. The demand for copper during World War II led to intensive mining that depleted the known deposits, and today Jerome is rapidly becoming a ghost town. Its rickety frame buildings, propped on stilts on the sheer slope of Mingus Mountain, recall the bygone era and are commemorated in Jerome State Historic Park, authorized in 1965.

From his ranch, El Potrero, located in the Santa Cruz Valley, early Arizona settler Pete Kitchen fought off Apaches, Mexican bandits, and American outlaws. He raised hay and vegetables, as well as large numbers of hogs.

## 5. Kitchen (El Potrero) Ranch, Arizona

*Location: Santa Cruz County, on U.S. 89, about 4 miles north of Nogales.*

Situated on the Santa Cruz River just north of the Mexican border, this was the best known pioneer ranch in southern Arizona during the 1850's and 1860's. Pete Kitchen, a newcomer to Arizona, established it in 1854. The ranchhouse, as much a fort as a home, became a rallying point and refuge for would-be settlers and travelers during the bloody Apache wars. Kitchen engaged in truck gardening and stockraising, especially hogs, and hired many Mexicans and Ópata Indians. Growing rich as a supplier of forts and stores from El Paso to Yuma, he was especially noted for his hams and bacon, considered to be the finest in the Southwest.

The original adobe building in which Kitchen lived until the 1880's is still intact. The present owner, Col. Gil Procter, has stabilized the walls and added a new roof. The more pretentious adobe ranchhouse that Kitchen later built is also still standing, and Procter uses it as a residence and museum. The museum is open to the public.

## 6. La Paz, Arizona

*Location: Yuma County, on an unpaved road off U.S. 70 about 6 miles north of Ehrenberg.*

In 1858 prospectors struck gold in the rich sands along the Gila River just east of its junction with the Colorado. The first placer gold rush in Arizona ensued, and miners established the boomtown of Gila City. In 1864, after the placers washed out, they moved upstream to the site of La Paz, where gold had been previously discovered. The mining camp of La Paz sprang into existence overnight. Set back from the river about 2 miles to avoid inundation by floods, it soon consisted of about 6,000 people and was probably the most important settlement in Arizona at the time. During a period of 7 years, the sands of the Gila yielded $8 million worth of gold. As other mining camps sprang up in the Hassayampa Valley, La Paz became a supply base to which river boats brought cargoes and from which wagon trains hauled supplies to inland settlements. In 1870 the Gila cut a new channel, and the town's port days ended. Miners exhausted the placers, and Ehrenberg became the new distribution center. Few remains of the ghost town of La Paz are extant today.

## 7. McMillenville, Arizona

*Location: Gila County, just off U.S. 60, about 18 miles northeast of Globe.*

In 1874 Charles McMillen and his partner, "Dory" Harris, accidentally discovered silver ore at the site of McMillenville. Immediately staking a claim, they named their mine the Stonewall Jackson. They concentrated on removing the surface deposits, though they noticed pay streaks of silver underneath. Unaware of the great value of their claim, they sold it for $160,000 to a California company. Soon prospectors crowded in and formed the town of McMillenville. The lusty camp reached its peak in 1880, when it consisted of a jumble of tents and adobe saloons, gambling casinos, stores, and hotels. In 1882 the ore thinned out, and the following year

many of the mines closed. Then, after an attack by the Cibecue
Apaches, who resented the intrusion on the San Carlos Indian Reservation, the miners moved away. Ruins of adobe buildings may be
seen today, but little remains of the mines or of the stamp mill.

## 8.  Mowry (Patagonia) Mine, Arizona

> *Location: Santa Cruz County, near the ghost town of Mowry,
> just off Ariz. 82, about 20 miles northeast of Nogales.*

Discovered in 1857 by a Mexican herder, this was one of the most
famous early silver mines in Arizona. Capt. R. S. Ewell and Col. J.
W. Douglass, the first owners, sold it in 1859 to Sylvester Mowry,
one of the Territory's pioneers, who prepared for large-scale production. By 1862 he was earning profits, but his outspoken Confederate sympathies led to his arrest by Gen. J. H. Carleton and
internment at Fort Yuma. In 1871 Mowry died in London, where
he had gone after his release to sell the mine. His heirs failed to
maintain the title. In 1875 some Tucson promoters took the mine
over and reworked it. In its lifetime the mine produced a total of
$1,500,000 in silver and lead.

Many mining remnants are scattered over the mountainside near
the ghost town of Mowry. Slag dumps, brick debris, and the remains of some building foundations, along with the rusting hulks
of chimney stacks, boilers, and smelting equipment, may be seen. A
group of abandoned buildings occupies a small valley below the
mine. Some, of adobe and obviously repaired, probably date from
Mowry's ownership; the others are of more recent construction.

## 9.  Rich Hill District, Arizona

> *Location: Yavapai County, about 7 miles east of U.S. 89, at
> Congress Junction.*

A long, light-colored streak from the top of present Rich Hill to its
base indicates the extent of mining activity in this district. Before
the miners abandoned the district late in the 19th century, every
bit of dirt had been overturned by gold seekers, who had pro-
gressed almost perpendicularly up the mountainside. Remains of
miners' cabins may still be seen on the mountaintop. At the base

of Rich Hill were three mining camps: Octave, Weaver, and Stanton. Octave was laid out in 1863. The Octave Mine, owned by eight men, began operations in 1893. Yielding millions of dollars worth of gold, it was active until World War II under various owners. Nothing remains of the camp today except stone foundations.

In 1862 prospectors discovered a small gold deposit on the surface at the east base of the mountain and rich placers of coarse gold at nearby Weaver Creek. A group of 100 Americans and 30 Mexicans removed $1 million worth of gold from the creek. By the 1890's the population of Weaver Camp was exclusively Mexican and the camp developed a reputation as a hangout for desperadoes. By 1896 the Mexicans had departed, and today only remains of burro corrals and the Boot Hill Cemetery may be seen.

Stanton Camp was formed at about the same time as Weaver. At its peak, the population was 2,000. Stanton gained a reputation similar to that of Weaver and was the scene of much violence. The remains are more substantial than those of Weaver or Octave. The site is privately owned.

## 10.  Silver King Mine, Arizona

*Location: Pinal County, on an unpaved road, 5 miles north of Superior.*

In 1872 two soldiers, who were helping to build a wagon road over the Pinal Mountains from Superior to Globe, discovered rocks of almost solid chloride of silver. No one exploited the deposit until 1875, when Charles Mason, Benjamin W. Regan, William H. Long, and Isaac Copeland rediscovered it. The four men organized the Silver King Mine and built stamp mills. A mining camp soon grew up. During the 1880's the mine yielded a seemingly inexhaustible flow of rich silver ore. During one 15-day period, 22 bars valued at $70,000 moved by mule from Pinal to the railroad at Casa Grande and then to San Francisco. For years the mine paid $25,000 a month in dividends, and its total output was $17 million. By 1886 the deposit began to thin out, and within 2 years all mining ceased.

The few buildings that are still standing house the lessees who work the mine on a small scale. Foundations and ruins of the mining camp and mine are scattered about the site.

## 11.   Swilling Canal, Arizona

*Location: Maricopa County.*

Ex-Confederate deserter and would-be mining promoter Jack Swilling probably started the conversion of the Salt River Valley from a desert into an agricultural area. Learning that prehistoric Indians had channeled the waters of the Salt and Gila Rivers into an extensive irrigation system, in 1867 he organized the Swilling Ditch Company at the mining town of Wickenburg. The company laid out a network of canals, which consisted of both new and renovated Indian ditches. Other companies moved into the area and helped build the irrigation system that formed the basic foundation of the Phoenix economy. Although no longer in use, the Swilling Canal may still be traced in places. It leaves the Salt River about a half mile east of the Joint Head Dam, near Pueblo Grande, and passes through Phoenix. The adobe building where Swilling organized his company is still standing in Wickenburg.

## 12.   Vulture Mine, Arizona

*Location: Maricopa County, on an unpaved road, 12 miles off U.S. 60–70, about 14 miles southwest of Wickenburg.*

Henry Wickenburg, an Austrian refugee who had arrived in Arizona in the year 1862 and first prospected at Yuma and La Paz, founded this gold mine the following year. He named it the Vulture because he was led to it by a circling scavenger of that species. Building an arrastra, he found that he could not operate it and also work the mine, so he allowed others to mine while he crushed the ore for a set price. Unaware of the value of the high-grade ore his mine was yielding and charging far too little for his services, he was victimized by associates who stole more ore than they paid him to process. In 1865 he sold his rights in the mine to the Phillips Company of New York for $85,000, of which he received $20,000 as a downpayment. In a dispute with the company, he lost that sum and never received the balance due him. Although after 1865 the mine changed hands many times, it produced total profits of $17 million and was responsible for the establishment of the nearby town of Wickenburg, in 1866 one of the largest in Arizona.

## 13.  White Hills, Arizona

> *Location: Mohave County, just off U.S. 93, about 50 miles northwest of Kingman.*

The Indians knew of mineral deposits in the White Hills vicinity, but they carefully concealed the information from the white men until 1892, when a friendly Indian helped Henry Shaffer discover some silver deposits. Shaffer and two of his friends began working mines and soon were shipping out silver ore at a profit of $1,000 per ton. Many lessees arrived and formed the town of White Hills, which grew to a population of 1,500. The streets were undermined by 27 miles of tunnels, and 15 mines were located within a 1-mile radius. In 1894 R. I. Root formed the White Hills Mining Company, but the following year this company sold out to an English concern for $1,500,000. The new owners built a 40-stamp mill and piped water from a spring 7 miles away. The spring was never able to meet mining needs. Yet between 1892 and 1899 the various mines returned to their owners from $3 million to $12 million in profits. By 1900 the mill was operating only half time. After peak production was reached in 1898, the town declined. It is now a ghost town that haunts the foothills of the Cerbat Range.

## 14.  Amador City, California

> *Location: Amador County.*

In 1848 prospectors discovered small placer deposits of gold on Amador Creek, began mining on a limited scale, and founded Amador City. Three years later they struck gold-bearing quartz veins, and quartz mining became the town's major industry once improved methods of working quartz evolved. In 1869 the leading mine, the Keystone, reached its peak production, but well into the 1880's it continued to yield considerable gold.

A few original buildings still stand in Amador City. These include a one-story stone store, now a museum; the Amador Hotel, a two-story frame structure; the Imperial Hotel, a two-story brick building, which has iron shutters and a balcony; and the Mine House, a large two-story brick building that was once the office and residence of the Keystone Mine superintendents and is now a motel.

## 15. Angels Camp, California

*Location: Calaveras County.*

James H. Carson and George Angel discovered placer deposits of gold near the site of this town in 1848. Angel established a trading post, and the mining camp that sprang up around the post became known as Angels Camp. After the miners exhausted the placers, they discovered gold-bearing quartz veins. By 1857, 11 quartz mills were operating. While visiting the camp in 1865, Mark Twain heard the tale that he soon fashioned into his famous short story "The Celebrated Jumping Frog of Calaveras County," which first

Familiar relics of the mining frontier are abandoned headframes and clusters of dilapidated shacks.

brought him national attention. Few original buildings have survived in the modern town of Angels Camp because of disastrous fires in 1856 and 1885. One of the few reminders of the city's past is a statue of Mark Twain, which stands in a small park.

## 16.   Auburn (Old Town), California

*Location: Placer County.*

Auburn—only about 20 miles away from Coloma, the scene of the first gold strike in California—was one of California's earliest mining camps. It was first known, for a few months, as North Fork Dry Diggings. As early as May 1848 prospectors were mining rich placers in the vicinity. In 1850 the town had a population of 1,500. Despite serious fires in 1855, 1859, and 1863, it continued to grow and was an important center for mine staging and freighting until 1865, when the Central Pacific Railroad reached it.

The original section of Auburn, now known as Old Town, lies at the head of the Auburn Ravine, bounded by Lincoln Way, Court, and Commercial Streets. Still standing are 10 brick and stone commercial buildings, one and two stories in height, which include the newspaper office, Masonic hall, bank, post office, firehouse, and several stores.

## 17.   Chinese Camp, California

*Location: Toulumne County.*

This town was founded in 1849 by a small group of Englishmen who were importing Chinese to work in the California mines. It soon became the headquarters for four of the six Chinese companies, or tongs, in the State. In 1855 its population reached a peak of 5,000. The following year a tong war occurred 2 miles to the west, where 900 members of the Yan-Wo Tong met 1,200 members of a rival faction, the Sam-Yap Tong. After 2 hours of combat, 4 were dead, 4 wounded, and 250 in jail.

Little of the original town remains today. A number of one-story stone buildings stand on the quiet main street, along with an occasional Chinese Tree of Heaven. The present post office, a one-story brick-and-stone structure, was originally built in 1854 as a two-story general store. St. Francis Xavier Catholic Church, a frame structure, was constructed in 1860.

## 18. Copperopolis, California

*Location: Calaveras County.*

Prospectors founded this town in 1861, the year after they struck a rich vein of copper ore. The Union Copper Mine and the Keystone and Empire Mines soon began operating. Between 1862 and 1865 the Copperopolis vicinity was the principal copper-producing area in the United States. Its ore moved by cart to Stockton, then by river boat to San Francisco, and finally by oceangoing vessels to Wales for smelting. By 1865 annual production in the Copperopolis area totaled $1,500,000. In 1866 a drop in the world price of copper brought mining to a halt, and the following year a fire destroyed much of the town. In the 1870's a rise in protective tariff duties caused a brief revival in mining, but the expanding output of the copper mines in Michigan could not be challenged. By 1872 the Copperopolis mines had been abandoned.

A few buildings erected in the 1860's are still standing, including the Federal Armory, the two-story brick warehouse and office of the Copper Consolidated Mining Company, and the brick Odd Fellows (I.O.O.F.) Hall.

## 19. Downieville, California

*Location: Sierra County.*

Set in one of the most rugged and elevated regions of California, Downieville was founded after gold was discovered at the site late in 1849. By the following spring, just after it became the county seat, some 5,000 miners had rushed to the vicinity and the town had become the center for the surrounding camps. In 1852 and 1858 fire destroyed much of it, but each time the residents rebuilt. In spite of fire, weather, and flood, a few brick and stone buildings dating from the 1850's and 1860's still stand along the main street, as well as five or six frame residences and two churches.

## 20.  El Dorado, California

*Location: El Dorado County.*

Mud Spring, later renamed El Dorado, was originally a watering place on the Carson Branch of the California Overland Trail. Then in 1849, when prospectors discovered gold placers in the vicinity, a booming mining camp and freighting center sprang up. In 1855 it incorporated as the town of El Dorado, but within 2 years began to lose population to other mining areas. Because a fire in 1923 destroyed much of the original business district, only a few structures remain today, including a frame hotel, a store, and a block of ruined stone walls of former buildings.

## 21.  Grass Valley, California

*Location: Nevada County.*

Prospectors discovered placer gold in 1849 near the site of Grass Valley, and a small camp sprang up in Boston Ravine. After the miners struck gold-bearing quartz the following year at Gold Hill, the town of Grass Valley grew up around the camp. Before the year ended, the first stamp mill in California and the Far West began operation, but after 2 years it went bankrupt. Improved techniques gradually evolved, however, and by 1856 five quartz mills and seven mines were operating. In 1880 the town's population was more than 5,000. Among the great gold mines in the world is the Empire, discovered in 1850 and now located on Colfax Road 1 mile southwest of town. Still in operation, it has more than 190 miles of tunnels and its deepest shaft is about 4,000 feet.

Because the inhabitants immediately rebuilt and kept modernizing after a fire in 1855 destroyed most of the buildings in the town, few original buildings have survived, though the town contains probably the most extensive mine dumps and surface mine structures in California. Among the most interesting of the older homes is that of Lola Montez, the famous actress and dancer of the mining era, who retired in Grass Valley.

## 22. Hock Farm, California

*Location: Sutter County, on the west bank of the Feather River, near Calif. 99, 8 miles south of Yuba City.*

Named for an Indian village on the Feather River, this farm was established in the winter of 1841–42 by John A. Sutter, who at first had an adobe ranchhouse erected on the west riverbank and later other buildings. By 1848 the herds consisted of 12,000 cattle, 2,000 horses, and perhaps as many as 15,000 sheep. In 1849, after being forced to sell his fort, Sutter moved to Hock Farm and erected a large Monterey colonial dwelling—a two-story frame-adobe house, where in 1850 his family joined him. At the time the farm consisted of 1,200 acres of land, of which about 200 were improved. Sutter resided there until 1865, when a fire destroyed the house. He then returned to the East, where he died in 1880. No remains of the Hock Farm buildings are extant, but the site is a Registered State Historical Landmark. A memorial is located in Yuba County, on the Garden Highway, 8 miles south of Marysville.

## 23. Hornitos, California

*Location: Mariposa County.*

Hornitos ("Little Ovens"), founded by Mexican miners in 1850, is one of the few camps in the Mother Lode country that still reflects the Mexican influence. Founded by Mexicans who had been driven out of nearby Quartzburg by an American vigilance committee, it was built in Mexican style around a plaza. When the placers at Quartzburg gave out, the Americans moved to Hornitos, which incorporated in 1861, and introduced law and order.

Well off the beaten track, the modern town retains much of its original atmosphere and setting. A number of buildings are unaltered, and a few of them are still occupied, mostly by Spanish-speaking people. Adobe-stone structures with massive iron doors stand along the narrow and unpaved streets. Among the 20 original structures, the most interesting are the post office, formerly a beer hall; the Wells-Fargo office, now maintained by the Native Sons of the Golden West; the one-story stone Masonic Hall; and the ruins of the D. Ghirardelli store.

## 24. Jackson, California

*Location: Amador County.*

The first settlers at the site of Jackson, when it was named Botilleas, were miners who arrived in 1849 after prospectors struck placers of gold in the area. Most notable of the deposits were located at Jackson Gate, 1 mile north of town, and at Tunnel Hill, 1½ miles to the south. By the end of 1850 the town had nearly 100 houses, but a fire ravaged it in 1862 and a flood in 1878. Many of the old buildings, however, are still standing along the narrow main street of the town, although nearly all of them have been altered with new fronts and neon signs. The Argonaut and Kennedy Mines, which yield gold-bearing quartz, are still operating.

One of the spectacular sights of the California Mother Lode country, at Jackson. These giant water wheels, 68 feet high, lifted tailings from the Kentucky Mine, in the background.

## 25.  Lassen's Ranch, California

*Location: Tehama County, off U.S. 99E near Vina, 21 miles south of Red Bluff.*

Peter Lassen, a blacksmith and native of Denmark, emigrated to the United States in 1829 and settled in Missouri. A decade later he moved to Oregon country, where he stayed a year before moving to Mexican California. In 1844 the Mexican Government made him a provisional grant of 5 square leagues (about 26,000 acres) in the northern Sacramento Valley that included the site where he had already built an adobe house and trading post. When explorer John C. Frémont visited the ranch in 1846, he found that Lassen had stocked it with cattle and was gradually bringing the land under cultivation with Indian labor. After being unsuccessful in efforts to promote a townsite on his ranch, Lassen sold it in 1852 and turned to trading and mining. In 1859 Indians killed him. No remains of the ranch are extant.

## 26.  Mariposa, California

*Location: Mariposa County.*

On learning of the discovery of gold at Coloma, in 1848 the famous soldier-explorer John C. Frémont "floated" his Mexican land grant of 44,386 acres, Rancho Las Mariposas, about 50 miles eastward to include mountain country that might contain precious minerals. In the summer of 1849, gold-bearing quartz veins were first discovered in California at his ranch, on the southern end of the Mother Lode. Frémont hired 25 Mexican miners and in August 1850 began operating a quartz mill, around which a small town grew up. Although by 1862 he had obtained some $3 million in gold, he profited little because of the chicanery of business associates, high operating costs, and legal battles over title to his ranch. In 1863 he lost control of the Mariposa. In the meantime the town had grown, in 1854 having become the county seat, and mining in the vicinity continued to attract settlers. By 1872 some $20 million had been extracted from the Mariposa mines.

Mariposa is still a prosperous town, but few early buildings remain. Probably the most interesting is the two-story frame court-house, which has functioned as such since its construction in 1854. Frémont's quartz mine, the Princeton, is located just south of the village of Mount Bullion, about 6 miles southwest of Mariposa on Calif. 49. His home (1851–61) is in Bear Valley, 12 miles northwest of the city on the same highway. At Bear Valley may be seen the ruined walls of his company store and the foundation stones of his house. Still standing there, too, are a block of two-story stone and adobe structures, including saloons, stores, and hotels, which were built in the 1850's.

## 27. Marsh Ranch, California

*Location: Contra Costa County, 1.6 miles on Marsh Creek Road, off Walnut Boulevard, 5.3 miles south of Brentwood.*

John Marsh, a native of Massachusetts, arrived in southern California in January 1836 and obtained a license to practice medicine from the Mexican Government. Moving 2 years later to northern California, he purchased the 17,400-acre Rancho Los Medanos (or Meganos) from José Noriega, and constructed a simple four-room adobe ranchhouse with a thatched roof. He raised cattle, sheep, and horses and engaged in some subsidiary farming. In 1856 he erected a new $20,000 home for his growing family. Called the Stone House, and designed by Thomas Boyd in Gothic and Italian villa styles, it was a large three-story stone-and-brick edifice and had a 65-foot tower. The same year, when Marsh was 52 years of age, he was murdered. The Stone House and 7.3 acres of the original ranch have been set aside as a county park. No remains of the original adobe ranchhouse are extant.

## 28. Marysville, California

*Location: Yuba County.*

This river-port town, lying at the head of navigation on the Feather River, the main tributary of the Sacramento River, was surveyed in the spring of 1849 by Charles Covillaud. Almost immediately it became an important steamboat landing and a major interior distributing point for the northern mines in the Sierra Nevada. By February 1850 it had 500 inhabitants, and about 1,000 miners were working in the immediate vicinity. Following the Civil War, mining declined and the construction of railroads caused a serious drop in Marysville's river trade. By 1880 the population had fallen to 4,300 from a peak of 8,000 in 1855. The town suffered in the early days from both fire and flood. Major conflagrations struck in 1851, 1854, and 1856. Four floods, in 1852–53, 1861–62, 1866, and 1875, destroyed many of the original buildings. Those that remain include the Yuba County Court House, St. Joseph's Catholic Church, and the Ramírez House. They are all brick structures in the Gothic Revival style.

### 29. Mokelumne Hill, California

*Location: Calaveras County.*

In 1848 a party of prospectors from Oregon Territory discovered gold near the site of this town, which arose the following year. In

This building in Mokelumne Hill, California, now an annex of the Leger Hotel, served as the Calaveras County Court House during the period 1852–79. Mokelumne Hill, a mining camp and trading center, was founded in 1850.

the 1860's, as the miners depleted the placers, the town began to decline and it suffered from damaging fires in 1854 and 1874. Today, little disturbed by modern intrusions, it is a good example of an early mining town. It still has a number of unaltered original buildings, including the two-story brick Calaveras County Court House, built in 1852 and used as a courthouse until 1866 and as an annex of the Leger Hotel since 1879; the frame Congregational Church, built in Greek Revival style in 1856; and the Odd Fellows (I.O.O.F.) Hall, a three-story brick building built in 1854 as an express office and acquired in 1861 by the Odd Fellows.

## 30. Murphys, California

*Location: Calaveras County.*

Daniel and John Murphy discovered rich placer gold beds on Angel's Creek in July 1848. The town that arose—not far from Angels Camp—was first known by the name of Murphy's Diggings, then as Murphy's Camp, and finally as Murphys. In 1855 the population reached its peak, but 4 years later fire destroyed much of the business district. Considerably isolated today, the town has survived with the setting largely unaltered. A number of the original buildings still stand, including the Mitcher Hotel, a large two-story stone structure equipped with iron doors and balcony, built in 1855; Thorpe's Bakery, a one-story stone building, constructed in 1856; two one-story stone stores dating from 1855; a Wells-Fargo express office; and a schoolhouse built in 1860.

## 31. Nevada City, California

*Location: Nevada County.*

After the discovery of placer deposits of gold at the site of Nevada City in September 1849, a small mining camp sprang up on Deer Creek. Because the placers proved to be rich, a major rush ensued and by the end of the first year the town had more than 400 buildings and a population of 2,000. An additional 8,000 men lived in a dozen nearby mining camps. When fire destroyed half the town in

Nevada City, California, was founded after prospectors discovered gold nearby in 1849. First known as Deer Creek Diggings and Caldwell's Store, it soon took the name of Nevada, or Nevada City. Courtesy, Bancroft Library, University of California.

1851, the citizens rebuilt with brick, but within a couple of years mining fell off, and the population declined. The development of techniques for the processing of quartz and the advent of hydraulic mining in 1856, however, led to a revival, and in 1880 the population numbered 4,022.

Today Nevada City is probably the best preserved mining town in northern California. Many brick and stone buildings dating from the middle 1850's still line its crooked, hillside streets, including Fire House No. 1, the National Hotel, and the assay office. This assay office correctly identified as silver the puzzling ore specimens from the Comstock Lode of Nevada.

## 32.  North Bloomfield, California

*Location: Nevada County, on an unpaved road, 19 miles north of Nevada City.*

In 1851 prospectors ran across placer deposits of gold at the site of North Bloomfield. A mining town, first named Humbug City for the creek on which it was located, sprang up the same year and by 1856 had 400 inhabitants. But until the invention of hydraulic mining progress was slow in the vicinity. In 1852 a Frenchman named Chabot used a hose without a nozzle on his claim at the nearby Buckeye Hill Mine to sluice away the gravel he had loosened with his pick. The following year Edward E. Matteson, adding a nozzle to a hose, invented hydraulic mining. The increased pressure provided by the nozzle eliminated costly pick and shovel work. Matteson first applied his invention at the American Hill Mine at neighboring Nevada City.

Improved by many individuals, the process was immediately adopted at North Bloomfield, which between 1855 and 1884 was the largest hydraulic mining center in California. To supply the vast quantities of water needed, the North Bloomfield Company constructed two large reservoirs high in the Sierra Nevada, 6,000 feet above sea level and about 3,000 feet above the town. A system of canals and flumes about 100 miles long transported the water.

North Bloomfield is now almost deserted, and only a few original frame structures remain. At the edge of town is the colossal pit of the Malakoff Mine, second only in size to the La Grange pit near Weaverville, Calif.

As mining technology advanced, the hydraulic method of loosening paydirt was invented. Here a "monitor" is being used near Yuba City, California. Courtesy, Wells-Fargo Museum, San Francisco.

### 33.  North San Juan, California

*Location: Nevada County.*

In 1853 prospectors discovered gold at San Juan Ridge, just north of the site of North San Juan. By 1859 the town had a population of 1,000 and consisted of 8 brick buildings, a church, a public school, 3 hotels, 2 restaurants, a brewery, 4 sawmills, an iron foundry, some 60 stores and saloons, and about 250 houses. Hydraulic methods were used to work the deposits on San Juan Ridge.

Today the town has a small population, but several original structures have survived, including four or five brick buildings. The most important are the Odd Fellows Hall (1860); the townhall (1857); and the frame Methodist Church (1856), built in the Greek Revival style.

### 34.  Placerita Canyon, California

*Location: Los Angeles County, on U.S. 6, about 6 miles east of Newhall.*

While looking in this canyon for stray cattle, on March 9, 1842, Francisco López y Arballo first discovered placer gold in commercial quantities in California. The deposits were worked mainly by Francisco García, an experienced miner from Sonora, Mexico, who brought others with him from his home state. By the end of 1843 the men had obtained about $42,000 worth of gold nuggets from nearby San Feliciana Canyon in the San Fernando hills, as well as an unknown amount from Placerita Canyon. After about 5 years they exhausted the deposits. Placerita Canyon is a Registered State Historical Landmark and also a State park.

### 35.  Placerville, California

*Location: El Dorado County.*

Placerville was one of California's earliest mining camps, for prospectors struck gold at the site in the summer of 1848. The camp that grew up was first known as Old Dry Diggings, but early in 1849, after the residents hanged several alleged robbers without benefit of trial, they renamed it Hangtown. The following year they again renamed it, as Placerville. When incorporated in 1854, the town had a population of 1,944. By 1856 gold production had fallen off, and two large fires swept the town, which began to decline. The citizens rebuilt with brick and stone. Their faith proved to be justified, for in 1860 the town became the gateway to the Comstock Lode area of Nevada. Also a major supply and transportation center for California mining camps, it was served by the first transcontinental telegraph line and was an important depot on the Carson Branch of the California Overland Trail, the Central Overland Mail and Stage Line, and the Pony Express.

Three men who later became famous began their careers at Placerville: Mark Hopkins sold groceries door to door, J. M. Studebaker built wheelbarrows for the miners, and Philip Armour ran a butcher shop.

On Main Street of modern Placerville are a number of buildings constructed about 1860: Placerville Academy, now the Ivy House; the Methodist Church; and St. Patrick's Catholic Church. The general setting of the town has been much altered by a superhighway and many modern buildings.

## 36.  Rancho Chico, California

*Location: Butte County, Sowilleno Avenue between Esplanade and Citrus Avenues, Chico.*

John Bidwell, a leader of the first organized party of overland emigrants to reach California, was later a successful agriculturist, horticulturist, and town builder. After his arrival in 1841, he entered the employ of John Augustus Sutter as soldier, bookkeeper, and manager and then became an officer in Frémont's California Battalion. In 1847 he acquired Rancho Chico, which consisted of approximately 25,000 acres, and the following year erected a small log cabin. Maintaining an experimental orchard, he eventually planted 65,276 fruit and nut trees on an 1,800-acre tract; and pioneered raisin growing and olive oil manufacture in the region.

In 1860, on his ranch, Bidwell founded the town of Chico, for

Ranchers built some of the finest homes in early California, such as John Bidwell's Italian villa mansion, headquarters of Rancho Chico.

which he donated much of the land. Five years later he retained Henry William Cleaveland, a San Francisco architect, to design a new home, a large two-story stone mansion. He began construction in 1865 and completed it 3 years later, at a cost of $56,000. He died in 1900. In 1921 the State of California acquired the mansion as a part of Chico State Normal School. In 1961 the California Division of Beaches and Parks took over the structure and made plans to restore it as a historic house and a State historical monument.

## 37. Rancho El Tejon, California

*Location: Kern and Los Angeles Counties, monument on U.S. 99, at Lebec.*

In 1852 Edward Fitzgerald Beale, a young U.S. Navy lieutenant who had served with distinction at the Battle of San Pasqual during the Mexican War in California, was appointed Superintendent of Indian Affairs for California and Nevada. He instituted a new Indian policy that called for the establishment of a series of small but well-defined reservations where the Indians were to be concentrated and taught farming and simple trades so that they could become self-supporting. In 1853 he launched his first reservation of this type, at Tejon, and the following year the Army founded Fort Tejon nearby to protect the Indians from the whites.

Removed as superintendent for political reasons in 1854, Beale turned to ranching in the San Joaquin Valley. Near Tejon, at a cost of about 5 cents an acre, he bought four contiguous Mexican ranchos (Castac, Liebre, El Tejon, and Los Alamos y Agua Caliente) and formed a 195,000-acre ranch. When the Tejon Reservation was disbanded in 1863, he invited the Indians to live on the ranch. By 1870 he was running more than 100,000 sheep, which were tended by 300 Indian shepherds. In addition to ranching, he also pioneered in irrigating the San Joaquin Valley. In this manner he cultivated 1,900 acres.

Beale died in 1893, and in 1912 his heirs sold the ranch to Harry Chandler. Part of the ranch is still in operation. The original ranch headquarters buildings have disappeared, as have the adobe quarters of the Indians. Fort Tejon State Historical Monument contains three restored adobe buildings—a barracks and two officers' quarters.

## 38. Rancho Jacinto, California

*Location: Glenn County, on an unpaved road, at Jacinto, 15 miles northeast of Willows.*

In 1867 Dr. Hugh James Glenn, who had come to California from Missouri in 1849 and for a while tried his luck in the goldfields, purchased this ranch, which originally consisted of a 7,000-acre Mexican grant dating from 1844. Adding to his holdings other lands in the vicinity, he soon owned 55,000 acres. On 45,000 of them he grew wheat, a task that required 108 teams of mules. Between 1874 and 1883 he was the leading wheat farmer in the United States. He also ventured into the cattle industry through partnerships. The firm of French and Glenn established a 132,000-acre ranch in Harney County, Oreg., which ran perhaps 30,000 cattle and 3,000 horses. With his nephew, E. W. Crutchers, Glenn also owned another large ranch in Paradise Valley, Nev., where another 15,000 cattle and 1,000 horses grazed. In 1883 Dr. Glenn was murdered. In the 1890's his California estate was subdivided into small farms, but the old Glenn mansion still stands at Jacinto.

## 39.  Rancho Las Flores, California

*Location: San Diego County, on Camp Pendleton Marine Corps base, 2 miles north of Oceanside.*

In 1841 the Mexican Government granted to Pio and Andrés Pico the ranchos San Margarita and Las Flores, which totaled 100,000 acres. On Rancho Las Flores, Pio Pico erected a large one-story adobe ranchhouse, which had a wide porch on two sides. Economic difficulties, however, forced him in 1864 to sell the two ranches to his brother-in-law, John Forster, who combined them with land he already owned in the vicinity to form one vast ranch of 187,000 acres.   Forster resided on the ranch until he died in 1882. During World War II, the land became a U.S. Marine Corps training base. The old ranchhouse, somewhat remodeled by the Marine Corps but maintaining in general its original appearance, is still standing.

## 40.  Rancho Los Cerritos, California

*Location: Los Angeles County, 4600 Virginia Road, Long Beach.*

This rancho was originally part of one of the first two provisional land grants made by the King of Spain in California for ranching purposes. In 1784 the King granted to Manuel Nieto all the land between the Santa Ana and San Gabriel Rivers and from the foothills of the San Gabriel Mountains to the Pacific Ocean. Nieto agreed to build a stone house and to maintain at least 2,000 head of livestock on the ranch. In 1834, when his heirs finally received full title to the 200,000-acre ranch from the Mexican Government, they divided it into five separate ranches. At the time John Temple, a young New Englander, married a granddaughter of the original owner, he acquired a twelfth interest in the ranch. In 1843 he became sole owner of the 27,000-acre Rancho Los Cerritos by buying out the other heirs, and soon was pasturing 15,000 cattle, 7,000 sheep, and 3,000 horses. Temple later acquired Mexican citizenship and became very wealthy. In the 1850's he was an important builder in the city of Los Angeles. He sold the ranch in 1866 to Flint, Bixby, and Company, which operated it as a sheep ranch until 1882, when the company subdivided it for real estate and town development purposes.

Rancho Los Cerritos ranchhouse was probably the largest and most impressive in southern California during the Mexican period. Now located within the city of Long Beach, it is one of the largest restored adobe structures in California.

The magnificent Los Cerritos ranchhouse, probably the most impressive in southern California during the Mexican period, is today the largest restored adobe structure in the region. Erected by Temple in 1844 in Monterey colonial style, it is now exhibited as a historic home by the city of Long Beach. Its central two-story portion is 100 feet long, and at each end are one-story wings, each 145 feet long. The wings are joined together by an adobe wall, which forms an enclosed patio. Unfortunately the original ranch setting has been destroyed almost completely by urban growth and the intrusion of Signal Hill district oil wells.

### 41.   Rancho Nipomo (William G. Dana Ranch), California

*Location: San Luis Obispo County, on U.S. 101, just south of Nipomo.*

William Goodwin Dana, a native of Boston and cousin of Richard Henry Dana, Jr., author of *Two Years Before the Mast*, emigrated to California in 1826 and settled at Santa Barbara. Two years later he married a Mexican girl and in 1835 became a naturalized Mexican citizen. In 1837 the Mexican Government granted him a 37,000-acre tract, Rancho Nipomo, upon which he settled in 1839. He resided in a large 13-room adobe house that he designed himself. Employing Indians, he stocked his ranch with cattle and engaged in the hide and tallow trade. For many years the Dana heirs owned the house and surrounding land. In 1954 the San Luis Obispo Historical Society acquired the old house and hopes to restore it.

### 42.   Rancho Santa Rita (Miller-Lux Headquarters), California

*Location: Merced County, on Calif. 152, about 13 miles east of Los Banos.*

In 1850 Henry Miller arrived in San Francisco, where he opened a butcher shop. In 1858 he formed a partnership with Charles Lux, another German immigrant. Five years later they purchased their first ranch—8,835 acres of Rancho Sanjon de Santa Rita—together with its "Double H" brand and 7,500 head of cattle. By 1866 Rancho Santa Rita had been extended until it was 68 miles in length. Using this ranch as a base, Miller and Lux began building the largest ranching empire on the Pacific coast. Acquiring thousands of acres in California, Nevada, and Oregon, by 1888 they owned 750,000 acres, two-thirds of which were fenced, and 100,000 cattle and 80,000 sheep. They ran a channel northward 30 miles from the San Joaquin River, 12 miles above its bend, to irrigate 500,000 acres of land. Only one original building has survived: a small one-story frame building at one time used as a store but now considerably altered. The once vast ranch has been reduced to an 1,800-acre farm.

## 43. San Bernardino Mormon Colony, California

*Location: San Bernardino County, Arrowhead Avenue and Court Street, San Bernardino.*

In 1851 Brigham Young directed Amasa M. Lyman and C. C. Rich to lead 500 Mormons from Salt Lake City to the vicinity of Cajon Pass in California and establish an agricultural colony and Mormon outpost. Upon their arrival, the Mormons purchased Rancho San Bernardino from the Lugo family for $77,000 and laid out the town of San Bernardino, along with adjacent farms. To protect themselves from possible Indian attacks, they erected a fort and stockade that measured 300 by 720 feet and enclosed about 8 acres of land. The settlement prospered until 1857, when Young ordered the colonists to return to Salt Lake City. Most of the settlers obeyed the order, and the San Bernardino colony was abandoned. No remains of the original fort survive, but the site is a Registered State Historical Landmark.

## 44. San Francisco, California

*Location: San Francisco County.*

The sleepy city of San Francisco, which had originated in 1835 as the Mexican village of Yerba Buena and which had been the site of a Spanish mission and presidio since the year 1776, was jolted by the discovery of gold at Coloma in 1848. At first, while the news was on the way eastward, the city was almost depopulated by a mass emigration of males to the goldfields. The next year, however, hordes of gold seekers from all over the world began to arrive. By 1850 the population was 25,000, many of whom had settled in the city instead of continuing on to the goldfields.

As the treasures of the mines poured in, the city became the economic capital of the Far West. Prices skyrocketed, lodgings became scarce, and vice and gambling prospered in the crowded and chaotic new metropolis. Portsmouth Square was studded with saloons and gambling halls, and gang warfare broke out on the dark streets. By 1855 the citizens had formed a vigilance committee. A

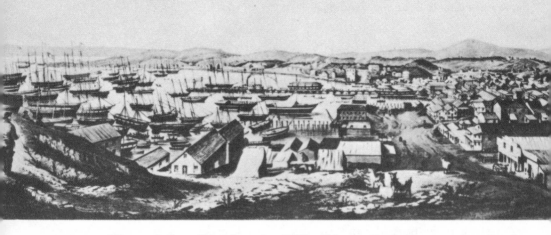

View of San Francisco in 1850, lithographed from a drawing by William B. McMurtrie. Courtesy, Bancroft Library, University of California.

series of fires, in 1849, 1850, 1851, and 1852, destroyed the tents and shanties of the first boom period, and a law of 1853 required that all buildings in the business district be constructed of brick and stone. Late in the century the Klondike gold strike brought new wealth and another boom. By 1903 the population was 425,000.

The great earthquake and fire of 1906 destroyed almost all of the original business district except for the section known today as Jackson Square. This section contains 10 brick and stone buildings dating from the 1850's and 1860's that have been carefully preserved and restored. Although used for modern commercial purposes, the buildings convey some of the flavor of early San Francisco. The Old United States Mint, located at the corner of Fifth and Mission Streets, is eligible to be registered as a National Historic Landmark.

### 45.  Santa Rosa Island (Vail and Vickers Ranch), California

*Location: Santa Barbara County, in the Pacific Ocean, about 30 miles south of Santa Barbara.*

In 1843 the Mexican Government granted the brothers Carlos Antonio and José Antonio Carrillo all of Santa Rosa Island, about 62,000 acres, for ranching purposes. The very next year the brothers, in turn, gave the island to two of Carlos' daughters, Mrs. A. B. Thompson and Mrs. John C. Jones, as a wedding gift. The ranch was then stocked with sheep. In the 1880's Alexander P. and W. Henry More of Boston purchased it and erected a New England-style framehouse and barns. The Mores were succeeded as owners in 1902 by the Vail & Vickers Cattle Company, which replaced the sheep with beef cattle. The island today is still a cattle ranch, and the house, stables, hay barns, and bunkhouses erected in the 1880's are still being used.

## 46. Shasta, California

> *Location: Shasta County, on U.S. 299, approximately 6 miles west of Redding.*

Between 1850 and 1852 miners formed a new gold-mining district at the head of Sacramento Valley, but it never achieved the importance of those in the Sierra Nevada. Shasta evolved in 1850 from Reading's Spring, a trading center that had been established the previous year to supply the isolated northwestern mining camps in the district. Supplies, which reached it by wagon, were packed over the mountains on mules. The period of the town's greatest prosperity was between 1852 and 1857, when more than 2,000 mules were transporting supplies to the mines. After 1857 the gold deposits began to play out, and in 1872 the California and Oregon Railroad bypassed the town. As a result the population, which in 1854 had reached 1,500, by 1880 had declined to 448. Fires in 1853 and 1878 destroyed many of the original buildings.

Today Shasta is a State historical monument that with three exceptions consists of crumbling walls and deteriorating foundations. Still intact are the two-story brick Masonic Hall and store (1853); and the one-story brick county courthouse (1855), which now serves as a museum. On a hill overlooking the town is a two-story framehouse that was once owned by Dr. Benjamin Shurtleff. Built in the Greek Revival style in 1851, it was prefabricated in Boston, shipped around the Horn to San Francisco, carried to Sacramento by river boat, and then freighted by wagon to Shasta.

## 47.  Sonora, California

*Location: Tuolumne County.*

A party of Mexican miners discovered rich placer deposits of gold on Woods Creek in August 1848, and nearby grew the town of Sonora Camp, or Sonora for short. Attracted by the deposits, other Mexicans, as well as Anglo-Americans, came into the area, and by 1849 the population of the town was 5,000. Known as the "Queen of the Southern Mines," Sonora was not without violence. In June 1850, when the Americans imposed a $20 tax on all foreign-born miners, most of the foreigners left at once. Ravaged by three fires—in 1849, 1852, and 1853—the town was rebuilt each time. By 1865 its mines were almost exhausted, and in 1880 its population was only 1,490.

Today the few original buildings that have survived have been considerably altered. The citizens have replaced most of the older structures with more modern ones. The outstanding building—one of the most beautiful in all the Mother Lode country—is St. James Episcopal Church, a graceful frame structure on North Washington Street. Completed in 1859, it is only 100 yards from the Big Bonanza Mine, reputedly the richest single-pocket mine ever discovered in California.

## 48.  Stockton, California

*Location: San Joaquin County.*

Lying on the lower San Joaquin River at the head of navigation, the river port of Stockton sprang into life in 1849–50. From there pack trains and wagons hauled supplies to the mining towns located in the interior. By the mid-1850's the town had some 200 framehouses, and in 1851 the first brick building was constructed. Today only three or four buildings of the gold-rush period survive. Among these are the two-story brick Forty-Niner Drugstore, located at the corner of Main and El Dorado Streets, erected about 1852; and the I.O.O.F. Hall, situated on the west side of El Dorado Street between Weber Avenue and Main Street, built in 1853.

## 49. Volcano, California

*Location: Amador County.*

Prospectors discovered placer gold at Volcano, or Soldiers' Gulch, in 1848, and a mining camp sprang up 2 years later. It quickly attracted a population of 5,000, but by 1855 the miners had almost depleted the rich deposits. Hydraulic mining came into use shortly thereafter, and the town gained a new lease on life. Well off the beaten path today, it preserves an authentic gold-rush flavor. Among the major surviving buildings from the 1850's and 1860's are the St. George Hotel, a three-story brick building; the two-story Odd Fellows and Masonic Hall; the Adams Express Office; two one-story saloons; and a store. All of these are of brick or stone construction.

## 50. Weaverville, California

*Location: Trinity County.*

John Weaver discovered gold on Weaver Creek in 1849. In mid-1850 miners established the town of Weaverville, which immediately became the county seat. By 1858, after two disastrous fires and rebuildings, the town had 25 stone and brick structures and had

Joss houses were places of worship for Chinese mineworkers. This one is at Weaverville, California.

reached its peak population of about 1,800. Like Chinese Camp, it was also the scene of a tong war, in the 1850's.

A considerable number of buildings have survived with relatively little change, including the courthouse, the Masonic Lodge, and several stores. A reminder of the 2,500 Chinese who once worked in the vicinity is the Weaverville Joss House, which was a temple of worship. Built in 1874 after a fire had destroyed the original, it is largely furnished with original funiture. Intricate imported Chinese carvings of fish and dragons decorate the exterior, and hand-painted tapestries lie beside an interior altar. In 1956 the building and its furnishings were donated to the State of California, which maintains them as a State historical monument.

### 51. Wolfskill Farm Site, California

*Location: Los Angeles County, Alameda Street between Aliso and Mary Streets, Los Angeles.*

William Wolfskill, a Kentuckian, formed a partnership in New Mexico with mountain man Ewing Young in the late 1820's. As a result, Wolfskill and George C. Young, leading a group of 20 men from Sante Fe to California in 1830–31, opened a new overland route that came to be called the Old Spanish Trail. Wolfskill settled permanently in California, where in 1838 he acquired a farm, later known as the Wolfskill Orchard Tract and located near the center of the present city of Los Angeles. He erected an adobe house and established the vineyards that were to make him rich and famous. A pioneer in the California wine industry, he helped supply the large market created by the gold rush. Also planting the first privately owned orange grove in California, he transplanted the trees from the abandoned gardens of San Gabriel Mission. After he died in 1866, his farm was subdivided as the city of Los Angeles expanded. In 1902 his adobe house was demolished. A portion of his farm is now occupied by the Los Angeles Union Railroad Station.

## 52. Aspen, Colorado

*Location: Pitkin County.*

Large quantities of silver ore lying in the debris on the sides of
Aspen and Smuggler Mountains attracted the earliest prospectors,
who came from Leadville, to the site of Aspen about 1879. Between
1880 and 1884 many mines were active in the area, some of which
became world famous. Large nuggets of high-grade ore netted
millions of dollars for stockholders. One of the largest bodies of
ore in the world was worked in the Comprise Mine, and more high-
grade ores were shipped from Aspen than any other camp in the
world. In 1889, when the town's population was more than 8,000—
and it had three daily newspapers, electric street lights, a telephone
exchange, waterworks, and two railroads—the output of the mines
in the vicinity was $10 million. By 1892, the population had risen
to 11,000, and the town boasted 6 newspapers, 10 churches, 3 banks,
and 3 streetcars. The average annual output of the lead and silver
mines was $6 million. In 1893, however, a depression occurred be-
cause of the collapse in silver prices. Mining continued on a smaller scale until the 1920's, when the ore thinned out and the mines
began closing down.

Four noteworthy structures of the early days have survived: the
Hotel Jerome and the Wheeler Opera House, both built in 1889;
the Catholic Church (1892) ; and the Court House (*ca.* 1890).
The city today is a ski resort and cultural center.

## 53. Boggsville, Colorado

*Location: Bent County, on an unpaved road, about 2 miles
southeast of Las Animas.*

Boggsville was the site of the first successful irrigation experiment
in southwestern Colorado and the cradle of the Colorado cattle
industry. It was established in 1860 by Thomas O. Boggs, who obtained a 2,000-acre tract of land from the original Vigil and St.
Vrain land grant. In 1867 Boggs joined with John W. Prowers, a

prominent cattle raiser who brought the first herd of cattle from Missouri into Colorado and settled at Boggsville, and Robert Bent to construct a 7-mile irrigation canal, known as Tarbox Ditch. This canal, on the Purgatoire River, a tributary of the Arkansas, irrigated 1,000 acres on the farms of the three men. Boggs sold his produce and livestock to nearby Fort Lyon. By the 1880's Prowers owned 10,000 head of cattle. The town thrived until 1873, when the Kansas Pacific Railroad bypassed it in favor of Las Animas. It then became a ghost town.

Only two significant structures, the Boggs and Prowers homes, have survived. The latter also served as a hotel, store, and stage station. Built of adobe, it is now unoccupied and in poor condition. The Boggs home, a 10-room one-story building, is in fair condition because of its 30-inch plastered walls.

## 54. Breckenridge, Colorado

*Location: Summit County.*

In 1859 Ruben Spalding and a party of 30 men discovered small amounts of gold in the Blue River. After building a blockhouse for protection against the Indians, they panned the river. They named their camp Breck*i*nridge in honor of the Vice President of the United States; later, after he sided with the Confederacy, they renamed it Breckenridge. In 1860 a rush occurred, and for 3 years the placer fields were the richest in Colorado, until they washed thin. The camp became the center of a group that had a combined population of 8,000. Late in the 1880's new strikes precipitated a second boom. During the 1890's a third boom occurred, when miners dredged the Blue River for placer deposits. Today the rock walls along the shore left by the dredging process may still be seen. Many of the buildings in the town date from the second or third boom and are excellent examples of mining-town architecture.

## 55. Chalk Creek Canyon, Colorado

*Location: Chaffee County, along Colo. 162.*

Between the 1870's and the end of World War I a number of gold-mining towns thrived in this canyon, located in the Arkansas River

Valley. They were served by the Denver, South Park, and Pacific Railroad. Alpine, the first, originated in 1875 to support the Tilden Mine. It was the point from which ore was shipped to Pueblo for smelting. The largest town in the canyon was St. Elmo, incorporated in 1880, which at one time had 2,000 inhabitants. Both Alpine and St. Elmo have a small population today.

Within a few miles of St. Elmo are two ghost towns, Romley and Hancock. Romley was founded about 1870, when the Mary Murphy Mine was active. The mine, which yielded a total of $14 million, ceased operations at the end of World War I. Hancock was once a bustling mining town of five stores, two sawmills, one hotel, and numerous saloons. It was also a railroad construction headquarters and transfer point for railroad passengers traveling to Gunnison.

## 56. Creede, Colorado

*Location: Mineral County.*

This town was founded by Nicholas C. Creede, a discouraged prospector who in 1890 and 1891 stumbled upon silver bonanzas at the townsite. Christening his mines the Holy Moses and Amethyst, Creede made a fortune from the rich ore. Hundreds of prospectors soon arrived via the branch line that the Denver and Rio Grande Western Railroad completed to the diggings. They formed a rough camp, called Jim Town for a short time, the forerunner of the town of Creede. By 1893 the population was about 8,000. Along with Aspen, Creede led Colorado in silver production, although periodically damaged by fires and floods. After 1893, when silver prices collapsed, most of the mines closed down, though they were far from exhausted. Mining resumed in the 20th century and has continued to the present day. The ramshackle Ford's Saloon, built by Bob Ford, reputedly the slayer of Jesse James, is still standing.

## 57. Fairplay, Colorado

*Location: Park County.*

In 1859 some prospectors reached the region of South Park and established Tarryall Camp, from which they barred all newcomers.

Dubbing the camp "Graball," the newcomers moved on and discovered gold in the gravel bars of the South Platte River. They organized a mining district and founded the town of Fairplay, so named because the camp boss demanded "fair play" for everyone. Two significant historic buildings are still standing in the modern town: The Community Church and the courthouse, both of which were built in 1874.

A non-profit corporation has reconstructed in Fairplay a replica of an old Colorado mining town, called South Park City. The town consists of old buildings and furnishings assembled from South Park, the mountain basin drained by the headwaters of the South Platte River.

## 58. Georgetown, Colorado

*Location: Clear Creek County.*

Prior to the Leadville strike in the year 1878, Georgetown was the most important mining town in Colorado. The first great boom occurred after 1859, when George and David Griffith discovered gold. Soon the valley around "George's Town" was alive with miners. In 1864 a prospector discovered a rich lode of silver, 2,000 miners arrived, and George's Town became a thriving community. In 1866 two camps half a mile apart agreed to combine under the name Georgetown, and 2 years later the county seat was moved to Georgetown from Idaho Springs. Georgetown—along with nearby Silver Plume—prospered until the 1890's, when the price of silver collapsed.

Among the remarkable historic buildings that have survived are: the Maxwell House, a typical Victorian house; the Hammill House, home of William A. Hammill, an influential citizen; the Protestant Episcopal Church, oldest Episcopal church in Colorado; the Hotel de Paris, famous throughout the West for its French wine and food; and two old firehouses. The Colonial Dames and the Colorado Historical Society are among the groups that have cooperated in preserving these quaint old buildings and opening them to the public.

## 59.   Iliff Ranch Headquarters Site, Colorado

*Location: Logan County, just east of the village of Iliff.*

John Wesley Iliff, son of a well-to-do farmer, left Ohio in 1856 and settled in present Kansas. Moving to Colorado during the gold rush of 1859 and eventually settling in the South Platte Valley, he entered the cattle business. By the early 1870's he owned 15,000 acres of land and 35,000 head of cattle. His main ranchhouse was near the present village of Iliff. After his death, in 1879, the ranch was broken up and the headquarters fell into ruins. The buildings had been destroyed by the beginning of the 20th century, and the ranch site is now a plowed field.

## 60.   Kokomo, Colorado

*Location: Summit County, on Colo. 91, about 12 miles north of Climax.*

In 1878 a group of Indiana prospectors, who found large silver deposits in the vicinity, founded this town. Two smelters, the White Quail and the Greer, processed the ore. Fire destroyed the town in 1881, when its population was 10,000, but the residents rebuilt. Mining slowly declined until only a few mines were active and the population of the town a few hundred. Today Kokomo is almost deserted. Significant surviving buildings are the Masonic Hall and the Community Church.

## 61.   Ouray, Colorado

*Location: Ouray County.*

This town was established in 1875, when prospectors discovered rich silver lodes nearby. Miners rushed to the vicinity, and Ouray incorporated 2 years later. It boomed during the 1880's, but the collapse of silver prices in 1893 cast a shadow over the future. The discovery of gold nearby in 1896 by Thomas Walsh, however, caused a revival. Walsh's Camp Bird Mine annually yielded $3 million or $4 million from 1896 to 1902. In 1902 Walsh sold the mine for $5,200,000 to a British syndicate, and it is still profitably operated. Ouray is a popular tourist resort and is still an active mining town. Among the buildings that are a reminder of the early days are the Beaumont Hotel, an ornate three-story white brick structure, and the Elks Hall.

## 62.  Silver Plume, Colorado

*Location: Clear Creek County.*

The picturesque mining town of Silver Plume was so named because the first ore discovered there, late in the 1860's, was shaped like a feather. Until the swampy flatland in the valley could be drained and cleared for a townsite, the miners erected their tents and cabins on the sides of the five mountains in the vicinity. By 1870 the town began to take shape. Rich mines, on tortuous mountain trails, were the source of silver, lead, copper, zinc, and gold. The most famous mine was the Pelican silver mine, discovered in 1868. In 1884 fire nearly destroyed the town, even though the residents obtained aid from nearby Georgetown. Slowly the landmarks of Silver Plume's early history have disappeared but many still remain.

## 63.  Boise, Idaho

*Location: Ada County.*

Boise, although never a mining camp, grew up as a result of mining activity in the region and became an important supply and agricultural center. It was originally known as Boise City. When prospectors discovered gold on the Clearwater River in 1860, miners rushed to Idaho country. Subsequent discoveries on the Salmon River and in the Boise Basin attracted more than 25,000 miners and created a great demand for agricultural produce. Boise, established in 1863 adjacent to Fort Boise, met this demand with irrigated farming and became a trading center.

Boise contains several excellent examples of pioneer homes, including the Coston, Pearce, and O'Farrell cabins. Also of interest are Fort Boise, Spanish Village, and the Stone Blockhouse. The United States Assay Office, built in 1870–71, is a Registered National Historic Landmark.

## 64.   Craig Donation Land Claim, Idaho

> *Location: Nez Perce County, on U.S. 95, about 8 miles south of Spalding.*

A native of Virginia and former mountain man, William Craig in 1840 settled among the Nez Percé Indians in the Lapwai Valley. He was the first permanent white settler in the Idaho country. The Indians liked him and he married one of them. For this reason he did not join the exodus of settlers from the region during the period of Indian troubles, in 1847–58, and in 1854 filed a land claim

Sawtell Ranch, on Henry's Lake in eastern Idaho Territory, 1872. For the time, these were almost palatial ranch quarters.

for 630 acres. During the gold rush into the Nez Percé Reservation in 1860–61, he served as adviser to the Indians and profitably operated ferries across the Snake River. After his death in 1869, part of his claim was divided into several smaller farms, but the remainder is still owned by his descendants. The site is indicated by a historical marker.

## 65. Elk City, Idaho

*Location: Idaho County.*

In 1861 a party of 22 miners from the town of Pierce discovered rich placer deposits on the South Fork of the Clearwater River. Several hundred miners rushed in and founded Elk City, the second mining camp in the Idaho country. Late in 1861 the town, which consisted of several saloons and 40 log cabins, supported about 2,000 miners in the vicinity. Around 1864 most of the white miners abandoned the shallow placers and Chinese took over. In 1892 the miners brought in hydraulic mining equipment and dredges to further work the placers. Elk City today is a tiny village that contains many summer cabins. No remains of mining buildings are extant, but for miles around are vast dumps left by the dredges.

## 66. Florence, Idaho

*Location: Idaho County, on a frequently impassable road, about 14 miles east of U.S. 95, just north of the Salmon River.*

One of Idaho's earliest and most short-lived mining camps, Florence sprang into existence in October 1861 following the discovery of gold placers on Miller Creek, which flows into the Salmon River. Thousands of miners poured in until January 1862, when heavy snows set in and trapped the residents, who slowly starved until the first pack trains broke through in the spring. In the fall of that year vigilante action was required to curb the lawless element. In 1863, just as the placers were giving out, the miners received news of the rush to the Boise Basin and by the next year most of them had left and been replaced by Chinese miners. Between 1861 and 1867 the area yielded about $9,600,000 in ore. Today the town has completely vanished; only scars of mining remain.

## 67.  Fort Lemhi, Idaho

>  *Location: Lemhi County, just east of Idaho 28, about 21 miles
>  southeast of Salmon.*

At this fort the Mormons made the first attempt to establish a
missionary and agricultural colony in present Idaho. In 1855 Brigham Young directed Thomas S. Smith and 26 other men to conduct missionary work among the Indians of Washington Territory.
At a site 379 miles northwest of Salt Lake City on a branch of the
Salmon River, which the missionaries named the Lemhi River for
a king in the *Book of Mormons,* they built Fort Lemhi of adobe
and wood and erected log cabins within. Outside they dug a few
small irrigation ditches so that farming could be carried on. The
Bannock Indians resented the intrusion. After several skirmishes,
early in 1858 Young directed the abandonment of the fort, which
was never reoccupied. The site is now marked by a stone monument. No surface remains of the fort are extant, but there are
traces of what might have been an irrigation ditch.

## 68.  Franklin, Idaho

>  *Location: Franklin County.*

Franklin, the first permanent white settlement in present Idaho,
was founded as part of a well-organized plan of Mormon expansion
by colonists from Utah under the leadership of Thomas Smart. Arriving in the southeastern corner of Idaho about 1 mile north of
the Idaho-Utah border in 1860, the colonists allotted tracts of land
and erected a log stockade. They also dug an irrigation ditch $3\frac{1}{2}$
miles in length to conduct water from Maple Creek to the fields
adjacent to the fort. Because of the hostility of the Bannock Indians, life at the little outpost was extremely hazardous for the first
3 years, until a U.S. Army force defeated the Indians at the Battle
of Bear River, about 12 miles north of the fort near the present
town of Oxford. As time passed the town of Franklin grew up
around the fort. The site of the fort is marked by a monument. A
museum exhibits a large collection of pioneer tools and relics. The
site of the Battle of Bear River, located 4 miles northeast of Pres-
ton on Idaho 34, is also marked by a monument.

## 69.  Idaho City, Idaho

*Location: Boise County.*

In the summer of 1862 gold placers were discovered at Elkhorn and Placerville in the Boise Basin. The following spring 16,000 miners rushed in and the basin became the most productive and heavily populated part of Idaho Territory. In January 1863 Boise County was created and the county seat situated at Bannack City, renamed Idaho City in February 1864. The town soon had a population of 6,000 and 250 places of business. A fire in 1865 destroyed the town except for the Catholic church, a theater, and the newspaper office of the *Idaho World.* Other fires occurred in 1867, 1868, and 1871, but each time the residents rebuilt the town. In the 1870's as the mines became depleted, the population declined and by the end of the decade was only 800.

Today the countryside for miles around is disfigured by tailing debris. Modern Idaho City is a small lumbering town. Only a few of the gold-rush buildings still stand, one of which was built in 1867 as a Wells-Fargo express office and now serves as the town museum.

## 70.  Kellogg, Idaho

*Location: Shoshone County.*

Discoveries of lead and silver ores near the site of Kellogg in 1885 transformed the mountain wilderness of northern Idaho into one of the world's leading sources of lead, silver, and zinc. In 1882 A. J. Pritchard had discovered gold in the vicinity. The following year a rush resulted, but the miners soon exhausted the easily worked placers and began to search for other metals. One of them, Noah S. Kellogg, in 1885 found pieces of silver ore mixed with lead and zinc near the head of Milo Creek Gulch. Obtaining the capital to develop his discovery, he immediately started tunneling at what came to be known as the Bunker Hill Mine. The mine, which by 1920 has passed through various hands, produced approximately $35 million in profits. In 1891 unions began to be formed in the mines

The Coeur d'Alene district of northern Idaho produced millions of dollars worth of silver and lead. A leader in this production was the Bunker Hill Mine, entered through the Kellogg Tunnel.

of the Coeur d'Alene area, the scene of some of the bloodiest violence between miners and mineowners in the West. In 1899 Federal troops had to be sent into the area.

Today the wild mountain setting of the Bunker Hill Mine is little changed since 1890, but the towns of Kellogg and nearby Wardner have been largely rebuilt and bear little resemblance to their original appearance. The mine, which is still worked, is not usually open to the public.


## 71.  Lewiston, Idaho

*Location: Nez Perce County.*

Named for Meriwether Lewis and founded in 1861 at the head of navigation on the lower Snake River, Lewiston became a river port and the major distributing center for the Idaho mining camps. Log cabins and warehouses soon replaced tents. The Oregon Steam Navigation Company, which had a monopoly on the Columbia and

Snake Rivers, carried passengers and freight upriver to Lewiston, from where they moved into the interior. Today Lewiston is a thriving lumbering town; no buildings of the mining period have survived.

## 72. Pierce, Idaho

*Location: Clearwater County.*

Pierce was the site of the discovery of gold in Idaho country. In 1860, the year the Federal Government signed an access treaty with the Nez Percé tribe, an Indian trader, Capt. Elias Davidson Pierce, discovered gold at Canal Gulch on Oro Fino Creek along the Clearwater River. By the end of 1861 some 10,000 miners had poured into the area and founded the bustling mining camps of Pierce, Oro Fino, Elk City, and Florence. Pierce had a population of more than 2,000. In 1863, after yielding a total of some $3 million, the placers in the vicinity began to decline and so did the population. Chinese miners began buying up claims and reworking the mines, and the town never died. Today it is a small lumbering center, which has few remains of the gold-rush days. The only remaining structure is the old county courthouse, located in the center of town. Erected in 1861–62, it is a small two-story wooden building. Now used for religious purposes, it is in good condition.

## 73. Pierce Ranch Site, Idaho

*Location: Cassia County, on U.S. 30S, just south of Malta.*

The Pierce Ranch, located in the Raft River Valley at the junction of the California and Hudspeth Cutoff overland trails, was typical of the small ranches established in the 1860's to supply the new mining towns of Idaho Territory with beef. Until 1885, when the Oregon Short Line Railroad began serving the area, such ranches could not reach major markets because of the prohibitively long drives required to reach railheads. J. Q. Shirley and Charles S. Gamble, who probably drove the first herd of cattle into Idaho, founded the Pierce Ranch in 1863. They drove the cattle from Wyoming via Fort Hall, Idaho. No remains of the ranch buildings have survived.

The mining towns scattered through the West contributed to the advance of the farming and ranching frontiers. Populations of such boomtowns as Silver City, Idaho, needed food.

## 74.  Silver City, Idaho

*Location: Owyhee County, on an unpaved road, 25 miles southwest of Murphy.*

In 1863 the discovery of gold placers on Jordan Creek along the Owyhee River by 30 prospectors from the vicinity of Boise City set off a rush of more than 2,500 miners. Later that year, when prospectors also found rich silver veins, thousands more arrived and founded in rapid order the towns of Boonville, Ruby City, and Silver City. Probably the most famous of the mines in the Silver City vicinity was the Poorman, discovered in 1865, on War Eagle Mountain. By 1866, when the town became the county seat, it had about 3,000 inhabitants. Then in the mid-1870's the mines began to decline, and by 1880 the total population of the county was only 1,600. The last of the Silver City mines did not close until World War II, after which the town was deserted.

More than 30 well-preserved frame structures still stand, including the Idaho Hotel. Containing 50 rooms, the hotel was built in Ruby City, a mile away, in 1865 and hauled by ox teams in three sections to Silver City.

Artist's sketch of the Abilene railhead in 1867. During that first year about 35,000 head of cattle moved eastward. Courtesy, University of Illinois Library.

## 75. Abilene, Kansas

*Location: Dickinson County.*

Abilene was the first of the great Kansas cowtowns. When the Kansas Pacific Railroad reached it in 1867, a few Texans began to drive Longhorns northward over the Chisholm Trail to the Abilene railhead. Joseph G. McCoy, an Illinois cattleman who recognized the economic potential of the Texas cattle drives, built stockyards in Abilene to accommodate 3,000 cattle. He advertised the market at Abilene throughout Texas, and soon cowboys were driving thousands of cattle northward.

At Abilene, a wild town during the 1860's, the newly paid cowboys spent their money in the gambling establishments, dancehalls, and saloons. After the town incorporated in 1869 a series of sheriffs attempted to maintain law and order. The mild-mannered but courageous Tom Smith was followed by the flamboyant "Wild Bill"

Hickok, one of the best known gunmen in the West and a hero of Eastern writers. In 1871, when the Santa Fe Railway extended its line from Emporia to Newton, the latter succeeded Abilene as the terminus of the Chisholm Trail.

Today Abilene is a prosperous modern town. A boulder on the post office lawn memorializes the terminus of the Chisholm Trail, over which more than 3 million head of cattle were driven in the 1860's and 1870's.

## 76. Dodge City, Kansas

*Location: Ford County.*

In 1871 H. L. Sitler constructed a sod house 5 miles west of Fort Dodge on the site of Dodge City, which later became "Queen of the Cowtowns." He invested in cattle, and his homestead became a stopping place for freighters and buffalo hunters. Later the same year Charles Myer built a trading post nearby and traded with the hunters. In 1872 a railroad construction company established headquarters at the site, and soon a clutter of tents and shacks constituted "Buffalo City." Later the same year a townsite was laid out and called Dodge City for the nearby fort.

After the buffalo were killed off, the cattle industry began. Within a decade after the Santa Fe Railway reached Dodge City in 1872, the town became the last of the four great cattle railheads in Kansas. Unlike Abilene, Newton, and Wichita, which were termini of the Chisholm Trail, Dodge City was on the Western, or Dodge City, Trail, which ran to Ogallala, Nebr. Texans drove vast herds of Longhorns to the Dodge City railhead. The saloons and dancehalls were the scenes of numerous brawls and shootings. Law enforcement officers such as Bat Masterson, Wyatt Earp, and Bill Tilghman sought to maintain law and order.

When the era of the great cattle drives ended, homesteaders took over and the economy became based on agriculture. Dodge City of today, a modern city of 12,000 population, bears little resemblance to the 19th-century town.

## 77. Newton, Kansas

*Location: Harvey County.*

When the Santa Fe Railway extended its line from Emporia to Newton in 1871, the latter city temporarily succeeded Abilene, located on the Kansas Pacific line, as the terminus of the Chisholm Trail and grew into a cowtown overnight. Saloons, dancehalls, and gambling houses sprouted from the plains. The city expanded rapidly until a connecting line was established from Wichita to Newton in 1872, after which it lost its key position as a cattle shipping point. Today Newton, a modern city and the county seat, serves as a trading center for the surrounding agricultural community.

## 78. Wichita, Kansas

*Location: Sedgwick County.*

In 1864 James R. Mead established a trading post near a small Wichita Indian village in Kansas on the site of the city of Wichita. Mead's partner was Jesse Chisholm, a half-breed Cherokee Indian, who pioneered the route into Oklahoma Territory that was later followed by the Chisholm Trail. The trail at first bypassed Wichita and ran to Abilene because of the railhead there.

After the Wichitas were removed to Oklahoma Territory in 1865, Mead's trading post became the nucleus of Wichita, which was platted in 1870. The following year the Santa Fe Railway reached the town of Newton and in 1872 Wichita, which became the new "cow capital" of Kansas for a decade. Texas cowboys arrived over the Chisholm Trail with thousands of cattle, and saloons, cafes, dancehalls, and shops opened to serve them. Scores of settler-farmers also arrived and property values soared. By 1882, wheat farming and fencing had stifled the cattle drives, whose terminus was relocated in Dodge City. Land values collapsed and Wichita began to decline. By the 1880's and 1890's, however, the grain industry had replaced the cattle industry, and Wichita became a trade and milling center.

## 79. Anaconda, Montana

*Location: Deer Lodge County.*

This city, whose history is closely associated with the development of the Anaconda Copper Company, has been the smelting center for the company since 1892. Laid out in 1883 by the company's founder, Marcus Daly, who selected the site because of its nearness to water and limestone, it was temporarily called Copperopolis until the postmaster discovered that another Montana town had the same name. Expanding with the copper industry, it vied with Helena for the State capital. Though Helena won the honor, Anaconda continued to prosper. An influx of Irish and Balkan immigrants increased the population until 1930, at which time it became stabilized. In the original section of the town may be seen some old log cabins and framehouses.

## 80. Diamond City, Montana

*Location: Meagher County, on an unpaved road, 23 miles northeast of Townsend.*

The mining camp of Diamond City, at the head of Confederate Gulch in the Big Belt Mountains, produced $10 million worth of gold. It was so named because of the layout of the first four cabins erected at the site. In 1864 three deserters from the Confederate Army in Missouri discovered gold near the mouth of the gulch. The news spread and a rush occurred. Nearly $2 million was obtained from placers before richer deposits were uncovered beneath. Prospectors next found rich deposits at the base of Gold Hill. Diamond City grew from a cluster of scattered cabins to a town of 10,000 people. A flume brought water from the mountains, and some of the houses had to be raised on stilts to prevent being swept away or buried in the tailings that filled the gulch. The gold was soon exhausted, however, and the city began to decline. By 1870 its population had dropped to 250 and by a year later to 64. Only a few foundations remain today.

## 81.  Elkhorn, Montana

> *Location: Jefferson County, on an unpaved road, about 10 miles northeast of Boulder.*

Elkhorn, today a typical ghost town, during its active years shipped out $14 million worth of gold, silver, and lead. Prospectors worked the area on a small scale prior to 1870, but did not form the town until the early 1880's. In 1883 the Elkhorn Mining Company bought the townsite and erected a new mill, which in a 10-month period yielded $183,000 in silver and $23,000 in gold. The town flourished throughout the 1880's and 1890's, and in 1889 the Northern Pacific Railway provided it with a rail connection. A couple of years later, however, mining became unprofitable and the town was abandoned. Many of the old frame buildings have survived, but they are in a rundown condition. The mine is occasionally worked by modern-day prospectors.

## 82.  Ford Ranch, Montana

> *Location: Cascade County, on U.S. 89, about 2 miles east of Sun River.*

In 1871 Robert Simpson Ford founded this ranch, one of the earliest in the rich range of Sun Valley, with cattle that he had driven from Colorado. In 1881 he contracted with the Canadian Mounted Police to supply beef to Fort McLeod, and also supplied the builders of the Canadian Pacific Railway. Later in his career he became the first president of the Montana Stockgrowers Association and established the Great Falls National Bank, which he operated until his death in 1914. The ranch is now occupied by his son. The remodeled ranchhouse and one of the barns, both built in the mid-1870's, have survived. The ranch is not open to the public.

Montana Territory ranch in 1872. Indicative of the primitive facilities are the chinked logs and dirt roof of the bunkhouse, which is conveniently located near the corrals. Courtesy, National Archives.

## 83. Fort Owen, Montana

*Location: Ravalli County, just off U.S. 93, about 1 mile northwest of Stevensville.*

This fort was the site of the first successful farming operations in Montana. In 1841 Father Pierre De Smet and six companions established St. Mary's Mission among the Flathead Indians. They brought oxen, wagons, carts, and plows with them from St. Louis and the following year began farming operations. By 1846 the farm had produced 7,000 bushels of wheat, 4,500 bushels of potatoes, and other vegetables. The livestock consisted of 40 head of cattle, horses, and other animals. In 1850 Maj. John Owen leased the mission property, after the missionaries had departed, and established a fort, which for a decade was the center of farming operations in the vicinity. A small portion of the fort has been restored, but most of the mission remains have disappeared. In 1956 the State of Montana founded Fort Owen State Monument.

## 84. Helena, Montana

*Location: Lewis and Clark County.*

Helena, once the third Territorial capital of Montana and now the State capital, originated in the gold-rush days and is still an active mining town. It owes its existence to gold discoveries in Last Chance Gulch in 1864. The first miners, ex-Georgians, erected tents and crude cabins against the slopes of the gulch. A trail formed by sluice tailings on which wagons entered the camp became the main street of today's Helena. As the town grew the inhabitants changed its name from Last Chance to Helena and erected permanent buildings.

By 1870, despite a bad fire the previous year, the town was the most important in Montana. In the 1870's the discovery of rich placer deposits of gold east of the Missouri River, gold to the south and to the west, and silver and lead to the southwest spurred Helena. Silver discoveries at Wickes, Corbin, and Elkhorn in the late 1870's and the early 1880's provided even further stimulation. The city incorporated in 1881 and was reached by the Northern Pacific Railway in 1883 and the Great Northern in 1887. The richest city per capita in the United States, it was the home of 50 millionaires. The fall of silver prices in 1893, however, brought an end to a flamboyant era. Since that time the mines have passed through slumps and booms.

The brick and stone buildings along Main Street and in the southern part of town are those that replaced the flimsy structures of the early mining camp. The massive stone mansions, with landscaped grounds and carriage houses in the rear, housed millionaires during the city's heyday. The newer residential sections reflect the prosperity of modern Helena.

## 85. Marysville, Montana

*Location: Lewis and Clark County.*

This town, founded in the mid-1870's, was one of the great gold-producing centers in Montana. It had a peak population of 2,000 in 1887 and was the goal of a race between the Great Northern and Northern Pacific Railways. The most famous mine in the vicinity, the Drumlummon, produced millions of dollars in profits for its various owners, who included Thomas Cruse, an English syndicate, C. W. Merrill, and the St. Louis Mining and Milling Company. Slowly the mines in the area played out, and early in the 20th century the town lost most of its population. A number of the old buildings are still standing, including the Drumlummon Mill, frame churches, a schoolhouse, and some stone and brick buildings. Marysville is now a ski center during the winter months.

## 86. Miles City, Montana

*Location: Custer County.*

Called the "cow capital" of Montana, Miles City is still in the heart of the State's range country and is an active cattle town. In the early days the south side of Main Street was a solid block of saloons, gambling dens, and dancehalls; the respectable citizens lived on the north side. An annual rodeo commemorates the historic era. Although none of the old buildings have survived, Miles City retains much of the old cowtown atmosphere.

## 87. N-Bar Ranch, Montana

*Location: Fergus County, on an unpaved road, about 20 miles southwest of Grassrange.*

One of the largest in east-central Montana, this ranch has been in continuous operation since the 1880's. In 1881 Thomas Cruse homesteaded and began ranching on Flatwillow Creek along the Musselshell River. After the catastrophic winter of 1886–87, he bought N-Bar cattle from the Niobrara Cattle Company and drove them from the Powder River to his ranch. At the end of the century he owned about 10,000 cattle and 35,000 sheep. The present ranch, undiminished in size, contains about 37,000 acres and is stocked with 1,400 cattle and 900 calves. The office, bunkhouse, and barn at the headquarters are original. The ranch is not open to the public. It is still in active operation.

## 88.   W-Bar (Pierre Wibaux) Ranch Site, Montana

*Location: Wibaux County, on Beaver Creek Road, 15 miles northeast of Wibaux.*

This ranch, established on a small scale in 1883 by the wealthy Frenchman Pierre Wibaux, was later one of Montana's largest ranches. In 1884 Wibaux built his residence, the White House, near his ranch headquarters. After the disastrous winter of 1886–87, he purchased many remnants of cattle herds from cattlemen who were forced to go out of business. At the peak of his operations, in the 1890's, he was one of the biggest ranchers in the United States. His 65,000 head of stock grazed a range that extended from eastern Montana into western North Dakota. When homesteaders came to the region early in the 20th century, Wibaux concluded his ranching operations and turned to mining. Today the ranch is still operated and is owned by Peter H. Scheiffer. It is not open to the public. All that remains of the Wibaux Ranch is a stone barn erected in the 1880's.

## 89.   Wickes, Montana

*Location: Jefferson County, on an unpaved road, 4 miles west of Jefferson City.*

The town of Wickes, founded in 1877, was named for George T. Wickes, a New York contractor and mining engineer who came to the vicinity with his partner, J. Corbin. The mining camps of Corbin and Wickes, 2 miles apart, were the center of an important mining area. The Alta was the largest mine, but the Gregory, the Ninah, and the Comet also provided good yields. Between 1884 and 1893 the Helena Mining and Reduction Company operated a lead-silver smelter at Wickes, the first in Montana. In 1886 the town consisted of 1,500 people and had 5 dancehalls and 22 saloons. It thrived until the end of the century, when the population left after the ores thinned out. Fires in 1900 and 1902 destroyed all the buildings. The Alta Mine, which is still being worked, has yielded $32 million worth of lead, gold, and silver.

## 90. Ogallala, Nebraska

*Location: Keith County.*

Ogallala, on the Union Pacific Railroad, was the original terminus of the Western Trail. The railroad set up cattle shipping facilities there in 1874, and within 2 years the Western Trail replaced the Chisholm Trail as the major northward artery for the Texas Longhorns. The cowboys camped on the banks of the river south of town, where the usual celebrating and fighting after the long drive took place. Boot Hill Cemetery, on a hill along the South Platte River, is a reminder of the cattle drives and the boisterous life associated with them. The trail to Ogallala was used until 1895, although around 1880 Dodge City, Kans., on the Santa Fe Railway, became the main terminus of the Western Trail.

## 91. Omaha, Nebraska

*Location: Douglas County.*

Like the city of St. Louis, Omaha was a bustling transportation, trading, and outfitting center for prospectors, miners, cattlemen, farmers, and emigrants. It was founded in 1854 opposite Council Bluffs, Iowa, jumping-off place for the Mormon Trail to Utah. By 1859 the newly founded city on the Missouri River was bustling, and its merchants carried on a thriving trade. Steamboats arrived daily; and, when the Union Pacific Railroad began to move west in the mid-1860's, the boom increased. The Union Stockyards and the great packinghouses, established in the 1880's, not only attracted scores of supporting industries and thousands of immigrants as laborers, but they also accommodated thousands of Western cattle. Floods in 1881 forced many Council Bluffs citizens to move to Omaha, and real estate prices soared. In the early 1900's the Omaha Grain Exchange was organized and the city became a central grain market. Despite a cycle of boom and depression periods, it continued to grow throughout the years. Today it is an industrial and commercial center in the heart of the farm belt.

## 92. Aurora, Nevada

*Location: Mineral County, on Nev. 3C via U.S. 95, about 30 miles southwest of Hawthorne.*

Founded in 1860, when three California prospectors found silver ore near the site, Aurora was one of the earliest mining camps in Nevada and marked the beginning of the eastward movement of the mining frontier from California into western Nevada. In 1863 it boasted a population of 6,000 and had 17 quartz mills, 20 stores, 12 hotels, and many boardinghouses and saloons. Mark Twain unsuccessfully tried his hand at mining in the vicinity. The mines began to play out in 1864, and disastrous fires in 1866 and 1873 further reduced the population of the town. By 1880 only 500 of the people remained, most of the others having moved to Bodie, Calif., about 12 miles to the southwest. After 1883 the town rapidly declined. During World War I the mines reopened briefly, but by 1930 only one inhabitant was living in the town. A few ruins of brick buildings and a school and a few abandoned framehouses may be seen today.

## 93. Austin, Nevada

*Location: Lander County.*

The rush of 10,000 miners to the site of Austin in 1863, following the discovery of silver by William Talcott, marked the advance of the mining frontier into central Nevada. From this base, where speculation was rife, important silver strikes were made subsequently at Eureka, Hamilton, and other places in southeastern Nevada. The town of Austin—366 brick, adobe, and frame buildings—became the county seat. In 1868 the mines in the area yielded a peak figure of $2,574,810. But thereafter production decreased, and most of the population moved to Eureka and Hamilton. When the Central Pacific Railroad passed 92 miles north of Austin, the city was no longer on the main artery of commerce and declined further. By 1900 it had only 600 inhabitants.

Mining jumped to central and eastern Nevada in 1863, when prospectors discovered silver near the site of Austin, shown here in the 1870's. Courtesy, National Archives.

Today only a two-block-long cluster of 13 original brick buildings on Main Street recall the town's former glory. Included are three brick churches, the International Hotel, the two-story courthouse, several one-story stores, and the former newspaper office. Reuel C. Gridley's former store now serves as the Austin Historical Museum.

## 94. Belmont, Nevada

*Location: Nye County, on Nev. 82, about 90 miles south of Austin.*

In 1865 an Indian discovered silver quartz veins at the site of Belmont. Miners rushed in, organized the Philadelphia Mining District, and founded the mining camp of Belmont. When the first of three stamp mills opened the following year, the camp already had a population of 1,500. Only a year later, it became the county seat. The mines in the vicinity reached peak operations in 1873–74 and then declined. They finally closed in 1885, and the population departed. In the early 1900's the county seat was moved to Tonopah.

Today Belmont is a ghost town. Still standing is the unused two-story brick courthouse, erected in 1874, as well as a few stone residences and a number of rundown framehouses. On the north side of town are the ruined walls and stack of the Combination Mill Company smelter.

## 95.  Carson City United States Mint, Nevada

*Location: Ormsby County, corner of North Carson and Robinson Streets, Carson City.*

This mint represented the recognition by the Federal Government of Nevada's importance on the mining frontier. In the 1860's the bullion output of the State was second only to that of California, and two decades later led the Nation. For the period 1861–80 it totaled more than $365,341,000. The Government established the mint at Carson City because the output of the Comstock Lode overtaxed the capacity of the San Francisco Mint. Construction of the building began in July 1866, and minting operations started little more than 3 years later. In 1893, by which time mine production had decreased, the Carson City Mint became a Federal Assay Office.

In 1939 the State of Nevada acquired the building and 2 years

The Carson City United States Mint, now operated as a museum by the State of Nevada, reflected Nevada's mineral wealth and was established by the Government when the output of the Comstock Lode overtaxed the San Francisco Mint.

later opened it as a museum. Little changed on the exterior, the building is well preserved today. It contains exhibits relating to all phases of Nevada's history. In the basement is a 300-foot tunnel that illustrates mining operations, and the former vaults contain exhibits demonstrating hoisting, drilling, and blasting operations.

## 96. Dangberg Ranch, Nevada

*Location: Douglas County, on Nev. 88, about 1 mile south of its junction with U.S. 395, just west of Minden.*

In 1853 Henry Dangberg crossed the Plains with a herd of cattle and established one of the first ranches in Nevada, in Carson Valley about 5 miles southeast of the Mormon agricultural colony of Genoa. Like the Mormons, he traded with the emigrants who were en route to California in the 1850's. Then the discovery of silver at the Washoe Dig around Virginia City further expanded his markets. Learning irrigation methods from the Mormons, Dangberg ditched his fields and grew hay. In 1864 he planted alfalfa, the first in Nevada. Selling his hay for $300 a ton, he profited more from farming than ranching. By 1879 his ranch, which comprised 4,648 acres and was watered by 40 miles of irrigation ditches from the Carson River, was valued at $60,000. Dangberg continued to expand his farming-ranching operations and when he died, in 1904, owned four ranches totaling about 36,000 acres. The original ranchhouse, much enlarged by additions in the 1860's and 1870's, is in excellent condition today. The ranch, still owned by the Dangberg family, is an outstanding example of diversified agriculture. It is not open to the public.

## 97. Eureka, Nevada

*Location: Eureka County.*

Prospectors from Austin discovered in 1864 the first significant silver-lead deposit in the United States not far from the site of this town. They immediately organized the Eureka Mining District. Because the ore was a new and special type and no one knew how to smelt it, no rush of miners into the area occurred. Finally in 1869

Maj. W. W. McCoy devised a small smelter that could process the ore, and miners formed the town of Eureka. In 1870 San Francisco capitalists incorporated the Eureka Consolidated Mining Company, and in 1871 London financiers formed the Richmond Consolidated Mining Company. Three years later the San Francisco group constructed the narrow gauge Eureka and Palisade Railroad to the site. By 1876, 19 smelters were working the ore. In the 1870's the district yielded $26,050,304 in silver bullion and 225,000 tons of lead, an amount large enough to influence the world price. The peak population of the town was 5,000, but by 1890–91 mining had exhausted the bonanza ore bodies and mine flooding was a serious problem. The smelters closed down and most of the population departed. On several occasions fires and floods damaged the town.

Only seven original structures are still standing, including the county courthouse, the Eureka *Sentinel* Building, and three churches. The town today has a population of about 400.

### 98. Genoa (Mormon Station), Nevada

> *Location: Douglas County, 3½ miles west of U.S. 395, about 15 miles southwest of Carson City.*

In June 1849 Hampden S. Beatie, en route from Salt Lake City to

Replica of the Col. John Reese cabin and stockade at Mormon Station (Genoa) State Park, Nevada. As the Mormons spread out from Salt Lake City, they established outposts such as this where they practiced farming and sold their produce to emigrants.

the California goldfields, arrived in the Carson Valley. Impressed with the spot, he decided to stay and erected a log cabin and a trading post to serve the thousands of emigrants passing by over the California Trail. In mid-1851 Col. John Reese and 18 other Mormons arrived in 10 wagons. Reese purchased the original cabin and also built a two-story log house and fort that served as a trading post and lodginghouse. Fencing and plowing 30 acres, he also began irrigated farming and sold produce to the emigrants. The little settlement that grew up, the first in Nevada, became known as Mormon Station; in 1856 it was renamed Genoa. Other Mormons continued to arrive until 1857, when Brigham Young ordered all Mormons to return to Salt Lake City. Although nearly depopulated by this exodus, Genoa survived and 2 years later had 150 inhabitants.

Reese's two-story log cabin, which also served as a Pony Express and Overland Stage station, stood until 1910, when fire destroyed it. Replicas of the station and stockade are now included in Mormon Station State Park, located on the original site of the cabin.

## 99.  Goldfield, Nevada

*Location: Esmeralda County.*

Goldfield, at the foot of Columbia Mountain, was the largest of the mining boomtowns of southwestern Nevada in the early 20th cen-

Gold Hill, Nevada, in the 1860's. Located not far from Virginia City, Gold Hill shared in the Comstock Lode boom. Leading mines in the town were the Imperial, Empire, Challenge, and Confidence. Courtesy, National Archives.

tury. Late in 1902 William Marsh and Harry Stimler staked the first claim in the vicinity and soon struck gold. The next year other prospectors made rich strikes. Laid out as a tent town in 1904, within 2 years Goldfield had a population of 15,000 and hundreds of brick and wooden structures. The mines in the vicinity reached their peak in 1910, when they produced more than $11 million. After that their yield declined steadily; in 1922 it was only $150,000. The following year a fire, driven by desert winds, destroyed 53 blocks of buildings in the center of the town, and in 1932 a flood destroyed many others.

Because of these disasters, coupled with the closing of the mines, only a few buildings of the mining era have survived. The most interesting are the Esmeralda County Courthouse and Firehouse No. 1, both two-story stone buildings erected in 1907. Also of interest is the Goldfield Hotel, a four-story brick-and-stone building built in 1910 at a cost of $500,000 and containing 200 rooms.

## 100.  Hamilton, Nevada

*Location: White Pine County, on an unpaved road, 12 miles south of U.S. 50, about 37 miles west of Ely.*

In 1865 a party of prospectors from Austin discovered silver at the site of Hamilton and founded the White Pine Mining District and a small mining town known as Cave City, which in 1868 they renamed Hamilton. A mill, which was erected in 1867, operated on a small scale for a few months until an Indian guided one of the miners to nearby Treasure Hill, which contained rich deposits of horn silver. As prospectors made other strikes and the news spread, Nevada experienced the greatest mining fever since the discovery of the Comstock Lode. The stampede to Hamilton moved the mining frontier 120 miles east of Austin into eastern Nevada. Approximately 10,000 men spent the winter of 1868–69 at the 8,000-foot altitude living in tents and caves.

Mining in the vicinity had a brief but spectacular history. Between 1869 and 1873 the mines yielded about $6,380,754. By 1875, however, all but one of them had ceased operations. The inhabitants of the town quickly departed, and by 1880 the population numbered only about 500. Fires in 1873 and 1886 destroyed most of the buildings, and Ely became the county seat. Today Hamilton is a ghost town; only a few ruins mark the original site. The most impressive of these are the stone walls of the two-story Withington Hotel.

### 101.  Las Vegas, Nevada

*Location: Clark County.*

The site of Las Vegas was a well-known camping area utilized by California emigrants traveling along the Mormon Trail to Los Angeles. The first settlers, in 1855, were Mormons sent from Salt Lake City by Brigham Young. He directed them to build a fort to protect emigrants and the U.S. mail route that had been newly established from Salt Lake City to Los Angeles. William Bringhurst and 30 other settlers built an adobe fort, 150 feet square and about 14 feet high, within which they erected log cabins. Outside, they constructed a dam, bridges, and fences. Reclaiming land by irrigation, they grew crops. They also unsuccessfully worked what they believed to be extensive lead deposits—actually galena, an ore-carrying silver—that were located about 18 miles to the southwest. They abandoned the mines when Young recalled all Mormon settlers to Salt Lake City in 1857. Remains of the fort may be seen in the city park on 5th Street.

### 102.  Mason Valley Ranch, Nevada

*Location: Lyon County, on an unpaved road, along the Walker River, 10 miles northeast of Yerington.*

This ranch was originally the headquarters of N. Henry A. Mason's ranch empire and after 1890 the center of Henry Miller's vast Nevada holdings. Mason, a Tennessean, emigrated to California in 1854 but 5 years later returned to Nevada, where he settled in what came to be known as Mason Valley. In 1860 he erected the first house in the valley, a small adobe tule-roofed ranchhouse, and began to supply the mining towns with beef. In 1871, using money that he obtained from Henry Miller, the California cattle king, Mason began buying ranches and expanding his range—selecting property along streams where he could control water rights. By 1880, when he owned more than 30,000 head of cattle and 90,000 acres, he was the largest rancher in Nevada. Drought and the severe winter of 1889–90 threw him heavily into debt, however, and in 1890 he sold out to Miller. The natural setting of the ranch is little changed today from the 19th century.

### 103.  Overland Stage Farm, Nevada

*Location: Elko County, on Nev. 46, about 60 miles southeast of Elko.*

In 1865 Ben Holladay's Overland Mail and Express Company established a farm in Ruby Valley, the first in eastern Nevada, to supply the company's Western Division. Because the division employed more than 79 men and utilized 268 horses, and since food and feed costs were high, the company decided to organize its own farm. The first harvest included 8,575 bushels of barley, 8,745 bushels of oats, 1,655 bushels of potatoes, 1,854 bushels of turnips, 1,000 bushels of carrots, and 78 bushels of beets. In 1867 the company erected a gristmill on the farm. The farm was in operation until 1869, when the company discontinued many of its routes because of the completion of the Central Pacific Railroad. The farm site is on the west side of Ruby Valley. No remains of the buildings can be seen, and the site is not marked.

### 104.  Pioche, Nevada

*Location: Lincoln County.*

In the winter of 1863–64 a Paiute Indian discovered silver ore at Meadow Valley, in southwestern Nevada. Shortly a group of miners formed the Meadow Valley Mining District (subsequently renamed the Ely District), but for 4 years mining was unproductive. In 1869 the miners founded the town of Pioche on the slopes of Ely Mountain and erected a smelter. The next year a rush occurred; the town underwent a boom and became the county seat. By 1874 its population was about 6,000. Between 1871 and 1873 production totaled $12 million, but after 1875 it rapidly declined and in 1885 ceased altogether. Fires in 1871, 1872, and 1876 destroyed much of the town, and a flood in 1874 swept away many other original buildings.

Based on railroad transportation and modern technology, mining revived in the 20th century and today Pioche is a small mining town. Few structures survive from the early days. The most impressive is the two-story stone-and-brick county courthouse, built in 1871 at a cost of $75,000 and now vacant.

## 105.  Rhyolite, Nevada

*Location: Nye County, on an unpaved road, 4 miles west of Beatty.*

Rhyolite was the third mining camp founded in southwestern Nevada in the early part of the 20th century. After prospectors struck silver at Tonopah in 1900 and gold at Goldfield in 1902, they pressed the search for valuable metals farther south. In 1904 Frank Harris and E. L. Cross struck gold and filed the first claim near the site of Rhyolite, named for the principal rock in the vicinity. By 1907 the town had a population of 7,000 and rail connections with Tonopah and Las Vegas. In 1910, after producing about $3 million in gold, the deposits played out, the people departed, and Rhyolite became a ghost town.

Surviving structures include the large and elaborate stucco passenger depot of the Las Vegas and Tonopah and Tidewater Railroad, erected in 1907 and now used as a nightclub; and the ruins of two large three-story stone and concrete office buildings that were built in 1908 and utilized as banks and stores.

## 106.  Ruth, Nevada

*Location: White Pine County.*

In the summer of 1900 Edward F. Gray and David P. Bartley, two young prospectors from Redding, Calif., came to try their luck at Ely, a gold-mining camp founded in 1868 but almost forgotten by the turn of the century. In the Robinson Mining District to the west, they took up two claims, the Ruth and the Kearsage,

Modern open-pit copper mine at Ruth, Nevada. Mining is still important to the Western economy.

which showed promising copper outcroppings, though Nevada at the time produced little copper. The value of the ore was such that the men obtained financing and in 1902 formed the White Pine Copper Company, which soon reorganized into the Nevada Consolidated Copper Company. The company established the Nevada Northern Railroad, 141 miles in length, and erected a smelter, which began operating in 1908. From 1907 to 1917 the Ruth Mine yielded 617,785 tons of copper and enabled the company to pay $75,770,882 in dividends. In 1933 the Utah Copper Company and the Kennecott Copper Corporation bought out the Nevada Consolidated Copper Company, and in 1943 the name was changed to Kennecott Copper Corporation, Nevada Mines Division.

The smelter erected in 1907–08 has been modernized and is still being operated at the town of McGill, 20 miles distant. The center of Ruth today is the vast Liberty copper pit, more than 1 mile in diameter and nearly 1,000 feet deep. The company-owned town and plant buildings are all modern structures.

## 107.   Star City, Nevada

> *Location: Pershing County, on Nev. 50, about 12 miles south of Mill City.*

Star City was once the largest mining town in northwestern Nevada. In 1861 Isaac Miller and José Thacker discovered silver ore and established the Sheba Mine in Star Canyon, on the eastern slope of the Humboldt Range. Miners moved in and founded the Star City Mining District and camp. By 1864 the camp had 1,200 inhabitants and was the largest in what was then Humboldt County. It had a stamp mill, two hotels, a Wells-Fargo express office, post office, and telegraph office. In 1868 the mines failed, and the population departed. Today all traces of the town have disappeared, and only the scars of mining remain.

## 108.   Sutro Tunnel, Nevada

> *Location: Lyon County, 1 mile north of U.S. 50, about 2 miles east of Dayton.*

In 1864 Adolph Sutro, a native Californian who operated a stamp mill in the Carson Valley, proposed to the Nevada Legislature adoption of his idea of digging a tunnel under the Comstock Lode to solve the problems of drainage, ventilation, safety, and access. He believed that the tunnel would drain the mines of water and prevent flooding. In 1865 the legislature granted him a 50-year franchise to construct the tunnel, wide enough for a double railroad track and more than 3 miles long. Sutro estimated the cost of construction at $3 million and set about raising the money, which he finally had to obtain from British sources. After many difficulties, in October 1869 construction began. Serious technical problems, the Panic of 1873, and political meddling hampered operations, but the crews finally completed the main tunnel, which was almost 4 miles long, in July 1878. Three years later they finished the 1½ miles or so of lateral branches.

The tunnel, one of the great engineering feats of the 19th century, cost a total of $2,096,556. It was completed too late, how-

One of the engineering wonders of the world, the Sutro Tunnel, completed in 1878 and running under the Comstock Lode to drain and ventilate the mines, was also one of the fiascos of the century, for it was completed too late to be of substantial value. Pictured in this modern photograph is the entrance.

ever, for by that time the Comstock mines were failing. In 1879 Sutro resigned as superintendent of the Sutro Tunnel Company and within a year disposed of his stock—before its value collapsed. Subsequently he invested in San Francisco real estate, made a fortune, and served as mayor from 1894 to 1898. In 1889 the English banking firm of McCalmont Brothers foreclosed the tunnel and operated it until the 1930's. Today the entrance is barred by an iron grill gate. The vicinity of the tunnel entrance is a jumble of frame buildings, car tracks and ties, timber, and rusting equipment.

## 109. Tonopah, Nevada

*Location: Nye County.*

In 1900 James Butler, a rancher from the town of Belmont, struck gold and silver at the site of Tonopah. Walter Gayhart of Austin laid out the town, which soon boomed. Most of the original owners of claims leased their mines to capitalists in return for 25 percent of the gross output. In 1903–4 the Tonopah and Goldfield Railroad provided a connection with the Southern Pacific terminal at Mina. In 1913 production reached a peak of $9,500,000, but by 1921 only four mines were in operation.

Tonopah is still a busy town, surrounded by the tailings, headframes, and mills of its boom period. It is the best preserved of the 20th-century boomtowns in southwestern Nevada. Among the more interesting structures are the Tonopah Club, formerly a gambling hall; the five-story Mizpah Hotel; and the huge yellow stone Nye County Courthouse. Small-scale mining is still done in the vicinity today.

## 110.   Unionville, Nevada

*Location: Pershing County.*

In 1861 prospectors from California began exploring what was then part of Humboldt County in Nevada, and two of them struck silver. A rush ensued and the miners organized the Buena Vista Mining District and the mining camp of Dixie. At the outbreak of the Civil War, the residents changed the name of the camp to Unionville, which served as the county seat of Humboldt County between 1862 and 1873. During its boom period the town had about 100 buildings and a population of 600, but after 1870 many of its inhabitants moved eastward to new silver camps. Of all the early boom camps in northwestern Nevada, Unionville is the only one in which any original buildings are still standing. Six of the original one-story miners' residences, in fair condition, are used today as dwellings.

## 111.   Williams Ranch, Nevada

*Location: Churchill County, on U.S. 50, at Eastgate.*

This ranch was typical of the 500 or so small stock ranches that were being operated in Nevada by 1885. Founded by George B. Williams in 1876 at Eastgate, which had been a stage station and stopping place for travelers since 1862, it ran cattle and sheep. In 1879 Williams erected a small one-story, tufa-block house that had a sod roof. In 1908 he built a second home, of similar construction but consisting of 12 rooms, adjacent to the original. Both structures are still standing, but have been altered considerably. The ranchhouse of 1879 is now a store and gas station.

## 112. Cerrillos Mining District, New Mexico

*Location: Santa Fe County, along N. Mex. 10, south of Santa Fe.*

This district, located in the Cerrillos Hills, Ortíz Mountains, and the northern foothills of the San Pedro Mountains, throughout the centuries has yielded modest quantities of gold, silver, coal, turquoise, and other minerals. It has been worked since prehistoric times, when the Pueblo Indians obtained turquoise. During the Spanish period, the Indians labored at the turquoise mines under the supervision of priests, but during the Pueblo Revolt (1680–92) they caved in the shafts and camouflaged the entrances.

In later times, activities in the district were concentrated in two

Grant Tunnel in the Cerrillos Mountains of New Mexico Territory. Eager miners dug thousands of such tunnels all over the West. From a Henry Brown stereopticon. Courtesy, Museum of New Mexico.

distinct locations: the Old Placer Area, to the east of the Ortíz Mountains, around the towns of Dolores and Galisteo; and the New Placer Area, west of the mountains, around Golden. In 1828 a Mexican herder discovered gold placers near present Dolores. In 1832 the source of the placers, a gold-bearing quartz vein, was found on a land grant of José Francisco Ortíz. Ortíz founded the Ortíz Mine and went into partnership with a skilled miner, Don Demasio López. The mine yielded $60,000 to $80,000 annually for some time, but Ortíz separated from López and could not make it pay himself. In 1864 he sold it to the New Mexico Mining Company, which erected stamp mills, utilized coal from the mines near the town of Madrid, and conducted profitable operations for several years. Finally the mine closed because of poor management.

In the New Placer Area a rush followed gold discoveries in 1839. A mining camp, Tuerto, grew up and by 1845 was the center of the area. Once the deposits were depleted, it became a ghost town and nothing remains of it today. In 1879 the discovery of sulphide, zinc, lead, and silver fostered the growth of Bonanza City and Carbonateville. A decade later Golden supplanted these two towns after a gold strike there.

Many remains of mining days have survived in the Cerrillos District. Rock foundations mark the sites of Carbonateville and Bonanza, which are surrounded by abandoned mineworks. Golden is a ghost town, but behind the small village of Dolores stands the abandoned works of the Ortíz Mine.

## 113. Chisum Ranch, New Mexico

> *Location: Chaves County, on U.S. 285, about 4 miles south of Roswell.*

This ranch on the Bosque Grande was founded by John Chisum, one of the great cattlemen. A Tennessean, Chisum emigrated to Paris, Tex., where he first worked as a county clerk. After the Civil War he drove three small herds of cattle to Little Rock and sold them to a packinghouse in which he held an interest. Facing bankruptcy when the packinghouse failed, he started a new drive up the Pecos River over the Goodnight-Loving Trail. Establishing his headquarters in the Pecos Valley at South Spring, he sold his first herd of 600 cattle at Fort Sumner and obtained a contract to deliver 10,000 more. Recognizing the riches of the Pecos Valley, he established a permanent ranch around his headquarters site, though he maintained cow camps at two other locations. Between 1870 and 1881 he had one of the largest cattle holdings in the world. His ranch extended from Fort Sumner on the Pecos 200 miles southward to the Texas line and at its peak ran more than 80,000 head of cattle. A prominent figure in Lincoln County, Chisum was involved in the Lincoln County War. Indian raids, rustlers, and competition from other ranchers finally diminished his power and wealth.

After Chisum died in 1884, J. J. Hagerman and a group of businessmen bought the ranch. In 1904 Hagerman remodeled the ranchhouse but left the main structure intact. Later he sold the ranch to Cornell University as an experiment station for range control and crop diversification. Today the ranch is operated as South Spring Dairy Ranch. No remains of the original ranch buildings have survived.

## 114.  Cimarron, New Mexico

*Location: Colfax County.*

Cimarron, still a cattle center today, has a colorful history. It was founded by Lucien B. Maxwell, owner of the 1,714,765-acre Maxwell Grant. A hunter and trapper from Kaskaskia, Ill., Maxwell was the son-in-law of Carlos Beaubien, who in 1841 with Guadalupe Miranda obtained from the Mexican Government a tract of land in present northeastern New Mexico that extended into south-central Colorado and whose ownership was to be litigated for many decades after the United States acquired the region from Mexico, in 1848.

In 1849 Maxwell settled on the tract, and the town of Cimarron grew up around his headquarters. In 1864, after buying out the remaining heirs on Beaubien's death, Maxwell built an adobe mansion and filled it with expensive furniture. Employing 500 peons and cultivating thousands of acres, he grazed vast herds of cattle and sheep, many of which he sold to Army posts. Often he started a rancher out by giving him a herd of cattle, sheep, or horses and a

Stone jail at Cimarron, New Mexico, built in 1874. Still a cattle center, Cimarron was once a lively cowtown.

small ranch to run on shares. Then the shareholder reciprocated by supplying surplus stock, hay, or grain to fill Government contracts. The discovery of gold on his land in 1867 ruined Maxwell, for he invested a fortune in the mining venture and it failed. In 1870 he sold his grant and moved to Santa Fe.

During Maxwell's ascendancy Cimarron was a lively and raucous cowtown. It was the agency for the Ute Indians; the cowboy capital of northern New Mexico; and an outfitting point for prospectors, trappers, and hunters bound for the mountains. "Buffalo Bill" Cody, who jointly owned a sheep ranch with Maxwell near Cimarron, organized his famous Wild West Show at the town.

Cimarron today has a historic atmosphere. The Don Diego Tavern, built in the 1870's and reputedly the scene of 26 killings, still stands and serves as a hotel. The warehouse for the Ute Agency, constructed in 1848, now houses a grocery store. The county courthouse, erected in 1854, is deserted.

## 115.  Elizabethtown, New Mexico

*Location: Colfax County, on N. Mex. 38, about 5 miles north of Eagle Nest.*

This town was the gold-mining center of the Sangre de Cristo Mountains. In 1866 prospectors discovered gold in the streams draining Baldy Mountain, and a small rush got underway. Two years later John Moore and T. G. Rowe laid out Elizabethtown, or E-Town for short. In 1870 the town had 7,000 inhabitants, but in the middle of the decade the placers began to give out and Indians in the vicinity became increasingly troublesome. Not until 1901 did the settlement again prosper. That year the Oro Dredging Company built an enormous dredge, which had a capacity of 4,000 cubic yards a day, and began profitable operations. The dredge operated for 4 years. Today Elizabethtown is a ghost town. A few people live in the decaying hulks of old buildings, and nearby are abandoned mineworks.

### 116. Hillsboro, New Mexico

*Location: Sierra County.*

In 1877 two prospectors discovered gold on the east side of the Black Range and soon opened the Opportunity and Ready Pay Mines. As other miners arrived in the area, a camp formed that was first known as Hillsborough and later Hillsboro. Despite its isolated location and vulnerability to Indian raids, all through the 1880's and 1890's it teemed with life. The mines produced more than $6 million in gold and silver. Although no mining is done in the vicinity today, the town has survived. It contains many old stone and adobe buildings that have been covered with other materials. Also of interest are the ruins of the large stone jail and the lower story of the old Sierra County Courthouse.

### 117. LC Ranch Headquarters, New Mexico

*Location: Grant County, Gila.*

In its heyday the LC Ranch, controlling a million-acre range that carried 60,000 head, overshadowed all others in southwestern New Mexico. In the late 1870's Tom Lyons, an Englishman who was reared in Wisconsin, came to New Mexico and formed a mining partnership with Angus Campbell, a Silver City prospector. In 1880 the partners sold their mining interests and bought the Nogales, or White House, Ranch, located 10 miles north of Gila.

Immediately they began to monopolize the water rights in the vicinity and eventually claimed all the range from the mouth of Duck Creek to above Mule Springs. In 1890 they moved the ranch headquarters into the town of Gila, where Lyons constructed a 25-room ranchhouse. Campbell, concentrating on irrigated farming on Duck Creek, directed the building of dams and reservoirs, while Lyons specialized in the cattle business. In 1885 he formed the Lyons and Campbell Ranch and Cattle Company, capitalized at $1,500,000, under the laws of the State of New Jersey. When Lyons died in 1917, the firm lost its driving force and was sold piece by piece until only the 5-acre headquarters complex remained. This property is owned today by Arthur L. Ocheltree, who is restoring the ranchhouse to its former grandeur.

## 118. Pinos Altos, New Mexico

*Location: Grant County.*

Col. Jacob Snively and a party of forty-niners, who had drifted back from California, discovered gold in 1860 near the site of this town. Despite Apache hostility in the vicinity, 1,500 miners arrived within 6 months and founded Pinos Altos. A series of raids culminated in a bloody battle in 1861, when Mangas Coloradas led 500 Indians against the town. Most of the miners fled, but Virgil Mastin remained and in 1866 formed the Pinos Altos Mining Company. By 1902 the mines in the vicinity, then controlled by Hearst interests, had produced $4,700,000 worth of gold. Large-scale operations subsequently shifted to the Silver City vicinity. Many abandoned mineworks are in the area of the town today, and some small-scale mining is done.

## 119. Santa Rita Copper Mine, New Mexico

*Location: Grant County, on N. Mex. 90, about 15 miles east of Silver City.*

This is the oldest active mine in the Southwest and one of the first copper mines to be developed within the boundaries of the United States. According to tradition, in 1800 an Apache chief guided José

Manuel Carrasco, commandant of a Spanish post in New Mexico, to the site. In 1804 Carrasco sold the property to Francisco Manuel Elguea, a wealthy merchant from Chihuahua, who obtained the Santa Rita del Cobre grant from the Crown to develop the mine. Using convict labor obtained through his influence with the Spanish Government, Elguea built a primitive smelting plant and an adobe fort for defense against Apache raids. For a time in the 1820's Sylvester Pattie, an American trapper, and some associates worked the mine under a lease from Elguea's widow. The mine then passed through many hands until the 1870's, when a group of Denver financiers purchased it. It is operated today by the Kennecott Copper Company. Several years ago the company removed the only surviving evidence of the Spanish period, an adobe fortress tower, to make way for new construction.

## 120.   White Oaks, New Mexico

> Location: Lincoln County, on an unpaved road, 11 miles northeast of Carrizozo.

Some cowboys found gold in the vicinity of Baxter Mountain as early as 1850, but a substantial strike was not made until 1879, when two prospectors began to work the North and South Homestake Mines. For the next three decades these mines, together with the existing Old Abe, poured forth a steady stream of rich ore. Laid out in 1880, White Oaks soon had churches, schools, hotels, newspapers, and a population of 4,000 people. During the 1880's it was one of the largest and most influential towns in the Territory. When the El Paso & Northeastern Railroad bypassed the town in 1899 in favor of Carrizozo, it began to die and today is almost deserted. Only a few brick and stone structures, including the bank and church, are still standing. The surrounding hills are marked with abandoned mine shafts and cluttered with mine wreckage.

## 121.   Medora, North Dakota

> Location: Billings County.

Still a typical cowtown, Medora was founded in 1883 by a wealthy

The Chateau de Mores, built in 1883 by the Marquis de Mores, a French nobleman turned Western rancher and Dakota neighbor of Theodore Roosevelt.

French nobleman, the Marquis de Mores, on the Northern Pacific Railway in the center of a rich cattle-grazing area along the Little Missouri River. The marquis chose the site for the headquarters of a meatpacking industry he planned to develop to avoid the shrinkage and other costs of shipping live animals to Eastern slaughterhouses. Incorporating the Northern Pacific Refrigerator Car Company, which planned to operate in five Territories and nine States and engage in the general transportation business, he built a packinghouse and cold-storage plant at Medora, capable of packing 150 head a day, and constructed cold-storage plants at a number of towns along the rail line. The town of Medora, which grew up around the plant, attained a peak population of about 400, in 1886.

The enterprise, which began operations in 1883, failed for a variety of reasons, but mainly because of the marquis' inexperience. In the winter months the marquis had to buy feed at exorbitant prices. Thousands of dollars had to be spent before any meat was sold. Moreover, Eastern packers undersold De Mores and forced ruinously low prices. De Mores ran sheep, but hundreds died. A foreigner, and a wealthy one at that, he was not popular in the community. Worst of all, he began to fence his land—a major sin in open-range country. After a fight with some local enemies, in which a man was killed, the marquis faced trial. Acquitted in 1886, by which time his meatpacking operation was a failure, he returned to Europe.

The ruins of the meat-packing plant are still in evidence today, and the smokestack has survived. The Chateau de Mores, home of the marquis, and the site of the meatpacking plant are administered by the State Historical Society of North Dakota. A portion of Medora is included in Theodore Roosevelt National Memorial Park.

## 122.  Guthrie, Oklahoma

*Location: Logan County.*

Guthrie commemorates the first "run" of the "boomer" movement, which opened the Indian Territory to white settlers. In the 1870's settlers on the Plains began to look covetously toward the rich Indian land in what is now Oklahoma. Agitation and political pressures began about 1879 and resulted in the opening a decade later of almost 2 million acres to settlement—the Oklahoma District. The time of the run from the Kansas border was high noon, April

A group of "boomers" in El Reno, not long after Oklahoma was opened to settlement in 1889. The Oklahoma rush was the last great land rush in the United States. Courtesy, National Archives.

22, 1889, when spirited horses and steamed-up locomotives stood ready to start the rush. By nightfall settlers had claimed every parcel of land; and Guthrie, 80 miles from the starting point, was a booming tent-and-shack city of some 15,000 people. Other cities founded at the same time were Oklahoma City, Kingfisher, and Edmond.

Guthrie, established around a Santa Fe Railway depot, became a prairie metropolis overnight and soon had a chamber of commerce, three newspapers, schools, churches, hospitals, a waterworks, and electrically lighted streets. It was the capital of Oklahoma Territory, organized in 1890, and of the State from 1907 until 1910, when Oklahoma City won the honor. The modern city has few physical reminders of its "boomer" origins.

## 123. 101 Ranch, Oklahoma

*Location: Kay County, just off U.S. 77, about 10 miles southwest of Ponca City.*

This ranch was founded by George W. Miller, a trader who had left Kansas in the early 1870's with 10 tons of bacon. He arrived in Texas with enough bacon to trade for 400 Longhorns, which he herded northward to a range in Quapaw Indian Territory and later sold at a handsome profit. Leasing 60,000 acres and founding the 101 Ranch, he made arrangements with the Ponca Indians, who were living temporarily with the Quapaws, to graze his cattle on Indian land. He kept on friendly terms with the Indians and eventually bought much land from them.

At the time Miller died, in 1903, he had sown 13,000 acres of wheat on his land, planted 3,000 acres of corn, and raised 3,000 acres of forage crops. His income ranged from $400,000 to $500,000 a year, and just before his death oil was found on his land. In 1908, the Miller Brothers 101 Ranch Wild West show, under the management of Miller's three sons, gave its first appearance at Ponca City. Devoting all their time to the show, which traveled around the country and featured such film cowboy stars as Tom Mix and Buck Jones, the brothers neglected the ranch. Between 1921 and 1931, oil prices fell, the show failed, and two of the brothers died. The third was unable to manage the ranch, which passed into receivership and was sold in parcels to subsistence farmers.

The most impressive remain is the White House, a three-story home Miller was building at the time of his death. Before that time the ranch headquarters was a dugout. Two miles west of the ranch is White Eagle Monument, erected by the Miller brothers in memory of the Ponca Indian chief who had dealings with their father.

## 124. Agency Ranch, Oregon

*Location: Malheur County, on an unpaved road, about 16 miles north of Juntura.*

This ranch was the headquarters of Henry Miller's cattle empire in eastern Oregon. In the early 1880's T. M. Overfelt, a pioneer in Oregon ranching, established a ranch on Trout Creek in Silvies Valley. Miller, the Pacific coast cattle king, impressed with Overfelt's capabilities, formed a silent partnership with him. Overfelt, using Miller's funds, conducted a large-scale land acquisition program under the name of Overfelt & Company. In the latter part of the 1880's, when the Government opened the Agency Valley Indian Reservation, in Malheur County, for occupation, the partners acquired the Agency Ranch. The Agency Valley region is still ranching country, but the original buildings of the Agency Ranch no longer exist.

## 125. Alvord Ranch, Oregon

*Location: Harney County, on an unpaved road, 35 miles south of Oreg. 78, about 69 miles southeast of Burns.*

In 1868 the Virginian John Devine arrived in the Harney Basin, in the southeastern part of Oregon, and laid claim to a range that totaled 150,000 acres of public land and stretched from the Nevada-Oregon line on the south to what is now the Owyhee Reservoir in the north. He located his headquarters at the Whitehorse Ranch and ran some 24,000 head of cattle. His influence and power were great until the catastrophic winter of 1889–90, when more than 75 percent of his stock perished, and he was forced to sell all of his holdings to Henry Miller, the California cattle king. Miller thereupon hired Devine as manager, but the two men did not get along and parted company. Nevertheless Miller presented Devine with the 6,000-acre Alvord Ranch, where Devine lived until he died in 1901.

This ranch, now consisting of more than 25,000 acres, is still an active spread and runs a large herd of cattle. Surviving original buildings include two stone one-story buildings, a creamery and granary-storehouse built in the 1870's, and a large stone-and-frame barn and corral erected about 1900.

## 126.  Auburn, Oregon

> *Location: Baker County, on an unpaved road, about 3 miles west of Oreg. 7, about 7 miles south of Baker.*

In 1861 prospectors first discovered gold in eastern Oregon, along the Powder River. As a result, miners from California and Nevada rushed in and the following year founded the mining town of Auburn. Soon becoming the county seat and having a population of 5,000, the town was the second largest in the State. Miners were at first handicapped by the lack of water, but the Oregon Steam Navigation Company financed the Auburn Ditch, constructed in 1862–63, which allowed the placers to be worked effectively. Within a few years, however, mining depleted the placers, and the population rapidly declined. After 1868, when the new town of Baker became the county seat, Auburn became a ghost town. No buildings have survived.

## 127.  Canyon City, Oregon

> *Location: Grant County.*

In 1861 prospectors ran across gold placers at Whiskey Flat on Canyon Creek along the John Day River about a half mile north of the site of Canyon City. Within 6 months nearly 1,000 miners arrived and established the town, which in 1864 became the county seat. By the next year the population was 2,500, but it soon began to decline as the placers became depleted. Fires in 1870 and 1937 destroyed most of the town. Among the few original structures remaining amidst modern buildings are the restored Joaquin Miller Cabin, home of the "Poet of the Sierra," now a museum; and the St. Thomas Protestant Episcopal Church.

## 128.  Fort William, Oregon

*Location: Multnomah County, on Sauvie Island in the Columbia River.*

This fort represented the second unsuccessful attempt by Americans to found a commercial colony in the heart of the Hudson's Bay Company's Columbia Department. But the men who came with Nathaniel J. Wyeth, in contrast to those who participated in the Astor effort at Fort Astoria, remained in the region. They were the first U.S. citizens to till the soil and establish permanent farms in the Oregon country. In 1834 Wyeth, though disappointed with a previous commercial venture in the region, returned from Boston with 20 men. Some of the party took up farms at Champoeg, in the French Prairie region. Wyeth erected a trading post that he named Fort William on Wappato Island, today called Sauvie Island. Failing in salmon fishing and packing and agriculture, in 1837 he sold the fort to the Hudson's Bay Company, which established a large dairy there. No surface remains of the fort have survived, but the site is marked with a granite stone and bronze plaque, located on U.S. 30, a half mile west of the fort site.

## 129.  French Prairie, Oregon

*Location: Marion County; the area extending from Champoeg south to Brooks on U.S. 99E.*

Although some farming had been done in the Pacific Northwest, at Astoria and Fort Vancouver, in conjunction with the fur trade, French Prairie was the first area that was settled exclusively for agricultural purposes. Étienne Lucifer, who in 1829 arrived at the prairie, in the rich Willamette Valley, was the first of a group of Hudson's Bay Company trappers to leave the company and turn to farming. Other farmers, mountain men, and missionaries soon arrived. By 1841, about 65 American and 61 French Canadian families were residing in the valley. Because of the agricultural successes at French Prairie and other nearby prairies in the Willamette Valley, this region was the main objective of the emigrants traveling over the Oregon Trail, who in 1843 arrived in large numbers.

Champoeg, one of the earliest settlements on the prairie, was the collection and distribution point for produce. Through a series of meetings, several of which were held at Champoeg, in 1843 the prairie settlers organized the Provisional Government of the Oregon Country, the first effective government in the Pacific Northwest. Because of the economic and political success of the community at French Prairie, the independent settlers gained the ascendancy over the British Hudson's Bay Company. This shift in power, plus continued heavy American immigration, helped establish the American claim to the territory north and west of the Columbia River, which Britain had previously claimed.

In 1844 the settlers established the seat of the provisional government, organized at Champoeg, at Willamette Falls. Yet Champoeg continued to grow, along with several new towns in the valley. By 1860 it had about 29 buildings and a population of 180 persons. A great flood in 1861, however, completely destroyed the town, except for the old Hudson's Bay Company grain warehouse, which has since disappeared. The settlers rebuilt the town on a new site on high ground about a half mile south of the river from its original location and renamed it Newellsville, which after 1880 declined and went out of existence. The original site of Champoeg continued to be used as a steamboat landing until about 1912.

In 1901 the State of Oregon erected a monument at the approximate site of the formation of the provisional government in 1843. Gradually the State acquired 159 acres of land in the vicinity and established a State park. None of the early structures remain, but the Champoeg Pioneer Historical Museum in the park contains relics, photographs, portraits, maps, and other items related to the history of pioneer settlement in the Willamette Valley and Oregon. Other early sites in the French Prairie region included the Willamette (Lee) Mission and the Joseph Gervais farm, but no visible remains of either are extant.

## 130.  French's "P" Ranch, Oregon

*Location: Harney County, on an unpaved road, 2 miles east of Frenchglen.*

In 1872 Peter French moved from California to Harney County, Oreg., to establish and manage a stock ranch for his business partner and father-in-law, Dr. Hugh James Glenn, the wheat and cattle baron of Jacinto, Calif. The French-Glenn Livestock Company eventually owned 132,000 acres in the county, including 500 miles of wire fence, and ran 30,000 cattle and 3,000 horses and mules. It utilized the railhead at Winnemucca, Nev., served by the Central Pacific Railroad, 250 miles distant. In 1897 another rancher killed French, after a long feud. In 1935 the "P" Ranch became a part of Malheur National Wildlife Refuge. The original ranchhouse, located near Frenchglen, has been demolished.

## 131.  Hanley's "Double O" Ranch Site, Oregon

*Location: Harney County, in Malheur National Wildlife Refuge, 35 miles southwest of Burns.*

The "Double O" Ranch was founded by William H. Hanley, who about 1870 arrived in Harney County. His 25,000-acre range lay to the west of the Jackass Mountains and Harney and Malheur Lakes, and extended north to Burns. Hanley was active in State politics. In 1941 the "Double O" Ranch became a part of Malheur National Wildlife Refuge. The only surviving buildings are a log shed, erected about 1878, and several barns built in 1908.

## 132.  Jacksonville, Oregon

*Location: Jackson County.*

Early in the 1850's Rich Gulch on Jackson Creek in the Rogue River Valley yielded gold to two California prospectors, James Cluggage and John R. Pool. The town of Jacksonville arose almost immediately. Before long, tents and log cabins gave way to frame buildings and then to brick structures. In 1853, when the town became the county seat, it had a population of about 900. Its early years were tempestuous; Indian attacks and the Rogue River Indian War retarded mining. In 1873 a fire destroyed much of the business section, but the residents immediately began rebuilding. The Oregon and California Railroad, however, bypassed the town in 1884 in favor of Medford, and the final blow came in 1927, when Medford became the county seat.

Today Jacksonville is a well-preserved 19th-century mining town. Still standing and in good condition are about 60 buildings, which represent a broad range of architectural types. Most of them are still being used for their original purposes. The Southern Oregon Historical Society maintains a museum in the former Jackson County Courthouse. The Beekman Bank, built in 1856, is also open to visitors. Because its original equipment has been preserved intact, it is a unique example of a frontier bank.

## 133. Pendleton, Oregon

*Location: Umatilla County.*

Surveyed and platted in 1870, even before it was designated as the county seat, this town grew slowly and became the cattle and wheat capital of the region. Throughout the 1870's and 1880's it was the assembly point for cattle drives east into Idaho, Montana, and Wyoming. When it was incorporated in 1880, the population had reached more than 1,000. By 1889, when the Oregon Short Line Railroad arrived, the population had trebled. Because of the railroad, cattle drives were no longer necessary, and the emphasis in the region was changing from cattle to wheat. Fires in 1893 and 1895 destroyed most of the original frame dwellings, which by 1900 had been replaced with the present brick and stone structures. Today Pendleton is the trading center for an extensive grain, sheep, and cattle area. The annual Pendleton Roundup, a rodeo instituted in 1912, commemorates the early days.

## 134. Waldo, Oregon

*Location: Josephine County, on an unpaved road, about 4 miles east of O'Brien.*

In 1851 a group of sailors who had deserted ship at Crescent City, Calif., discovered placer gold on the East Fork of the Illinois River in the southwestern part of present Oregon, about 3 miles north of the California-Oregon border. Oregon's first mining camp, originally named Sailors' Diggings and later Waldo, sprang up to support the 2,500 prospectors who arrived and pitched their tents. Within a year other small mining camps had been established in the vicinity. By 1855 Waldo, then a town of wood, stone, and brick, had a population of 500 and was the largest in the area. The following year it became the county seat. After reaching its zenith in the 1860's, it declined. In 1876 the county seat was moved to Kerbyville, a virtual death warrant for Waldo. Today almost nothing remains of the town.

## 135. Central City, South Dakota

*Location: Lawrence County.*

In 1877 several mining towns in the Black Hills that had a combined population of 10,000 assumed the common name of Central City, although one town in the group became known as Central City. Having a population of 3,000, it included 4 newspapers, 16 mills that were in operation night and day during the boom years, and many other businesses. Its residents organized the first public school system in Dakota Territory. In 1883 Deadwood Creek flooded and washed away the placer workings. Soon afterwards a fire broke out and destroyed a large part of the town, parts of which its residents never rebuilt. Today some deep stone foundations may be seen in lots that are overgrown with weeds. Only a small number of buildings survive from the era of mining operations. These buildings, which provide the town with some degree of historic atmosphere, sit amidst modern structures.

The Custer expedition en route to the Black Hills in 1874. For years prospectors had heard rumors that the Black Hills contained gold. The expedition confirmed the rumors and set off the last great rush of the mining frontier. Courtesy, National Archives.

## 136. Custer, South Dakota

*Location: Custer County.*

The oldest town in the Black Hills and the first boomtown in the State, Custer is located on French Creek near the site where in 1874 Horatio N. Ross discovered gold. Ross was a prospector accompanying Gen. George A. Custer's expedition that explored Dakota Territory. Even though the Sioux Indians had possession of the area, the next year prospectors moved in and established a camp known as Stonewall, in honor of "Stonewall" Jackson. The U.S. Army, which occupied the area, ordered them to leave. In December 1875, when the troops withdrew, the miners returned and formed the town of Custer; and 2 years later the Government signed a treaty with the Indians.

In 1876 the population of the town was 5,000, but after the discovery of profitable placer mines at Deadwood it dwindled to less than 100. Settlers were later attracted to the area, however, and the arrival of the Burlington Railroad in 1890 fostered the town's development. Only a few early structures have survived, but several monuments commemorate the early days.

### 137.   Galena, South Dakota

*Location: Lawrence County.*

A group of prospectors who sought placer gold but found rich veins of silver instead founded Galena in 1876. They staked out two claims, the Florence and the Sitting Bull. Despite the opening of mills and a small smelter, the town grew slowly because of its isolation. A legal battle in the 1880's over mining properties brought about its demise. A brief revival occurred between 1895 and 1897, when silver prices were high. Later the town was a summer resort, but now has only a few residents.

### 138.   Hill City, South Dakota

*Location: Pennington County.*

Founded in 1876, the year after prospectors struck gold along Spring Creek, this town had hardly been established when news of the gold strike at Deadwood depleted its population. Some of the miners later began to drift back and discovered gold lodes, a few ranchers settled in the valley, and the town started to grow once again. In 1883 prospectors found tin in the vicinity and staked out claims. An English corporation, the Harney Peak Consolidated Tin Company, bought up all the promising claims, but after a few months of successful mining operations in 1892 abandoned the area. Most of the population drifted away, but in modern times the town revived.

### 139.   Rochford, South Dakota

*Location: Pennington County.*

In 1876 three hunters from Deadwood accidentally discovered

deposits of gold in the vicinity of this village. Soon swarms of prospectors arrived and formed a mining district and the town of Rochford. Some 500 resided in the town and 500 more camped in the nearby hills. By 1879 two 20-stamp mills, the Evangeline and the Minnesota, were operating in the vicinity. The Standby Mine, which had a 40-stamp mill and other elaborate facilities, was the most extensively developed property. The town consisted of more than 200 buildings. In the 1880's the mills closed down and most of the residents departed. A few ruins of gold-rush buildings may be seen in the modern town.

## 140. Rockerville, South Dakota

*Location: Pennington County, on U.S. 16, about 12 miles east of Hill City.*

This town was second only to Deadwood in Dakota Territory in the richness of its gold placers. In 1876, not long after a prospector found gold in the vicinity, a stampede of miners occurred. During the dry winter season they had to transport their rockers by hand-cart to the nearest pool or stream to rock out their load. During the rest of the year hundreds of rockers were in use along the banks of Rockerville Gulch.

In 1880, when operations reached their peak, the Black Hills Placer Mining Company laid a flume to the diggings from a dam 2 miles above Sheridan, 15 miles away. The flume, in operation for 2 years, made possible the recovery of $500,000 worth of gold. In 1881 the Rockerville Gold Mining Company built a 1,100-foot bed-rock flume on the hill below the town, but it was unsuccessful. By 1883, mining had practically ceased, and the camp had been desert-ed. Today only a dilapidated cabin and a few other remains may be seen in the ghost town of Rockerville.

## 141. Roubaix, South Dakota

*Location: Lawrence County.*

In 1876 prospectors struck gold on the banks of Elk Creek near the site of the town of Perry, later renamed Roubaix. A one-stamp mill served the Uncle Sam Mine. In 1880, after the mine had changed hands several times, its owners closed it down when it filled with water. The town almost died. In 1899 Pierre Wibaux, a wealthy Frenchman, arrived and took possession of the Uncle Sam, which he operated under the name of the Clover Leaf Mining Company. He renamed the reinvigorated Perry for his hometown in France, Roubaix. After only a few years of profitable operation, however, the mine again flooded and Wibaux was forced to abandon it. A fire destroyed many of the buildings, and the mine was not operated again except for a brief period in the 1930's by the Anaconda Copper Company. In 1947 it was sold for taxes. Only a few people live in the town today.

## 142.  Sheridan (lost site), South Dakota

*Location: Pennington County.*

This town originated in 1875 as a mining camp called Golden City after prospectors discovered placers in the meadows along Spring Creek. The very next year the residents chose a new name, Sheridan. The town became the county seat and accommodated the first Federal court west of the Missouri River. It was an important station on the Deadwood-Denver stageline and a regular stopping place for Brig. Gen. George Crook and his troops on their patrols through the Black Hills. Rapid City acquired the county seat in 1878, the coming of the railroads brought about the demise of the stage business, and the productivity of the placers in the vicinity lessened. Sheridan became a ghost town. In 1938 construction of a dam across Spring Creek started and the reservoir, Sheridan Lake, submerged the town.

## 143.  Clarendon, Texas

*Location: Donley County, on Tex. 70, about 6 miles north of New Clarendon.*

One of the earliest settlements in the Texas Panhandle, Clarendon was founded as a temperance colony in 1878 by Lewis H. Carhart, a Methodist minister. The cowboys dubbed it "Saint's Roost" because deeds contained prohibition clauses. Surrounded by huge ranches, the town became the commercial center of the county. A stageline provided service to Dodge City. When the Fort Worth and Denver Railroad bypassed the town in the late 1880's, the residents abandoned it and established a new settlement 6 miles to the south on the rail line. The site of the old town lies on the Bugbee Ranch, north of New Clarendon. The sole surviving structure, a one-story framehouse, has been moved to the Bugbee Ranch headquarters.

## 144.  Fort Griffin, Texas

*Location: Shackelford County, on U.S. 67, about 15 miles north of Albany.*

Established by Col. Samuel D. Sturgis in 1867 on a hill overlooking the valley of the Clear Fork of the Brazos River, Fort Griffin became a link in the chain of military posts along the Texas frontier. At the bottom of the hill grew a wide-open frontier town, known as The Flat, whose visitors included outlaws such as Billy the Kid and lawmen such as Bat Masterson and Pat Garrett. Supply and shipping center for a section of the southern Plains buffalo country, it shipped bales of hides to Eastern markets. As the buffalo hunters completed their slaughter and troops from the fort pacified the Plains, Goodnight, Loving, Adams, and other well-known cattlemen pushed their holdings northwest from the town. In 1881 the Army abandoned the fort, which had been of lesser importance than its sister forts on the northwest frontier of Texas, Forts Concho and Richardson, and the town declined.

Fort Griffin is today a State park. A few remains of the fort may be seen, and the sites of some of the buildings are marked. A granite shaft erected by the Texas Centennial Commission in 1936 stands in the center of the parade ground. Ruins of the nearby town, which is in private ownership, are particularly interesting.

## 145.  Horsehead Crossing, Texas

*Location: At the Pecos River boundary of Pecos and Crane Counties, about 65 miles southeast of Pecos City.*

This crossing of the Pecos River was a landmark on the Goodnight-

Modern view of Horsehead Crossing, Texas, well-known landmark on the Goodnight-Loving Trail, used not only by Texas cattle drovers but also by Indians, forty-niners, emigrants, surveyors, and U.S. Army troops.

Loving Trail, but it was known and used long before the Texas cattle drives, perhaps even by early Spanish explorers. It was traversed by Indians following the Great Comanche War Trail to and from Mexico; forty-niners, emigrants, and surveyors; passengers on the Butterfield Overland Mail route; Texas cattlemen driving herds to California to feed the miners after the 1849 gold rush; U.S. Army troops transporting supplies to military posts and Indian agencies in Arizona and New Mexico; and Texas cowboys driving feeder stock to the northern and western ranges over the Goodnight-Loving Trail. Charles Goodnight and Oliver Loving had blazed the trail in 1866 from central Texas into New Mexico and Colorado Territories.

In private ownership today, the crossing is in much the same condition as it was in cattle-drive days. Isolated from main travel routes, it is virtually lost in the barren desert.

## 146.  Matador Ranch, Texas

*Location: Motley County, on U.S. 62, about 3 miles south of Matador.*

This ranch was founded in 1879 when H. H. Campbell and A. M. Britton formed a partnership, acquired range rights from a buffalo hunter, and bought 8,000 head of cattle. Prospering until 1882, they sold the ranch to the Matador Land and Cattle Company, Ltd., of Dundee, Scotland. Under the management of Murdo Mackenzie, the Matador became one of the largest enterprises in Texas. By 1910 the company owned 861,000 acres in Texas and had leased another 650,000 acres to the north. Some 66,000 head of cattle stocked these ranges. During a time of heavy British investment in American cattle, the Matador was one of the most successful of the British-owned ranches. In 1951 Lazard Brothers, an American syndicate, bought the ranch, which has since been subdivided.

The core of the old ranch, occupying 190 sections, is now owned by Fred C. Koch of Wichita, Kans. Only four buildings now

Group of Matador Ranch cowhands. Texas cowboys made substantial contributions to the open range cattle industry. Courtesy, Russel Jones, Photographer, Jacksboro, Texas.

extant antedate 1906: An old stone bunkhouse; a deserted stone icehouse; ruins of a windmill, milkhouse, and wellhouse; and a small white frame building. The major complex of stone buildings now at the ranch headquarters was built in 1918 by the Scotch owners.

Hard-working cowhands always welcomed mealtime. Scene on the Matador Ranch, Texas, about 1900. Courtesy, Russel Jones, Photographer, Jacksboro, Texas.

## 147.  Mobeetie (Old), Texas

*Location: Wheeler County, on Tex. 152, about 30 miles east of Pampa.*

Mobeetie was an active trading and social center of the cattle country in the Texas Panhandle. In the 1880's it vied with Tascosa for the reputation of the toughest town in the region. Originating as a trading post in 1875 to serve the troops at nearby Fort Elliott, by 1879 it had grown into a village, populated largely by gamblers, dancehall people, and buffalo hunters; and had become the county seat of the newly organized Wheeler County. A damaging storm in 1898 and failure to obtain railroad service caused the town to decline, and in 1907 Wheeler gained the county seat. When the Panhandle and Santa Fe Railroad bypassed Mobeetie in 1929, a new town sprang up 2 miles to the north, and the old one became a ghost town. The stone jail, built in 1886, is the principal surviving building.

## 148. T-Anchor Ranch, Texas

*Location: Randall County, on U.S. 87, just north of Canyon.*

The second ranch in the Texas Panhandle, established the year after the JA Ranch, the T-Anchor was founded in 1877 by Leigh Dyer, brother-in-law of Charles Goodnight. Dyer used timber from Palo Duro Canyon to construct the first log cabin in the Panhandle. The following year he sold the ranch to the firm of Gunter, Munson, and Summerfield, which in 1883 sold it to an English firm, the Cedar Valley Lands and Cattle Company. At the time the T-Anchor consisted of 225 sections of land and 24,000 head of cattle. In 1902 the owners divided the ranch into small sections and sold them to farmers and ranchers.

Early ranches were primitive by today's standards. The T-Anchor Ranch was founded in 1877 by Leigh Dyer, a brother-in-law of Charles Goodnight. The ranchhouse is preserved by the Panhandle-Plains Historical Society of Canyon, Texas.

Dyer's simple log cabin still stands on 80 acres of the T-Anchor land, owned and operated by West Texas State University as an experimental farm. The cabin is maintained under the supervision of the Panhandle-Plains Historical Society of Canyon.

### 149.  Tascosa, Texas

> *Location: Oldham County, on Tex. 385, about 22 miles north of Vega.*

Tascosa, now a ghost town, was formerly one of the liveliest and toughest towns in the Texas Panhandle, a distinction that it shared with Mobeetie. It originated as a sheep camp that was called Plaza Atascosa. In 1876 a blacksmith shop and general store opened for business, followed quickly by a saloon that served the thirsty riders on the cattle and freight trail that crossed the Canadian River at Tascosa Ford. Some of the riders were Pat Garrett, Bat Masterson, Billy the Kid, Charlie Siringo, and Frank James. Bypassed by the Fort Worth and Denver City Railroad in 1887, the town was abandoned. In 1939 the Maverick Boys' Ranch took over the site and for a headquarters utilized the old courthouse building, an original stone structure. The boys have marked the foundations of buildings and indicated their former uses. Visitors are welcome.

### 150.  XIT Ranch, Texas

> *Location: Hartley and Deaf Smith Counties; sites at Channing and Escarbada.*

Largest of the pioneer ranches in the Texas Panhandle, the XIT originated because of a unique financial arrangement. The Chicago firm of Taylor, Babcock, and Company, founder of the Capitol Syndicate, received more than 3 million acres in the Panhandle from the State of Texas in return for constructing the capitol building in Austin. In 1885 the firm, with English backing, established the XIT Ranch and located the headquarters in the town of Channing. The ranch, which consisted of seven divisions, ran 110,721 head of cattle. In 1887 the company set up a branch operation in Montana, where it sent cattle each year for finishing.

Surviving buildings of the Escarbada Division Headquarters of the XIT ("Ten in Texas")—one of the most famous ranches in Western history. The XIT encompassed 10 counties.

Though prospering at first, in 1901 it began to sell land to meet its financial obligations. By 1912 it had disposed of its assets to small ranchers and farmers.

The headquarters building at Channing still stands and is used as a private residence, but it has been altered beyond recognition. In the 1890's Escarbada was a lively division headquarters. The foreman and his hands lived in a two-story plastered stone building that still stands on the present Reinauer Brothers Ranch.

## 151. Alta, Utah

*Location: Salt Lake County, on an unpaved road, about 18 miles east of Sandy.*

In 1864 soldiers found silver in Little Cottonwood Canyon, and 3 years later prospectors formed the mining camp of Alta on the side of Mount Baldy. After J. B. Woodman founded the Emma Mine in 1869, a boom occurred. The Emma shipped its ore in ox-drawn wagons to Ogden, from where it moved by rail to San Francisco and then by ship to Wales for smelting. In 1871 investors formed the Emma Mining Company of Utah. Within a few months Eastern investors poured $375,000 into the company, renamed the Emma Mining Company of New York, and it soon gained an

international reputation. In 1872 British capitalists purchased it
and again renamed it, as the Emma Silver Mining Company, Ltd.,
of London. That same year, however, cave-ins rendered the mine
worthless.

The population of the town at the time was 5,000, and it included 2 breweries, 6 sawmills, and 26 saloons. After the Emma
failed, most of the miners remained to work other veins. Between
1871 and 1877, the mines yielded more than $13 million in ore. In
1893, because of the decline in silver prices, mine after mine closed
down. Several avalanches in the 1880's destroyed much of the town,
but in 1904 prospectors found a new ore body and the town came
back to life. Today it is a modern ski resort and has few remains
from the mining days.

### 152.  Bingham Canyon, Utah

*Location: Salt Lake County, on Utah 48, about 20 miles south-
west of Salt Lake City.*

As early as 1848 Mormons discovered gold and silver deposits in

Mining operations at Bingham Canyon, Utah. Loaded cars traveled
from mines in the canyon by gravity to the smelter and depot in the
valley. Horses pulled the empty cars back up to the mines. Courtesy,
Utah State Historical Society.

this canyon, but church officials feared the inevitable rush and prohibited dissemination of the information. In 1862, however, Col. Patrick E. Connor, Army commander of the District of Utah, learned of gold, silver, and lead deposits in the canyon and promptly broadcast the news. Prospectors rushed in and staked out the mining camp of Bingham Canyon. By 1870 the gold placers had given out, but completion of a railroad into the canyon made lode operations for silver and lead profitable. The drop in silver prices in 1893 brought silver and lead mining to a standstill, but a subsequent rise in the price of copper led to renewed interest in the district. In 1903 the Utah Copper Company was organized. Using open-pit mining methods, it has been operating in the canyon ever since. Today the town of Bingham Canyon looks like many other mountain mining towns. A single main street meanders up the canyon between houses perched on the flanking slopes.

## 153. Cove Fort, Utah

*Location: Millard County, on U.S. 91, about 30 miles south of Fillmore.*

Cove Fort, like Pipe Spring, was established under the direction of Brigham Young as a way station for travelers between the Mormon settlements of southern Utah and northern Arizona. Erected in 1867 by Ira N. Hinckley, it lay on a heavily traveled road that linked Salt Lake City with the Virgin River Valley of northwestern Arizona. Nearby Cove Creek supplied water for irrigating the truck gardens that provided produce. Constructed of basalt blocks laid with lime mortar, the fort consists of two rows of five rooms facing each other across a closed courtyard, whose walls are equipped with loopholes and firing parapets. It is open to the public.

## 154. Goodyear Cabin, Utah

*Location: Weber County, Tabernacle Park, Ogden.*

This cabin commemorates the activities of mountain man Miles Goodyear, who founded the first permanent settlement by whites in Utah west of the Wasatch Mountains, and was one of the first to carry on agricultural pursuits. It was part of a trading post called Fort Buenaventura, which in 1846 Goodyear established on the Weber River on the site of Ogden. When the Mormons arrived in the Great Salt Lake basin in 1847, they persuaded Goodyear to sell out. Capt. James Brown and his family, the new occupants, extended Goodyear's cultivated acreage. A cottonwood log cabin that once was a part of Fort Buenaventura is still standing. It has been moved from the original site, near the Union Pacific depot in Ogden, to Tabernacle Park.

### 155.  Mormon Irrigation Sites, Utah

*Location: Salt Lake County, Salt Lake City.*

The Mormons were the first Anglo-Saxons to irrigate extensively in the West and make the desert bloom. They introduced irrigation wherever they settled and influenced others to do likewise. Arriving in the Great Salt Lake basin in 1847 and finding the soil too dry to plow, they immediately built a dam at one of the two nearby creeks flowing down from the Wasatch Mountains and diverted the water to their fields. Soon the farms prospered.

Rejecting the English common law system of riparian rights and drawing on the Spanish Doctrine of Appropriation, the Mormons developed a policy of land survey and distribution of water based on individual need and capacity. All fields adjoined an irrigation ditch connected with the main creek. A committee planned the principal ditches, whose construction was participated in by all users on the basis of the amount of land tilled. Each farmer then dug smaller trenches to his own plot. The church rigidly controlled use of the water, and each farmer received just enough for his needs.

The original irrigation sites, along what is now City Creek in downtown Salt Lake City, have been obliterated. In the heart of the city, however, stands a monument, executed by the Utah sculptor Mahonri Young, commemorating the Mormon irrigation achievement.

Pioneer Monument, at the mouth of Emigration Canyon, Salt Lake City, pays tribute to all Utah pioneers, especially the hardy Mormons who settled in the Great Basin and made it bloom.

## 156. Park City, Utah

*Location: Wasatch County.*

In 1869 some soldiers stumbled onto silver, lead, and gold deposits near the site of this town. The following year they opened the Flagstaff Mine, and miners poured into the area. A line of tents and shacks at the bottom of Provo Canyon became the camp of Park City. The Ontario Mine, staked out in 1872, brought in substantial capital. Even major fires in 1882 and 1898 failed to retard the town's progress and by the time of the silver "crash," in 1893, the population was 6,000. Despite the crash, some mining continued, and by 1915 several mills were again in operation. Still an active mining town, Park City has produced more than $250 million worth of gold, silver, copper, lead, and zinc.

### 157.  Silver Reef, Utah

> *Location: Washington County, about 1½ miles off U.S. 91, 4 miles south of New Harmony.*

In 1866 a prospector discovered silver in the vicinity of the future town of Silver Reef, but he did not develop his find until 1870, at which time he and some friends formed the Harrisburg Mining District and began small-scale operations. In 1874, when prospectors staked out the Leeds claim on White Reef, a sandstone ledge, a small camp originated nearby that came to be known as Silver Reef because of the numerous silver strikes in the area. It reached its peak between 1877 and 1880, when stores and hotels, a bank, a church, and a Wells-Fargo office lined the busy street.

By 1880 a few companies owned most of the mines. The next year the price of silver fell, water seeped into the mines, and stockholders demanded a cut in miners' wages—resulting in a conflict that led to lessee operation of the mines. Between the years 1892 and 1903, the mines shipped $250,000 worth of bullion and produced a total of $10½ million worth of silver ore. Today the town is in ruins. Rotted wooden sidewalks, remnants of adobe and stone walls, and sage-clogged streets characterize the landscape.

### 158.  Clark Cabin, Washington

> *Location: Walla Walla County, at Log Cabin Farm, on Wash. 3, about 2 miles south of Walla Walla.*

This cabin was erected in 1859 by Ransom Clark, a farmer who supplied produce to nearby Fort Walla Walla, established 3 years earlier. The market broadened greatly in 1860 when prospectors struck gold at Orofino. By 1862 Walla Walla was an outfitting center, as well as a winter home for Idaho miners. The cabin is an excellent example of a pioneer farm home in the Northwest. It is a one-story structure that consists of two rooms, separated by a breezeway. This style of pioneer architecture is known as the "dog-run." The original fireplaces have been removed from the cabin, which has been moved about 100 feet from its original location.

## 159. Conconully, Washington

> *Location: Okanogan County.*

In 1886 two prospectors, who had earlier discovered gold along the edge of Salmon Creek, began working the Homestake and Toughnut Mines above the town of Ruby. Their activity lured others, and within a few months Salmon City came into existence. It grew fast because of the abundance of water and the richness of the diggings, and in 1888 was renamed Conconully. In that year it lost a battle with Ruby for the county seat. Suffering many disasters, including a fire in 1892, a flood in 1894, and a depression in 1893, it never fully recovered. Since 1915 it has had only a small population.

## 160. Cowlitz Farm, Washington

> *Location: Lewis County, on an unpaved road, just north of Toledo, along the north bank of the Cowlitz River.*

The Hudson's Bay Company contributed substantially to the development of farming in the Northwest by forming, in 1839, a subsidiary, known as the Puget's Sound Agricultural Company. One of two farms the company established, Cowlitz was highly successful. In 1841 it produced 8,000 bushels of wheat and 4,000 bushels of oats, as well as barley, peas, and potatoes, on nearly 1,000 fenced acres. The farm was in operation until 1853–54, when armed American settlers took possession and the British withdrew. In 1869 the United States awarded the Hudson's Bay Company $200,000 as compensation for the farm property. The area is still devoted to farming, but no buildings of the Cowlitz Farm have survived.

At Fort Nisqually the Puget's Sound Agricultural Company, a subsidiary of the English Hudson's Bay Company, raised cattle, sheep, and garden produce—long before Americans settled in the Northwest. Pictured here is a reconstructed blockhouse and the stockade, located in Point Defiance Park, Tacoma, Washington.

### 161. Fort Nisqually, Washington

*Location: Pierce County, Point Defiance Park, Tacoma.*

Fort Nisqually (Nesqually) farm, founded in 1840, was one of two established by the Puget's Sound Agricultural Company, a subsidiary of the Hudson's Bay Company. The fort, built in 1833 by Archibald McDonald as a fur-trading post and shipping center, had been the first permanent white settlement on Puget Sound. Soon the Fort Nisqually farm was operating a large dairy, running several hundred head of cattle, and growing wheat, peas, and oats. In 1845, when the herds included 2,280 cattle and 5,872 sheep, the farm exported to England nearly 10,000 pounds of wool, as well as hides, horns, and tallow. That same year the first Americans arrived in the vicinity, founded farms at Tumwater, and soon began encroaching on Fort Nisqually land, but the Hudson's Bay Company retained possession of the farm until 1869, when the United States acquired it, along with Cowlitz Farm.

The original site of Fort Nisqually—at Dupont, about 15 miles south of Tacoma on Sequalachew Creek—is now marked by a small granite monument. There are no surface remains, but two original log buildings, the factor's house and the granary, are now exhibited at Point Defiance Park in Tacoma. These two buildings are the only surviving examples of Hudson's Bay Company structures in the United States. Eight other buildings, two blockhouses, and the stockade have been reconstructed in the park.

## 162.  Jackson Cabin, Washington

*Location: Lewis County, just to the east of U.S. 5, at Mary's Corner.*

This cabin was the home of the first American settler north of the Columbia River, John R. Jackson, a native of England who arrived in the Oregon country in 1844 and staked out a claim about 10

John R. Jackson was the first American to settle north of the Columbia River, in 1844, and 4 years later he completed his cabin, which has been restored. In 1851 a group of American settlers met at the cabin, then used as a courthouse, to agitate for Territorial status.

miles north of Cowlitz Farm. In 1847–48 he completed a small cabin and eventually acquired some 2,200 acres of land. He raised grain, vegetables, and livestock for market, kept a public house, and participated in politics. In 1851 a group of American settlers met at his house, which had been converted to a courthouse the previous year, and began agitation for Territorial status. Jackson died in 1873.

In 1915 the cabin was donated to the Washington State Historical Society, which has restored it as a museum and historic home. One-and-a-half stories high, it is built of peeled logs with hand-split cedar boards above the first floor and a long, low porch across the front.

### 163.  Old Fort Colvile Site, Washington

*Location: Stevens County, on Wash. 22, about 6 miles north of Kettle Falls.*

Old Fort Colvile, also known as Fort Colville, was a fur-trading post, agricultural colony, and important way station of the Hudson's Bay Company. Named after Andrew W. Colvile, a governor of the Northern Department, and built in 1825 to complete the line of posts linking the company's forts in Canada with those in the Oregon country, it became the central supply post for all the forts in present northeastern Washington and the first agricultural center there. Consisting of high picket walls, equipped with bastions, it was well prepared to withstand Indian attacks. Within the walls were dwellings and storehouses.

In 1855, after the discovery of gold in the vicinity, Americans began arriving. When the gold supply there and in nearby British Columbia ran out, the disappointed miners turned to other endeavors. Some chose to farm and squatted on Fort Colvile lands. The Hudson's Bay Company, however, did not withdraw from the post until 1871, when the U.S. Government paid its claims. The site of old Fort Colvile has been inundated by Franklin D. Roosevelt Lake. A few remains of new Fort Colville, a U.S. Army post established in 1859, may be seen 3 miles west of the town of Colville.

## 164.   Republic, Washington

*Location: Ferry County.*

When the discovery of gold on Granite Creek in 1896 near the site of this town caused the northern section of the Colville Indian Reservation to be opened to miners, a rush occurred and a lively tent camp sprang up that was first called Eureka and then Republic after the leading mine. It soon included 50 log and canvas shacks, 5 stores, 3 blacksmith shops, numerous other businesses, 3 assay offices, and several saloons. As early as 1900 it was one of the largest towns in eastern Washington and included 28 saloons, an opera house, and many balconied false-fronted stores. Stage service connected it with Spokane and other points. In recent years half of the State's silver output has been mined in the vicinity. A fire in 1938 destroyed most of the picturesque landmarks of the early period, and the modern town shows little evidence of its origin.

## 165.   Ruby, Washington

*Location: Okanogan County, on an unpaved road, 13 miles northwest of Okanogan.*

Early prospectors illegally operated in the area of Ruby Mountain on the Moses Indian Reservation, but the real rush came after 1886, when the Government opened the reservation as part of the public domain. More than a thousand prospectors rushed in and struck silver and small amounts of gold. In 1887 they organized the Ruby Mining District. The associated town grew rapidly until stores and log houses lined both sides of a 1/4-mile-long street. It became the county seat after a clash with nearby Conconully and continued to prosper until 1893, when the silver market collapsed. After the population departed, ranchers removed or tore down most of the buildings, and a fire in 1900 destroyed most of the remains. Today only a line of weathered foundations, hidden in brush and grass, indicate Ruby's main thoroughfare.

## 166.   Snipes Cabin, Washington

*Location: Yakima County, Sunnyside City Park, 4th Street and Grant Avenue, Sunnyside.*

Benjamin E. Snipes, one of the early cattle kings of Washington, was a North Carolinian who arrived in 1854 at The Dalles, Oregon Territory. The following year he acquired a small herd of cattle from an Army captain at Fort Dalles and obtained a range in the Horse Heaven Hills in Washington Territory. Four times—in 1856, 1861, 1862, and 1863—he made 800-mile drives to the mines in British Columbia to sell his beef to the gold seekers. He supplied U.S. Army Forts Dalles, Simcoe, and Walla Walla. To feed his cattle during the winters, he developed a series of hay ranches between the Yakima and Columbia Rivers, so situated that his control of the water gave him uncontested use of thousands of acres of public land.

In 1864 Snipes married and 3 years later built a fine two-story brick house at The Dalles, which fire destroyed in 1886. That same year he began investing heavily in Seattle real estate, and built and resided in a large home at 11th and Madison Streets. Next venturing into banking, he established banks at Ellensburg and at Roslyn. The Panic of 1893 swept away his fortune, estimated at $1 million, and he returned to The Dalles, where he died in 1906.

Snipes' ranching headquarters had been located on the north bank of the Yakima River at the base of Snipes Mountain, about 8 miles southwest of Sunnyside. The original ranchhouse, erected in 1859, was a crude one-story log cabin, which had mud-plastered walls and a sod roof. Removed from its original site, it is now exhibited in Sunnyside City Park.

## 167.   Atlantic City, Wyoming

*Location: Fremont County, on an unpaved road, about 22 miles south of Lander.*

One of the most significant mining camps in Wyoming, Atlantic City sprang up in 1868, the year after prospectors from nearby

South Pass City discovered the Atlantic Ledge. Before long about 300 prospectors were living in a camp on Rock Creek that came to be known as Atlantic City. Surrounded by gold lodes and placers, the town grew to a population of 2,000, and boasted Wyoming's first brewery and an opera house. Because of Indian depredations, the residents demanded a garrison, and in 1870 the U.S. Army established Fort Stambaugh, about 1½ miles away. By 1878, however, the town had been abandoned, even though seven mills were still in operation. Today the gray, weathered buildings are deserted and vacant.

## 168. Cheyenne, Wyoming

*Location: Laramie County.*

Cheyenne, the cow capital of Wyoming, originated in 1867, when the Union Pacific Railroad selected it as a company townsite. Settlers rushed in even before the railroad began to sell building plots. Within a matter of months, the population was 4,000, and thousands of tents, shacks, dugouts, and covered wagon boxes lined the

Main street of Cheyenne, Wyoming Territory, in 1869, the same year that the first Texas Longhorns arrived. A typical cowtown, Cheyenne boomed after the Union Pacific Railroad founded it, in 1867. Courtesy, National Archives.

streets. The arrival of the rail line late in the year attracted a new variety of settlers. Because of the lawlessness, the citizens maintained a vigilance committee until the rail line moved west in 1868 and much of the transient population traveled along with it. That same year the town became the county seat of the newly organized Laramie County.

By 1869 Longhorns were arriving in the vicinity from Texas, and the next year the first Wyoming cattle were loaded at Cheyenne for the European market. By the mid-1870's the Cheyenne Plains had been stocked; the Wyoming Stock Growers Association founded; and Cheyenne was the capital of a vast cattle-ranching region. English cattlemen settled there and formed the Cheyenne Club, which made policies affecting the cattle industry throughout the West. The town outfitted prospectors going to the Black Hills and provided them with stage transportation. By 1880, the population was 3,456; by 1897, 10,000. Cheyenne today is the capital of the State. The annual Frontier Days Celebration commemorates its early history.

## 169. Douglas, Wyoming

*Location: Converse County.*

In 1886 the Fremont, Elkhorn, and Missouri Valley Railway announced plans to extend westward from Chadron, Nebr., up the Platte River. Settlers, in anticipation, established "Tent Town" on the banks of the Platte River, just north of its confluence with Antelope Creek. The town soon had three streets and many businesses, including a newspaper. When the railway decided to locate the station and the associated townsite 10 miles east of Fetterman on the opposite side of the river, the inhabitants moved to the new location, which was named in honor of Stephen A. Douglas.

In 1887 Douglas became the county seat. Because of the abundance of water and the fine grasses in the region, in the 1880's many cattlemen founded ranches, on which Texas Longhorns soon grazed. After the disastrous winter of 1886–87, many large ranches failed and the population of Douglas dwindled from 1,500 to 400. Homesteaders took over some of the cattle lands, and agriculture as well as the cattle industry came to support the town.

## 170. Encampment, Wyoming

*Location: Carbon County.*

Trappers used the site of Encampment as a rendezvous and camping ground. In 1877 ranchers settled in the area, and 2 years later prospectors found small quantities of copper. In 1897 a prospector established a copper mine that sparked the boom in the area and reinvigorated the towns of Ellwood, Battle, Rambler, Copperton, and Dillon. In 1899 the Rudefeha Mine began operations near the site of Encampment, or Grand Encampment as it was first known. As soon as it proved successful, a townsite was laid out close to Grand Encampment Creek. George Emerson promoted the town in the East. He also formed the North American Copper Company and bought the Rudefeha Mine, renamed it the Ferris-Haggarty, and sold thousands of shares of stock.

Between 1903 and 1908 the population of the booming town reached 2,000. In 1905 a smelter that had been erected in 1899 was enlarged, and an independent company started constructing the Saratoga Encampment Railroad to link the town with the main line of the Union Pacific Railroad. In 1906 fire destroyed a mill at the smelter and the town began to decline. By 1908, when the railroad line was completed, the smelter had closed, and the drop in copper prices forced mine after mine to cease operations. The same year the Ferris-Haggarty Company was indicted for overcapitalization and fraudulent stock sales, and within 3 years the population of the town was only 200. After that time, the town became a ranching center. Several buildings from the boom days are still standing.

## 171. Laramie, Wyoming

*Location: Albany County.*

The first settlements near the site of Laramie, in the 1860's, were road ranches along the Overland Trail that supplied hay and emergency provisions to stage companies, freighters, and emigrants. When the Union Pacific Railroad built its line along the west slope of the Laramie Mountains early in 1868, a tent town of 500 residents grew up on the bank of the Laramie River. The railroad company platted a townsite and sold lots. The first train brought the transients that had been living in Cheyenne, but Laramie did not long remain the end of the line and in only a few months had a far more stable population. Late in 1868 the Dakota Territorial Legislature created Albany County and made Laramie its seat, but before long the increasing lawlessness in the town forced the legislature to dissolve its government and place it under the jurisdiction of the Federal courts. This status continued until 1874, when the Wyoming Territorial Legislature reincorporated the town.

In 1868 only a few cattle belonging to the road ranches grazed on the Laramie Plains, and within 2 years the road ranchers left the country or turned to cattle breeding. In 1871, however, Texans arrived with herds of Longhorns. Stories of the rich Laramie Plains reached the East, and wealthy Englishmen acquired choice ranches in the area, built mansions in Laramie, and organized many clubs. After the "crash" of ranching in the 1880's, most of them left, but a few stayed on. For a time miners recovered some gold in the mountain gulches west and south of town. The modern city of Laramie is proud of its historical heritage.

## 172. South Pass City, Wyoming

*Location: Fremont County.*

After several unsuccessful mining attempts along the Sweetwater River, in 1867 prospectors discovered placers of gold. Others rushed in and established South Pass City. Soon having a population of 700, the town included 5 hotels, 3 meat markets, 2 bakeries, 4 law firms, and 13 saloons. By the end of 1868 the population had risen to about 4,000 and the town had become the seat of Sweetwater County. By 1872 it was the largest in the Territory, but mining declined and within 6 years it was a ghost town; it lost the county seat to Green River, and most of the mines were abandoned. About a block of buildings have survived. Some of the false-fronted stores date back to the 1860's. A handful of people still reside in the town.

# SUGGESTED READING

ADAMS, ANDY. *Log of a Cowboy*. Boston: Houghton Mifflin, 1903. This classic piece of Western fiction, written by a former trail boss, provides a vivid account of a great cattle drive. Authentically portrays the cowboy and trail life.

ATHEARN, ROBERT G. *High Country Empire: The High Plains and Rockies*. New York: McGraw-Hill, 1960. A first-rate history of the region drained by the Missouri River, comprising the States of Colorado, Kansas, Montana, Nebraska, North and South Dakota, and Wyoming. Emphasizes broad regional developments.

ATHERTON, LEWIS E. *The Cattle Kings*. Bloomington: Indiana University Press, 1961. A readable and interpretive account of the great cattle drives and the open range cattle industry on the Plains.

BRANCH, DOUGLAS. *The Cowboy and His Interpreters*. New York: D. Appleton-Century, 1926. A reliable work on the cowboy and what has been written about him.

BUCK, SOLON J. *The Agrarian Crusade—A Chronicle of the Farmer in Politics*. Vol. XLV of *The Chronicles of America* series, ed. by Allen Johnson. New Haven: Yale University Press, 1920. Traces the agrarian crusade and its political implications from the Granges, through the Greenback and Populist phases, to its climax in the battle for free silver.

CAUGHEY, JOHN W. *Gold is the Cornerstone*. Berkeley: University of California Press, 1948. Surveys all aspects of the California gold rush. Accords special attention to the economic, social, political, and cultural results.

CLELAND, ROBERT G. *Cattle on a Thousand Hills*. San Marino: Huntington Library, 1941. One of the best works on the cattle industry in California.

DALE, EDWARD E. *The Range Cattle Industry*. Norman: University of Oklahoma Press, 1930. A standard work. Traces the development of the ranch industry on the Plains from the close of the Civil War to the 1920's.

DICK, EVERETT. *The Sod-House Frontier*. New York: D. Appleton-Century, 1937. An original synthesis that surveys the entire process of agricultural settlement on the Great Plains. Presents a sympathetic and realistic account of the living conditions, social life, and obstacles faced by the farmers. Descriptive rather than interpretive.

———. *Vanguards of the Frontier—A Social History of the Northern Plains and Rocky Mountains from the Fur Traders to the Sod Busters*. New York: D. Appleton-Century, 1941. Deals mainly with the pre-settlement phase. Traces the activities of the mountain men, frontier soldiers, missionaries, Indian agents, railroad builders, buffalo hunters, and cattlemen. Topics covered include the Santa Fe trade, Mormon migration, mining camps, stagecoach travel, trail driving, and sheep raising.

DOBIE, J. FRANK. *The Longhorns*. Boston: Little, Brown, and Company, 1941. A genial Texan who had a unique literary style, Dobie excelled in describing the range life he knew and loved. A companion work to this volume is *The Mustangs* (1952).

FRANTZ, JOE B., and JULIAN E. CHOATE, JR. *The American Cowboy—The Myth and the Reality*. Norman: University of Oklahoma Press, 1955. Separates fact from fantasy in cowboy lore, and analyzes various literary treatments of the cowboy.

GARD, WAYNE. *Frontier Justice*. Norman: University of Oklahoma Press, 1949. Discusses feuds, range wars, vigilante activities, and the rise of law and order in the West.

GREEVER, WILLIAM S. *The Bonanza West—The Story of the Western Mining Rushes, 1848–1900*. Norman: University of Oklahoma Press, 1963. A readable but scholarly treatment of the major mining rushes.

HALEY, J. EVETTS. *Charles Goodnight, Cowman and Plainsman*. Norman: University of Oklahoma Press, 1949. An excellent biography of one of the most colorful and important figures in the range cattle industry that also provides much information on ranching in general.

HIBBARD, BENJAMIN H. *A History of Public Land Policies*. New York: Macmillan Company, 1924, rev. ed. 1939. One of the most authoritative histories of public land policy in the United States.

HICKS, JOHN D. *The Populist Revolt.* Minneapolis: University of Minnesota Press, 1931. Treats agrarian unrest in the Middle West and the Great Plains and the political reactions of the farmers. Examines the conditions that produced the Populist movement, its supporters, and its contributions to political and economic reform.

HUFFMAN, ROY E. *Irrigation Development and Public Water Policy* New York: Ronald Press, 1953. Presents the history of irrigation and river basin development in the United States. Analyzes the nature and administration of water rights and the relation of irrigation to land policy.

McCOY, JOSEPH G. *Historic Sketches of the Cattle Trade of the West and Southwest,* ed. by Ralph P. Bieber. Glendale: Arthur H. Clark Company, 1940. One of the founders of the open range cattle industry reminisces about its beginnings.

OSGOOD, ERNEST S. *The Day of the Cattleman.* Minneapolis: University of Minnesota Press, 1929. An outstanding work on the cattle industry. Emphasizes the economic influence of the industry.

PAUL, RODMAN W. *Mining Frontiers of the Far West, 1848–1880.* New York: Holt, Rinehart and Winston, 1963. A broad study of Western mining. Stresses the importance of science and technology in advancing the mining frontier.

PELZER, LOUIS. *The Cattlemen's Frontier.* Glendale: Arthur H. Clark Company, 1936. Soundly analyzes the economics of the cattle industry and the attitudes of the cattle barons.

ROLLINS, PHILIP A. *The Cowboy.* New York: C. Scribner's Sons, 1922, rev. ed., 1936. Among the many accounts of the cowboy's life and the development of the ranch industry, this one by a former cowboy has stood the test of time.

SHANNON, FRED A. *The Farmer's Last Frontier.* Vol. V of *The Economic History of the United States.* New York: Farrar and Rinehart, 1945. One of the best accounts of all phases of the farmers' frontier.

SMITH, HENRY N. *Virgin Land—The American West as Symbol and Myth.* Cambridge: Harvard University Press, 1950. One of the few books that discusses the treatment of the agricultural West in American literature.

TOWNE, CHARLES W., and EDWARD N. WENTWORTH. *Shepherd's Empire.* Norman: University of Oklahoma Press, 1945. Tells the story of the sheep industry in the West from the days of the conquistadors to the present.

WEBB, WALTER P. *The Great Plains.* Boston: Ginn and Company, 1931.

This influential book discusses the effects of climate, geography, fencing, and water upon the development of the land and settlement patterns.

WOLLE, MURIEL S. *The Bonanza Trail—Ghost Towns and Mining Camps of the West.* Bloomington: Indiana University Press, 1953. An exceptionally valuable work for those interested in the present condition of the mining towns and ghost towns of the West. The author traveled 70,000 miles by automobile throughout the 12 mining States.

# NOTES

1. San Bernardino Ranch, Ariz.: John R. Bartlett, *Personal Narrative* . . . (New York, 1854); Frank C. Lockwood, *Pioneer Days in Arizona— From the Spanish Occupation to Statehood* (Tucson, 1932); J. J. Wagoner, "History of the Cattle Industry in Southern Arizona, 1540– 1940," University of Arizona Bulletin, Social Science Bulletin No. 20 (Tucson, 1952); Rufus K. Wyllys, *Arizona—The History of a Frontier State* (Phoenix, 1950).

2. Sierra Bonita Ranch, Ariz.: Will C. Barnes, *Arizona Place Names* (Tucson, 1960); Bert Haskett, "Early History of the Cattle Industry in Arizona," *Arizona Historical Review,* VI (1935); Richard J. Hinton, *The Hand-Book of Arizona* (San Francisco, 1878); Edward H. Peplow, Jr., *History of Arizona* (3 vols., New York, 1958), II; Wagoner, "History of the Cattle Industry in Southern Arizona."

3. Tombstone, Ariz.: Walter N. Burns, *Tombstone—An Iliad of the Southwest* (New York, 1929); Historic American Buildings Survey, National Park Service, 30 photos, 7 sheets (1937); Aubrey Neasham, "Special Report on the Proposed National Historic Site of Tombstone, Arizona," MS Report, National Park Service (1941); John M. Myers, *The Last Chance—Tombstone's Early Years* (New York, 1950); L. D. Walters, *Tombstone's Yesterdays* (Tucson, 1928).

4. Bodie, Calif.: Ella M. Cain, *The Story of Bodie* (San Francisco, 1956); Harold Kirker, *California's Architectural Frontier* (San Marino, Calif., 1960); Rodman W. Paul, *California Gold—The Beginning of Mining in the Far West* (Cambridge, 1947); Muriel S. Wolle, *The Bonanza Trail—Ghost Towns and Mining Camps of the West* (Bloomington, Ind., 1953).

5. Coloma, Calif.: John W. Caughey, *Gold is the Cornerstone* (Berkeley and Los Angeles, 1948); William S. Greever, *The Bonanza West—The Story of the Western Mining Rushes, 1848–1900* (Norman, Okla., 1963); Aubrey Neasham, "Sutter's Sawmill," *California Histori-*

*cal Society Quarterly,* XXVI (1947) ; Rodman W. Paul, *Mining Frontiers of the Far West, 1848–1880* (New York, 1963), and *California Gold;* Hero E. Rensch, "Marshall Gold Discovery State Park, Coloma, California—A Preliminary Research Study, 1852–1865," California Division of Beaches and Parks mimeographed report (Sacramento, 1962).

6. Columbia, Calif.: Historic American Buildings Survey, National Park Service, 18 photographs, 13 sheets (1934–36) ; Kirker, *California's Architectural Frontier;* Paul, *California Gold;* Lyle F. Perusse, "Gothic Revival in California, 1850–1890," *Journal of the Society of Architectural Historians,* XIV, No. 3 (October 1955) ; Elizabeth G. Potter, "Columbia, Gem of the Southern Mines," *California Historical Society Quarterly, XXIV* (September 1945) ; Wolle, *Bonanza Trail.*

7. New Almaden, Calif.: Edgar H. Bailey, "The New Almaden Quicksilver Mines," *Geologic Guidebook of the San Francisco Bay Counties,* Bulletin 154, Division of Mines (San Francisco, 1951) ; Hubert H. Bancroft, *History of California* (7 vols., San Francisco, 1884–90), VI and VII; Donald C. Brown, "The New Almaden Quicksilver Mines," unpublished MA Thesis, San Jose State College, Calif. (1958) ; Kenneth M. Johnson, *The New Almaden Quicksilver Mine, with an Account of the Land Claims Involving the Mine and Its Role in California History* (Los Gatos, Calif., 1963) ; Paul, *California Gold;* Henry W. Splitter, "Quicksilver at New Almaden," *Pacific Historical Review,* XXVI (1957).

8. Old United States Mint, Calif.: *A History of Public Buildings Under the Control of the Treasury Department* (Washington, 1901) ; A. L. Himmelwright, *The San Francisco Earthquake and Fire* (New York, 1906) ; John A. Hussey, "Old United States Mint Building, San Francisco, California," MS Report, National Park Service (1956) ; Kirker, *California's Architectural Frontier;* Benjamin E. Lloyd, *Lights and Shades in San Francisco* (San Francisco, 1876) ; George Tays, "The First United States Branch Mint in California," California State Registered Historical Landmark Series No. 87 (Berkeley, 1936).

9. Sutter's Fort, Calif.: Bancroft, *History of California,* IV and V; Paul C. Phillips, *The Fur Trade* (2 vols., Norman, Okla., 1961), II; James P. Zollinger, *Sutter—The Man and His Empire* (New York, 1939).

10. Warner's Ranch, Calif.: Robert G. Cleland, *Cattle on a Thousand Hills* (San Marino, Calif., 1941) ; Roscoe P. and Margaret B. Conkling, *The Butterfield Overland Mail, 1857–1869* (3 vols., Glendale, Calif., 1947), II; Joseph J. Hill, *The History of Warner's Ranch* (Los Angeles, 1927) ; J. J. Warner, "Reminiscenses of Early California, 1831–1846,"

*Annual Publications, 1907–08,* Historical Society of Southern California (Los Angeles, 1909).

11. Central City, Colo.: Caroline Bancroft, *Historic Central City* (Denver, 1953); Muriel S. Wolle, *Stampede to Timberline—The Ghost Towns and Mining Camps of Colorado* (Boulder, 1949).

12. Cripple Creek, Colo.: Wolle, *Stampede to Timberline.*

13. Durango-Silverton Narrow Gauge Line, Colo.: Lucius Beebe and Charles Clegg, *Narrow Gauge in the Rockies* (Berkeley, 1958); David L. Hieb, "Preliminary Report, Narrow Gauge Railroad, Colorado," MS Report, National Park Service (1959); Stewart H. Holbrook, *Story of American Railroads* (New York, 1947).

14. Leadville, Colo.: Wolle, *Stampede to Timberline.*

15. Silverton-Telluride Mining District, Colo.: Wolle, *Stampede to Timberline;* Works Progress Administration (WPA), *Colorado—Guide to the Highest State* (New York, 1941).

16. United States Assay Office, Idaho: John A. Hussey, "Former U.S. Assay Office, 210 Main Street, Boise, Idaho," mimeographed report, National Park Service (1961), and "Building Most Valuable—The Story of the Idaho Assay Office," *Idaho Yesterdays,* V, No. 1 (1961); Greever, *Bonanza West;* Dorothy O. Johansen and Charles M. Gates, *Empire of the Columbia* (New York, 1957); Paul, *Mining Frontiers.*

17. Bannack, Mont.: Wolle, *Bonanza Trail.*

18. Butte, Mont.: Joseph Kinsey Howard, *Montana—High, Wide, and Handsome* (New Haven, 1943).

19. Fort Benton, Mont.: Hiram M. Chittenden, *History of Early Steamboat Navigation on the Missouri River* (New York, 1903); Paul F. Sharp, *Whoop-Up Country* (Minneapolis, 1955).

20. Grant-Kohrs Ranch, Mont.: Merrill G. Burlingame, *The Montana Frontier* (Helena, 1942); Larry Gill, "From Butcher Boy to Beef King—the Gold Camp Days of Conrad Kohrs," *Montana, The Magazine of Western History* (Spring 1958); Louis Pelzer, *The Cattleman's Frontier* (Glendale, Calif., 1936); Mari Sandoz, *The Cattlemen* (New York, 1958).

21. Virginia City, Mont.: Wolle, *Bonanza Trail.*

22. Virginia City, Nev.: Myron Angel, *History of Nevada, with Illustrations and Biographical Sketches of its Prominent Men and Pioneers* (Oakland, 1881), reprinted with an introduction by David F. Myrick (Berkeley, 1958); Greever, *Bonanza West;* Olaf T. Hagen, "Report on Planning for the Preservation and Development of Virginia City, Nevada," MS Report, National Park Service (1940); Oscar Lewis, *Silver Kings—the Life and Times of Mackay, Fair, Flood, and O'Brien, Lords of the Nevada Comstock Lode* (New York, 1947); Eliot Lord, *Com-*

*stock Mining and Miners,* U.S. Geological Survey, Monographs, IV (Washington, 1883), reprinted with an introduction by David F. Myrick (Berkeley, 1959) ; George D. Lyman, *Ralston's Ring—California Plunders the Comstock Lode* (New York, 1937) ; Paul, *Mining Frontiers;* Grant H. Smith, *The History of the Comstock Lode, 1850–1920,* University of Nevada Bulletin, XXXVII, No. 3, Geology and Mining Series No. 37 (Reno, 1943) ; Cecil G. Tilton, *William Chapman Ralston, Courageous Builder* (Boston, 1935) ; Mark Twain, *Roughing It* (Hartford, 1872) ; William Wright (Dan De Quille, pseud.), *The Big Bonanza: An Authentic Account of the Discovery, History, and Working of the World-Renowned Comstock Lode of Nevada* (San Francisco, 1876), reprinted under the title *The Big Bonanza,* Oscar Lewis, ed. (New York, 1947).

23. Deadwood, S. Dak.: Wolle, *Bonanza Trail.*

24. JA Ranch, Tex.: Harley T. Burton, *A History of the JA Ranch* (Austin, 1928) ; J. Evetts Haley, *Charles Goodnight, Cowman and Plainsman* (Norman, Okla., 1949) ; L. F. Sheffy, "The Old Home Ranch Site," *Panhandle-Plains Historical Review,* XIX (1946).

25. King Ranch, Tex.: Frank Goodwyn, *Life on the King Ranch* (New York, 1951) ; Tom Lea, *The King Ranch* (2 vols., Boston, 1957).

26. Swan Land and Cattle Company Headquarters, Wyo.: Robert H. Burns et al., *Wyoming's Pioneer Ranches* (Laramie, 1955) ; John Clay, *My Life on the Range* (Norman, Okla., 1962).

27. Tom Sun Ranch, Wyo.: John K. Rollinson, *Wyoming Cattle Trails* (Caldwell, Idaho, 1948).

28. Old Sacramento, Calif.: Joseph A. Baird, Jr., "The Architectural Legacy of Sacramento," *California Historical Society Quarterly,* XXXIX, No. 3 (September 1960) ; Bancroft, *History of California,* VI; Roy S. Bloff, *Pony Express—The Great Gamble* (Berkeley, 1959) ; Carroll D. Hall and Hero E. Rensch, *Old Sacramento—A Report on its Significance to the City, State, and Nation, with Recommendations for the Preservation and Use of its Principal Historical Structures and Sites,* in Parts I, II, and III, California Division of Beaches and Parks (Sacramento, 1958–60) ; Kirker, *California's Architectural Frontier;* Aubrey Neasham, "Old Sacramento, Inventory of Historical Buildings," Historical Report No. 2, California Division of Beaches and Parks (Sacramento, 1962) ; Paul, *California Gold* and *Mining Frontiers.*

29. Lincoln, N. Mex.: Charles F. Coan, *A History of New Mexico* (3 vols., Chicago, 1925), I; Emerson Hough, *The Story of the Cowboy* (New York, 1924) ; William A. Keleher, *Violence in Lincoln County, 1869–1881* (Albuquerque, 1957) ; Ralph Emerson Twitchell, *The Leading Facts of New Mexico History* (2 vols., Cedar Rapids, 1914).

# CRITERIA FOR SELECTION
# OF HISTORIC SITES
# OF EXCEPTIONAL VALUE

1. Structures or sites at which events occurred that have made a significant contribution to, and are identified prominently with, or which outstandingly represent, the broad cultural, political, economic, military, or social history of the Nation, and from which an understanding and appreciation of the larger patterns of our American heritage may be gained.

2. Structures or sites associated importantly with the lives of persons nationally significant in the history of the United States.

3. Structures or sites associated significantly with an important event that outstandingly represents some great idea or ideal of the American people.

4. Structures that embody the distinguishing characteristics of an architectural type specimen, exceptionally valuable for a study of a period style or method of construction; or a notable structure representing the work of a master builder, designer, or architect.

5. Objects that figured prominently in nationally significant events; or that were prominently associated with nationally significant persons; or that outstandingly represent some great idea or ideal of the American people; or that embody distinguishing characteristics of a type specimen, exceptionally valuable for study of a period style or method of construction; or that are notable as representations of the work of master workers or designers.

6. Archeological sites that have produced information of major scientific importance by revealing new cultures, or by shedding light upon periods of occupation over large areas of the United States. Such sites are those which have produced, or which may reasonably be

expected to produce, data affecting theories, concepts, and ideas to a major degree.

7. When preserved or restored as integral parts of the environment, historic buildings not sufficiently significant individually by reason of historical association or architectural merit to warrant recognition may collectively compose a "historic district" that is of historical significance to the Nation in commemorating or illustrating a way of life in its developing culture.

8. To possess national significance, a historic or prehistoric structure, district, site, or object must possess integrity:

For a historic or prehistoric structure, integrity is a composite quality derived from original workmanship, original location, and intangible elements of feeling and association. (A structure no longer on the original site may possess national significance if the person or event associated with it was of transcendent importance in the Nation's history and the association consequential.)

For a historic district, integrity is a composite quality derived from original workmanship, original location, and intangible elements of feeling and association.

For a historic or prehistoric site, integrity requires original location and intangible elements of feeling and association. (The site of a structure no longer standing may possess national significance if the person or event associated with the structure was of transcendent historical importance in the Nation's history and the association consequential.)

For a historic object, integrity requires basic original workmanship.

9. Structures or sites which are primarily of significance in the field of religion or to religious bodies but are not of national importance in other fields of the history of the United States, such as political, military, or architectural history, will not be eligible for consideration.

10. Birthplaces, graves, burials, and cemeteries, as a general rule, are not eligible for consideration and recognition except in cases of historical figures of transcendent importance. Historic sites associated with the actual careers and contributions of outstanding historical personages usually are more important than their birthplaces and burial places.

11. Structures, sites, and objects achieving historical importance within the past 50 years will not as a general rule be considered unless associated with persons or events of transcendent significance.

12. Structures, sites, and objects proposed for addition to the National Park System must also meet standards of suitability and feasibility.

# ACKNOWLEDGMENTS

*Advisory Board on National Parks, Historic Sites, Buildings, and Monuments (1960–64)*

Stanley A. Cain, University of Michigan.
Edward B. Danson, Jr., Museum of Northern Arizona.
Marian S. Dryfoos, *The New York Times.*
Harold P. Fabian, Utah State Park and Recreation Commission.
Melville B. Grosvenor, National Geographic Society.
E. Raymond Hall, University of Kansas.
John A. Krout, Columbia University.
Frank E. Masland, Jr., Carlisle, Pa.
Edward J. Meeman, Memphis, Tenn.
John B. Oakes, New York City.
Sigurd F. Olson, Ely, Minn.
Paul L. Phillips, United Papermakers and Paperworkers.
Earl H. Reed, American Institute of Architects.
Fred Smith, Newark, N. J.
Robert G. Sproul, Berkeley, Calif.
Robert L. Stearns, Denver, Colo.
Wallace E. Stegner, Los Altos Hills, Calif.
Carl I. Wheat, Menlo Park, Calif.

*Consulting Committee for the National Survey of Historic Sites and Buildings (1960–64)*

J. O. Brew, Peabody Museum of Archaeology and Ethnology.
Ralph H. Gabriel, American University.
Robert R. Garvey, Jr., National Trust for Historic Preservation.
Eric Gugler, American Scenic and Historic Preservation Society.
Richard Howland, Smithsonian Institution.

## ACKNOWLEDGMENTS

Frederick Johnson, Robert S. Peabody Foundation for Archaeology, Phillips Academy.

Waldo G. Leland, American Council of Learned Societies.

Earl H. Reed, American Institute of Architects.

S. K. Stevens, Pennsylvania Historical and Museum Commission.

Louis B. Wright, Folger Shakespeare Library.

### National Park Service

Herbert E. Kahler, Chief (retired), Division of History and Archeology.

Roy E. Appleman, Historian, Division of Interpretation and Visitor Services.

Joseph P. Cullen, Staff Historian, Division of History Studies.

Dr. John A. Hussey, Regional Historian, San Francisco.

Richard E. Morris, Editorial Assistant, National Survey of Historic Sites and Buildings.

John W. Walker, Staff Archeologist, National Survey of Historic Sites and Buildings.

### State and Private Organizations

Mrs. Clara S. Beatty, Director, Nevada State Historical Society, Reno.

H. D. Bugbee, Clarendon, Tex.

Albert Culverwell, Historian, Washington State Park Commission, Olympia.

William S. Evans, Jr., Curator, Los Cerritos, Long Beach, Calif.

Adlai Feather, Mesilla Park, N. Mex.

Russell W. Fridley, Director, Minnesota Historical Society, St. Paul.

Maurice Frink, Executive Secretary, State Historical Society of Colorado, Denver.

Mrs. Alice G. Good, Director of Library and Archives, Phoenix, Ariz.

Dr. Emil W. Haury, Arizona State Museum, Tucson.

Mrs. Isabel M. Haynes, Yellowstone Park, Wyo.

Miss Lola Homsher, Executive Secretary, Wyoming State Historical Society, Cheyenne.

Michael S. Kennedy, Director, Montana Historical Society, Helena.

Mrs. Edna G. Landin, President, Tombstone Restoration Commission, Tombstone, Ariz.

Dennis McCarthy, Director, Arizona State Parks Board, Phoenix.

C. Boone McClure, Director, Panhandle-Plains Historical Society, Canyon, Tex.

Nyle H. Miller, Secretary, State Historical Society of Kansas, Topeka.

Dr. A. R. Mortensen, Director, Utah State Historical Society, Salt Lake City.

Dr. Aubrey Neasham, State Historian, California Division of Beaches and Parks, Sacramento.

Dr. James C. Olson, former Superintendent, Nebraska State Historical Society, Lincoln.

Dr. William J. Peterson, Superintendent, State Historical Society of Iowa, Iowa City.

Glenn W. Price, Executive Director, The Westerners Foundation, Stockton, Calif.

Gil Procter, Kitchen's Ranch, Nogales, Ariz.

Frank D. Reeve, Department of History, University of New Mexico, Albuquerque.

Russell Reid, Superintendent, State Historical Society of North Dakota, Bismarck.

Will G. Robinson, Secretary, South Dakota State Historical Society, Pierre.

Paul A. Rossi, Director, Gilcrease Institute of American History and Art, Tulsa, Okla.

Dr. Carl Russell, Orinda, Calif.

Roscoe Sheller, Sunnyside, Wash.

Dr. Floyd C. Shoemaker, Secretary, State Historical Society of Missouri, Columbia.

Miss Irene Simpson, Wells Fargo Museum, San Francisco.

Mrs. Agnes Wright Spring, Historian, State Historical Society of Colorado, Denver.

H. J. Swinney, Director, Idaho Historical Society, Boise.

Dr. K. Ross Toole, former Director, Historical Society of Montana, Helena.

Thomas Vaughan, Director, Oregon Historical Society, Portland.

Dr. W. W. Wasley, Arizona State Museum, Tucson.

Dr. Merle Wells, Historian, Idaho State Historical Society, Boise.

Robert C. Wells, King Ranch, Kingsville, Tex.

Arthur Woodward, formerly with the Los Angeles Museum, Los Angeles.


NOTE: The eight F. Jay Haynes photographs included in this volume appeared in FOLLOWING THE FRONTIER *with F. Jay Haynes, Pioneer Photographer of the Old West,* by Freeman Tilden (New York, Alfred A. Knopf, Inc., 1964). They are reproduced through the courtesy of Alfred A. Knopf, Inc., and The Haynes Foundation.

# Index

☆ U.S. GOVERNMENT PRINTING OFFICE : 1968 O—294–106